T0380440

GENERAL BIBLE KNOWLEDGE

Systematic Theology

Bishop Willie J. Duncan Ph.D.

authorHOUSE®

AuthorHouse™
1663 Liberty Drive
Bloomington, IN 47403
www.authorhouse.com
Phone: 1 (800) 839-8640

Published by AuthorHouse 12/28/2015

ISBN: 978-1-5049-6488-3 (sc)
ISBN: 978-1-5049-6489-0 (e)

Library of Congress Control Number: 2015920016

Print information available on the last page.

Any people depicted in stock imagery provided by Thinkstock are models,
and such images are being used for illustrative purposes only.
Certain stock imagery © Thinkstock.

This book is printed on acid-free paper.

GENERAL OUTLINE

VOLUME I

VOLUME II

VOLUME III

VOLUME IV

VOLUME I

TEXTBOOK
GENERAL BIBLE KNOWLEDGE

CONTENTS

PREFACE

This course will consist of the study of General Bible Knowledge. My effort is to walk the student through the Bible in various subjects. The course will begin with a logical study of the arrangement of the Books of the Bible.

We will examine the Ages, Dispensations and Covenants. You will learn how to study the Bible effectively rightly dividing the word of truth.

In this course, you will study the Godhead. You will learn about the Prophecy of Daniel and Revelation. We will walk through Church History and capture the expectations of the Rapture of the Church.

The Muskegon Institutes' **ostensible purpose is** that each student would **embrace a burning desire to continue in the study** of the **Word of God** effectively, and our goal is that each student would learn how to **apply the knowledge acquired** from this course. Please study all the Biblical references given. This will enhance your learning capability. Consider it a blessing for being a part of this course.

Dr. W. J. Duncan
The Author

MUSKEGON BIBLE INSTITUTE INC.
GENERAL BIBLE KNOWLEDGE
STUDY COURSE PROCEDURE

CHAPTER ONE

(FIRST TEN WEEKS)
THREE TIME PER WEEK

FIRST WEEK

1. You must learn the Books of the Bible and the divisions thereof in order.
2. You must learn the Dispensations and Covenants.

SECOND WEEK

1. You must learn the creative story and be able to compare the Seven Feast Days of the Lord with the Seven Days of Creation.

THIRD WEEK

1. You must learn the answer to the twelve questions on the subject. "Thy Word is True: Proven by the scriptures from your memory.

FOURTH WEEK

1. You must study the course on the Godhead.

FIFTH WEEK

1. You must write a three-page report on, How God is Father, Son, and Holy Ghost, and yet be one.

SIXTH WEEK

1. You must study the Names of God. You must be able to quote at least ten names with their meanings and where they are found.

To pass this section you must pass the test questions that are recorded in the test booklet.

1. The Divisions of the books of the Bible.
2. Dispensations and Covenants.
3. The Mystery of the Godhead.
4. The Names of God.

PROPHECY

SEVENTH WEEK

1. You must be able to define the word Prophecy in your own words.
2. You must explain the approach of the use of the term political prophecies.
3. You must be able to discuss Satan's "I Wills" verses God's "I wills"

EIGHT WEEK

1. You must study the whole book of Daniel and give a summary of the Book.

NINTH WEEK

1. You must be able to remember the Hebrew names of Daniel and his friends. You must also remember the Chaldean names.
2. You must be able to tell the dream of Nebuchadnezzar and what it means. Also name the order of the kingdoms.

TENTH WEEK

1. You must be able to tell the vision of Daniel and what this vision represent in the succession of Kingdoms.
2. You must be able to explain the origin of the Anti-Christ from their visions.
3. You must answer the questions on Bible Prophecy in the test session.

CHURCH HISTORY
SECOND TEN WEEKS
(Revelation)

FIRST WEEK

1. Give a brief summary of Revelation.
2. Put to memory the seven periods of Church History, including their fates if any.

SECOND WEEK

"Apostolic Age"

1. You must study the contents and doctrines of the apostolic warnings and prophecies given by the Apostles concerning the rise of false doctrines and false churches.

THIRD WEEK

"Persecuted Age"

1. You must study the times of the Christian Martyrs and that, which led to the persecution of the Church.
2. You must study the various men who arose in this period and their doctrinal opinions, which were developed.

FOURTH WEEK

"Pergamian Age"
(Imperial)

1. Give a brief history of the nation of Rome.
2. Give a report on the doctrines of the Nicolatans.

FIFTH WEEK

1. Give a research paper on the council of Nicaea.

SIXTH WEEK

"The Thyatirian Age"
(Catholic)

1. You must study the origin of the Catholic Church.
2. Study the result of the "Dark Age" in the Christian Church.

SEVENTH WEEK

1. You must study the difference between Manuscripts, Copies, and Translations.
2. Who was the Massoretes?
3. What is a Version?

EIGHT WEEK

"The Sardian Age"
(Reformation)

1. You must determine, "What event brought about the Reformation Period.
2. Some main Leaders of the Reformation Period.

NINTH WEEK

"Philadelphia Age"
(Wesleyan)

1. Examine the origin of various churches of this age. Could they be justified in the light of the Holy Scriptures?

TENTH WEEK

"Laodician Age"
(Pentecostal's Revivals)

1. You must be able to explain the spirit of this age.
2. You must be able to give a brief History of the Pentecostal Revivals beginning in 1901 to date.
3. Write a 5,000 words report on what you have learned in the various subjects throughout this course.

The Questions are listed at the end of each course Volume

BIBLE STUDY COURSE

THE DIVISIONS OF THE BOOKS OF THE BIBLE

(OLD TESTAMENT)	(MAJOR PROPHETS)	(HISTORY)
		ACTS
(LAW)	ISAIAH	
GENESIS	JEREMIAH	(PAULINE EPISTLES)
EXODUS	LAMENTATIONS	
LEVITICUS	EZEKIEL	ROMANS
NUMBERS	DANIEL	1 CORINTHIANS
DEUTERONOMY		2 CORINTHIANS
	(MINOR PROPHETS)	GALATIANS
(HISTORY)		EPHESIANS
	HOSEA	PHILIPPIANS
JOSHUA	JOEL	COLOSSIANS
JUDGES	AMOS	1 THESSALONIANS
RUTH	OBADIAH	2 THESSALONIANS
I SAMUEL	JONAH	1 TIMOTHY
2 SAMUEL	MICAH	2 TIMOTHY
I KINGS	NAHUM	TITUS
2 KINGS	HABAKKUK	PHILEMON
I CHRONICLES	ZEPHANIAH	HEBREWS
2 CHRONICLES	HAGGAI	(GENERAL EPISTILES)
EZRA	ZECHARIAH	
NEHEMIAH	MALACHI	JAMES
ESTHER		I PETER
	(NEW TESTAMENT)	2 PETER
(POETRY)	(GOSPELS)	I JOHN
		2 JOHN
JOB	MATTHEW	3 JOHN
PSALMS	MARK	JUDE
PROVERBS	LUKE	(PROPHECY)
ECCLESIASTES	JOHN	REVELATION
SONG OF SOLOMOM		

INTRODUCTION TO GENERAL BIBLE KNOWLEDGE

KING JAMES VERSION

The Study of the Bible is one of the **most fascinating** and **rewarding endeavors** that any of us can ever take. For in these pages of the Holy writ are the treasures of wisdom, knowledge, and understanding. We will receive **prolong** life physically and **Eternal life** spiritually, if we continue our **study in the Word of God.** We will be exposed to **the knowledge** of all things. Moreover, we will be apt to **comprehend** quite easily on all subjects, taught by **God** and **man.**

The books of the bible are **arranged logically,** and **not** chronologically. That is as they relate to **subjects** and contents, rather than **dates** and **periods** each was written; meaning **all law** books are grouped together, all **history books** are grouped together, **all gospels** are **grouped together** and so on.

They are **divided** under **various** topics. There are **ten divisions** of the Bible, **which are as follows:** Law, Israel's **History,** Poetic, **Major** Prophets, **Minor** Prophets, The **Gospels,** History (The **Acts) Pauline** Epistles, **General** Epistles, and **Prophecy.**

The books in the **Law Division** contain **specific moral codes** that regulate the **behavior** of man toward man and God. The lessons in the HISTORICAL books teach us concerning THE RISE and FALL OF THE NATION OF ISRAEL. The POETIC books are the FOLKLORES and LITERATURE or writings of the **people of Israel**. The subject listed as: Major Prophets are the prophets who wrote **longer books,** and the Minor Prophets wrote **shorter books**. The **Gospels** are biographical **accounts** of the **birth, life, death** and **resurrection of Jesus.** The BOOK OF ACTS **gives thirty years** of CHURCH HISTORY. The **Pauline Epistles** are the letters written to the CHURCH and OFFICERS. The GENERAL EPISTLES are so called because they DO NOT address any SPECIFIC CHURCH or PERSON. **Revelation** is the last of the PROPHETICAL books.

The Bible also can be **divided** under the **Headings such as:** The **Old Testament** is the **New** Testament CONCEALED. The **New Testament** is the **Old** Testament REVEALED. The **Old Testament** is the **New** Testament CONTAINED. The **New Testament** is the **Old** Testament EXPLAINED. The **Old** Testament is **the** SHADOW. The **New** Testament is **the** BODY. The **Old** Testament is **the** PREPARATION. The **Gospel** is **the** MANIFESTATION. The **Book of Acts** is **the** PROCLAMATION. The **Epistles** are **the** EXPLANATION, and; **Revelation** is **the** CONSUMMATION.

The term Testament suggests that the **testator makes a will effective at his death.** All **wills** must be **enjoined** with the death or **blood** of the **Testator** (Heb. 9:16). In the **Old Testament** the **Testator** DID NOT DIE, only **animal blood** was shed. In the **New Testament,** the **Testator** HAD TO DIE to **free man** from the **penalty of sin.** GOD being the TESTATOR **purchased** the **church** with his **own blood** (Acts 20:28; 1 John 3:16). The Bible can be divided into other divisions such as **Ages, Dispensations, Covenants,** etc.

THE SCRIPTURE SPEAKS OF THREE AGES IN TIME SUCH AS:

1. **THE ANTE-DILUVIAN AGE**
2. **POST-DILUVIAN AGE, AND**
3. **AGE OF AGES**

AND SEVEN DISPENSATIONS:

1. **INNOCENCE**
2. **CONSCIENCE**
3. **HUMAN GOVERNMENT**
4. **PROMISE**
5. **LAW**
6. **GRACE**
7. **MILLENNIUM**

AGES OF THE BIBLE

AGE - an age **is a period** between TWO GREAT PHYSICAL CHANGES in the earth's surface (Genesis 7:11; Zech. 14:4, 10; 2 Peter 3—KJV)

DISPENSATION - a dispensation **is a** moral or PROBATIONARY PERIOD in which God dealt or **deals with man.**

ANTE-DELUVIAN AGE – From 'THE FALL OF MAN' to the FLOOD

POST-DELUVIAN AGE - From the FLOOD to the SECOND COMING OF JESUS CHRIST
AGE OF AGES - From the SECOND COMING OF CHRIST to the END OF TIME, which includes the MILLENNIUM.

THE DISPENSATIONS OF THE BIBLE

MAN'S INNOCENCE - this dispensation extends from the **creation of Adam** to the **expulsion** from the garden (Genesis 1:26, 27; 2:16, 17; 3:6, 22-24).

IT HAS TO DO WITH GOD MAKING MAN TO BECOME HIS SON. Prior to this time, God had **no son.** "And God said, Let us make man in our image, **after our likeness:** and let them have dominion **over the fish of the sea**, and over the fowl of the air, and over the cattle, and over all the earth, and over every creeping thing that creepeth upon the earth.

"So God created man in his own image, in **the image of God created he him;** male and female created he them." (Genesis 1:26, 27) To further **show that God made man his son,** God gave him the dominion over **all the earth**, and that he should pursue it. This is the **Father giving** the **inheritance to his son.**

The book of **Psalms** tells it **more emphatically** by saying, "**What is man,** that thou art mindful of him? And the son of man, that thou visitest him? For thou hast made him a **little lower** than the angels, and hast **crowned him with glory** and **honour**".

Thou madest him to have dominion **over** the **works of thy hands;** thou hast put **all** things under **his feet:** All sheep and oxen, yea, and the beasts of the **field;"** (Ps. 8:4-7)

This truly **shows that man is God's son.** Though made a little lower than Angels, man is **genuinely God's Son. Christendom** has made one of the **greatest** mistakes in biblical **interpretation** in determining the **Son of God** by ascribing to Jesus Christ Eternal **Son-ship.** When in all actuality **the son-ship** that **Jesus took on** was **that of the position** that **Adam once had.**

Note, in particular, the unique testimony: "For unto the **angels** hath **he not** put in **subjection** the world to come, whereof we speak. [6]But **one in a certain place testified,** saying, **What is man,** that thou art **mindful** of him? Or the **son of man,** that thou **visitest** him? Thou madest him a **little lower than the angels;** thou **crownedst** him with **glory** and **honour,** and didst set him over the **works of thy hands:** Thou hast put all things in subjection under his feet. For in that he put all in subjection under him, **he left nothing** that is **not put under him.** "But **now,** we **see not** yet **all things** put under him. "But we **see Jesus, who was made a little lower** than the **angels** for the **suffering of death,** crowned with **glory** and **honour;** that He **by the grace of God** should **taste death** for every man." (Heb. 2:5-9—KJV)

This passage in Hebrews tells us that **man was made a little lower** than Angels, yet God saw fit to **put all things under his feet.** This **shows** that **Adam is Son of God.** The **angels** were **not given** this **privilege** though greater in nature. "For unto **which of the Angels** said he **at any time,** Thou **art my son, this day have I begotten thee?** And again, I will be to him **a Father,** and **he shall be to me a Son?**" (Heb. 1:5)

So when **Adam sin** and **lost** his **position as son,** Jesus **himself** took **the position** of man. In Hebrews 2:7, **Adam is made** a little lower than **angels;** and **took** on the **form** of **the son of God** with **all things** being **put under him.**

The **scriptures** show that **man lost that position,** and then brought in the point saying: "But **we see Jesus, who** was **made a little lower than the angels for the suffering of death,** crowned with **glory** and **honour;** that he **by the grace of God** should **taste death for every man.**" (Heb. 2:9)

The **son-ship** that **Jesus assumes** was only for the **purpose of destroying** the **enemy** of **man,** which is **death.**

"Forasmuch then as the **children** are **partakers** of **flesh** and **blood,** he also himself likewise **took part of the same;** that **through death he might destroy** him that had the **power** of **death, that is, the devil**; And deliver them who through fear of death were all their lifetime subject to bondage." (Hebrews 2:14-15; Phil. 2:5-9)

Christ must stay in the position of son ship until the last enemy is destroyed. "Then *cometh* **the end,** when he shall have **delivered** up the **kingdom to God,** even the **Father; when he shall** have put down **all rule** and **all authority** and **power.** For he must **reign,** till he hath put **all enemies under his feet.** The **last enemy** *that* shall be **destroyed** is **death.** For he hath put all things under his feet: But when he saith **all things** are put under him, it is manifest that **he is excepted,** which did put all things under him."(1 Cor. 15:24-27)

This is the **same** language of the scripture found in **Genesis 1:26-28** when God did **at the first put all things under man.** And gave him the power to **pursue** and **subdue** the earth. But Adam **lost that position** and **Christ came** and **took the place** of man to **restore** him to his former **position.**

When Adam sinned he **lost all** that was granted unto **him in the son-ship,** and **Satan became the god of this world** (2 Cor. 4:4; St. Luke 4:6). After hearing that Jesus was Son of God, **Satan** made an effort to **take away from Jesus his Son-ship** just as he did unto **Adam.** All things were already given unto Jesus as God gave to **Adam.** Jesus said, "**All things are delivered unto me of my Father;** and **no man knoweth the Son,** but the Father; neither knoweth any man the Father, **save the Son,** and he to whomsoever **the Son will reveal** him.

Jesus must **reign** as **Son** until the **last enemy** of **man is destroyed.** This is **death** itself. After this completion, **Jesus** will **turn** the **kingdom back** to **God,** and the **position** of **son-ship** unto **man** and he will **return** to his **pre-incarnate-state** as the **Eternal God.** This will fulfill the scripture in **Revelation 21:6-7.**

"And he said unto me, it is done. I am Alpha and Omega, the beginning and the end. I will give unto him that is **athirst** of the fountain of the water of life **freely.** He that **overcometh** shall inherit **all things;** and I will be his **God,** and **he shall be my son.**"

CONSCIENCE - This dispensation deals with **man knowing good** from **evil.** That is, if he did good or evil, his **conscience** would let them **know.** That ended with a Judgment in a flood (Genesis 3:7, 22; 6:5, 11, 12; 7:11).

The term **conscience means** that one **knows with oneself,** what **he has done.** This is the time **without the law** of the Ten Commandments. There is a law written in the **hearts of men** that give the **sense** to **know** between **right** and **wrong.**

"For when the **Gentiles,** which have not the law, do by nature the things contained in the law, these, having not the law, are a law unto themselves. Which shew the work of the law written in their hearts, their **conscience** also **bearing witness,** and their **thoughts** the mean while accusing or else **excusing** one another.

HUMAN GOVERNMENT - In this dispensation, **man tried to build a society without God**. They tried to build a tower called **Babel** to make **a name** for them. This dispensation ended with the **confusion** of tongues (Genesis 9:12; 11:1-4, 5—KJV)

This dispensation is the **era of time where the earth** was given a **new chance to exercise** discipline. **Noah** and his **three sons** were challenged to **repopulate** the earth; therefore, this dispensation and population **emanated** from three progenitors **Shem, Ham,** and **Japheth.**

Shem: __meaning RENOWN, FAMOUS, or NAMED. His name is suggestive of a **religious connotation**. It is **true** that **from** the **Semites** most of the **world religions** are arrived. He is considered as being the **father** of the **yellow races**. From which we get most of our **world religions**. **Abraham** is the **most famed religious figure**. From his descendants spring **three great world religions** such as: JUDAISM, CHRISTIANITY, and ISLAM. All of them trace their **allegiance to father Abraham**. It is very true that **God used his promise** that he made to **Abraham:** That through **his seed shall all the people be blessed.** From Jesus, we have the establishment of the **gospel** for all mankind by which he **told** his **disciples** to **preach** to **every creature** under heaven, so that **all** may **have a chance to be saved.**

All **racial** distinctions became **obvious**, after a **long period** from being **separated** upon the **different continents** over the face of the **whole** earth. "**Remember** the **days** of **old**, consider the years of many **generation:** ask thy father, and he will **shew thee;** thy **elders,** and they will **tell** thee. [8]When the **most High** divided to the nations their **inheritance**, when he **separated** the sons of **Adam**, he set the bounds of the people according to the number of the children of Israel." (Deu. 32:7) In previous time, all were of the **same nationality** and **language**. "And the whole earth **was of one language**, and of **one speech**." (Gen. 11:1; Mal. 2:10; Acts 17:26) **Ham occupied Africa. Egypt,** which is in Africa, is **called** the **land of Ham. It's interesting to note** that, "**Israel** also **came** into **Egypt;** and **Jacob sojourned** in the land of Ham." (Psalm 105:23) From **Ham** we have, on the most part, the **black Race;** who from this day until now, **dwells in Africa:** Ham means Hot! His name is suggestive of the **hot climate** where most of his **descendant** resides. His **pigmentation of skins, texture of hair,** or **thickness of lip,** etc., are **not** the **result** of a **curse**, but more or **less** have received **hereditary** or **environmental adaptability** over the period of **thousands of years**. The same things are the case of the **development** of other races and **ethnic** distinctions. The **Hamites** are **not** the **only ones** that are **black**. In fact, most of the **populations** of the **earth** are **black** and of **a darker** complexion.

Ham__ is attributed as having developed HUMAN GOVERNMENT. Nimrod the first human governor was the son of Cush, who was the son of Ham (Gen. 10:6-7). **Miz-ra-im** is attributed as having **found Egypt in Africa**. It is a known fact that the **Egyptians** were among **the first** in **civilization**. This is well attested throughout the **world history. Cush is** considered to have established **Ethiopia**, which **is in Africa**. Africa then can be classified as the **cradle of civilization**. One the **most prestigious thing in Africa** is to be **a Chief of a tribe**: meaning a king.

Japheth__the meaning of this name is ENLARGEMENT. This is suggestive of their development in the area of SCIENCE and PHILOSOPHY. It is a **known fact**, that the descendants of **this son** are the **Caucasians**, the **Romans**, the **Greeks**, **Scandinavians**, **Russians**, etc., with their **ethnicity** and racial features. The bible says, "For the **Jews** require a sign, (religious), and the **Greeks** seek after **Wisdom**."__Philosophy (1 Cor. 1:22)

It is quite **evident** that the **Greeks** are historically involved with **Philosophy**, **science** and **technology**. Men like **Euclid, Aristotle, Plato**, etc. are long ago **clad** in such efforts. Even unto this day, these **descendants** are engaged in **education** more than any **other race.**

MAN UNDER PROMISE

MAN UNDER PROMISE - In this dispensation, **God entered into a covenant** with **one** man **named Abram,** whom **God called** out from the heathen and **made** an **unconditional promise** unto him and **his seed. This dispensation ended** with the **children of Israel** in bondage **in Egypt.** The book of **Genesis** began with the **words:** "**In the beginning God created...**" but ended with "**in a coffin in Egypt.**" (Gen. 1:1; 50:26; 12:5; 15:5; 26:3; 28:12, 13; 13:14-17; Ex. 11:13, 14) Anytime there **is a promise**, it is required that **faith** should be **invoked** that the hearer might **believe** and be the **recipient** of **such promises.** Here, it is noted under **this dispensation** that, **Abraham believed God**, and it was **accounted** unto him for **righteousness.** This is true for everyone who **believes** shall be **blessed** with **faithful Abraham** (Gal. 3:9).

LAW

LAW - This dispensation is sometimes REFERRED TO AS LEGAL. In this time, God gave the children of Israel **a list** of "THOU SHALT NOTS", but they **continued to sin**. This dispensation ENDED **on the** CROSS OF CALVARY, with Jesus giving His LIFE for the sins of the world (Ex. 19:1-8; Rom. 10:5; Gal. 3:10; Rom. 3:19, 20). **The Law only teaches** us **how to deal** with **God** and **man.** It briefly summed up with **one word** that is **Love.** In fact, **Love to God** and **Love to man.** The first portion deals with **our relationship** with **God,** and the second portion deals with our **relationship** with man (Matt. 22:36-40**).**

GRACE

GRACE – This is the dispensation where GOD MAKES MAN TO BECOME RIGHTEOUS WITHOUT ANY EFFORT on man's part. "For by grace are ye saved through **faith;** and that not of yourselves; it is the **gift of God:**" This dispensation **closes in three phases as follows:**

(1) The **Rapture** –is when God takes the church from the earth (1 Thess. 4:16, 17).
(2) The **Tribulation** Period –when Israel goes through a great trial and troublous time, along with the **whole world** (Matt 24:21, 22; Zeph. 1:5-18; Dan. 12:1; Jer. 30:5-7;Zech. 14:1**).**

(3) The **Second Coming** of Christ – this is the time He comes in great power and glory to set up the **Millennium** kingdom and the restoration of Israel (Matt. 24:29, 30; 25:31-46).

THE MILLENNIUM - This is the time when CHRIST AND HIS SAINTS SHALL REIGN a THOUSAND (1000) years in PEACE and happiness over the **restored nation of Israel** and the **Gentiles.** This is the time when **Satan** shall be **bound** for a THOUSAND (1000) years (Acts 15:14-17; Isa. 2:1-4; Chapter 11; Rev. 19:11-21; 20:1-6)**. It ends up at the** time when the **Devil is loosed after being bound for a Thousand years**. It ends with the **White Throne Judgment** (Rev.20: 3, 7-15; Rev. 21 and 22). AMEN! AND AMEN!

SOME MAIN CHARACTERS OF THE SEVEN DISPENSATIONS

INNOCENCE	LAW	GRACE
ADAM	MOSES	JESUS
EVE	AARON	PETER
(DEVIL)	JOSHUAH	JAMES
CONSCIENCE	SAMUEL	JOHN
ADAM	UNITED KINGDOM	PAUL
EVE	SAUL	TIMOTHY
ENOACH	DAVID	TITUS
NOAH	SOLOMON	MILLENNIUM
SHEM	DIVIDED KINGDOM	JESUS
HAM	REHOBOAM	SAINTS
JAPHET	JEROBOAM	ISRAEL
HUMAN GOVERNMENT	JOHORIAKIM	GENTILES
NOAH	(POST EXILIC)	
SHEM	EZRA	
HAM	NEHIMIAH	
JAPHET	ZERUBABEL	
NIMROD	INTER-TESTAMENT	
PROMISE	MACABEAN	
ABRAHAM	HEROD THE GREAT	
SARAH	MEDIA-PERSIA	
HAGAR	GRECIA	
ISHMAEL	ALEXANDER THE GREAT	
ISAAC	JULIUS CAESAR	
ESAU	AUGUSTUS CAESAR	
JACOB	JOHN THE BAPTIST	
ISRAEL	JESUS CHRIST	

HOW TO STUDY OUR BIBLE

KING JAMES VERSION

In order to understand the Bible, we must **rightly divide** the **Word** of **truth**. The apostle Paul advised Timothy to: "**Study** to **show** thyself approved unto GOD, a workman that needeth not to be ashamed, rightly dividing the Word of truth." (2 Tim.2: 15) The Bible is the **Revelation of God**, the **fall of man**, and **the way of salvation** (St. John 5:39; Rom. 3:10; St. John 20:30, 31).

It deals with THREE **places:** *Heaven, Earth, and Hell*, and THREE **classes** of **people:**

1. JEW
2. GENTILES, and
3. SAINTS.

It was written over a period of about sixteen hundred (1600) years, from 1492 B.C. to about 100 A.D. The language of the Bible in a limited sense, is of THREE kinds as follows:

1. SYMBOLIC ——**Daniel 7:1-8**
2. FIGURATIVE —**Matthew 8:22**
3. LITERAL ——**Matthew 12:1**

There are THREE **things** we must **avoid** doing **concerning the scriptures**, such as:

1. MIS-INTERPRETATION
2. MIS-APPLICATION
3. DIS-LOCATION

In the **teaching** of the Bible, there are **Parables** and **Allegories**. A parable is a **comparison** using **literal** speech, or things to portray **a definite truth**. A **Symbol** is the using of **fake images to reveal** or portray a definite truth. The **four winds** in Daniel, chapter seven, are a SYMBOLIC EXPRESSION. In Job, the thirty-eighth chapter, it actually happened.

THE SEVEN SPEECHES OF THE BIBLE

What an **interesting observation**, when we are **able to see**, that the **Bible speaks** unto us in SEVEN **different** ways. I don't mean in verbal language, as **Hebrew, Greek,** or **Latin;** but rather, in **Seven rhetorical** speeches such as

Symbolism————Daniel 7:1-8
Figurative————Matthew 8:22
Literal————Matthew 5:1
Parables————Matthew 13:11
Allegories————Galatians 4:24
Biblical Contrasts—1 Samuel 9:1; 16:1
Biblical Implications—Genesis 12:1-6; 16:1
(Firstly, Secondarily, Thirdly)

No one will be able to **understand** the Bible, as he should, until he has **mastered** these **speeches**. Many mistakes are made **because** of **wrong interpretations** of the **Scriptures.**

The term speech is to be understood with the definition of as the power of expressing or communicating thoughts by speaking. A message is given sometime after speaking by a comparative and subliminal approach.

Jesus said in Matthew 22:29, **"Ye do err, not knowing** the **scriptures,** nor the **power of God."** In St. Luke 24:25 Jesus said, "O fools and **slow of heart to believe all** that the prophets **have** spoken... ⁴⁴These are the words which I spake unto you, while I was yet with you, that **all things must be fulfilled,** which were **written** in the **law of Moses,** and *in* the **Prophets,** and *in* the **Psalms,** concerning **me.** ⁴⁵ "Then opened he their **under-standing,** that they might **understand** the **Scriptures," (St.** Luke 44-45)

Peter said, concerning Paul's writings: ¹⁵"And account that the **longsuffering** of our Lord is **salvation;** even as our beloved **brother Paul** also according to **the wisdom given** unto him hath **written unto you;**

As also in **all his epistles,** speaking in them of **these things;** in which are some things **hard to be understood,** which they that are **unlearned** and **unstable wrest,** as *they do* also the **other Scriptures,** unto their own destruction." (2 Pet. 3:15-16)

For instance, this is how one could **mis-understand** the **Word** of God. **Note in particular,** the following **Scriptures:**

"And when his disciples were come to the other side, **they had forgotten** to take **bread.** Then Jesus said unto them, ⁶"Take heed and beware of the **leaven of the Pharisees** and of **the Sadducees.** ⁷And they reasoned among themselves, saying, it is because we have **taken no bread**. ⁸Which when Jesus perceived, he said unto them, "O ye of **little faith,** why reason ye among yourselves, because **ye have brought no bread?"**

⁹Do ye **not yet understand**, neither remember the five loaves of the five thousand, and how many baskets ye took up?..¹¹How is it that ye **do not understand** that I spake it not to you **concerning bread**, that ye should beware **of the leaven of the Pharisees** and of the Sadducees.

¹²Then understood they how that he bade *them* **not beware of the leaven of bread,** but of the **doctrine** of the **Pharisees** and of the **Sadducees."** (Matt. 16:5-12)

The thing that was present in the **minds of the disciples** was, that they were discussing that they **had forgotten to bring bread.** When Jesus made mention of leaven, they immediately felt that Jesus was talking about **physical bread,** because **leaven** is **associated** with bread. But Jesus was talking about leaven in a **figure of speech.** As **natural leaven** is very **influential on dough,** so is **false doctrine** very **influential** on **people.**

In St. John 8:43, **Jesus said: "Why** do ye **not understand** my **speech?"** even because ye **cannot hear** my word." The Lord said, "GIVE EAR, O ye heavens, and I will **speak;** and **hear,** O earth, the **words** of my mouth. **My doctrine shall drop as the rain, my speech** shall **distil as the dew,** as the **small rain** upon the **tender herb,** and **as** the **showers** upon the **grass:"** (Deu. 32:1-2)

Understanding the language of the **figure of speech,** will help you **understand** the **sense** of the **woman hiding leaven** in **three measures of meal** (Matt. 13:33). This too has to do with **false doctrine.**

Therefore, we **must study** the Bible under **the headings** of **Symbolisms, Parables, Literals, Allegories, Contrasts,** and **Biblical Implications.** This is an **interesting** approach **to the study** of the **Word of God.**

SYMBOLISM

Symbolism, is the study of a thing that is **presently known** to you. It is the method of **taking** that thing and **its characteristic,** to portray a **spiritual truth.** By this method, there is no need for a **lengthy, worded presentation.** A picture is **worth a thousand words.** Therefore, symbolism **is a** process of making **complex things** to be **understood in a simple way.**

An example of **symbolistic** speech is given in **Daniel the seventh chapter.** It **is striking** to **note the dream:**

"IN THE first year of **Belshazzar king of Babylon** Daniel had a dream and visions of his head **upon his bed:** then he **wrote the dream,** *and* **told the sum of the matters.** ²Daniel spake and said, I saw in my vision by night, and, behold, the **four winds** of the heaven strove upon the **great sea."**

And **four great beasts** came up **from the sea,** diverse one from another. ⁴The first *was* like a lion, and had **eagle's wings:** I beheld till the wings thereof were plucked, and it was lifted up from the earth, and made **stand upon the feet as a man**, and a man's **heart was given to it**.

And behold another beast, a second, **like to a bear**, and it **raised up itself on one side,** and it had three ribs in the mouth of it **between the teeth of it: and they said** thus unto it, **Arise, devour much flesh.**

[6]After this I beheld, and lo another, **like a leopard**, which had upon the back of it **four wings of a fowl;** the beast had also **four heads;** and **dominion was given to it.**" (Dan. 7:1-7)

This is a speech in **symbolism**. The **Lion** is a symbolism of a **quality government** rule by **one person. A lion is a king of the beast.** So, therefore, it demonstrates that Babylon is the **Lady of Kingdoms** (Isa. 47:5). Every **fragment** of the symbolism is applicable:

The sea__Suggest the same geographical area.
The Four Winds__Diversity of the kingdoms as the four winds are.
There will be only four different Universal Kingdoms.
Strove upon the great sea___Wars and commotions of the kingdoms.
The Lion__Quality of Government.
Eagle wings__Quality of government in flight.
Standing upon feet as a man suggests the kingdom is brought to humility.

Bear__**Inferior in quality, but stronger.** Raising up itself on one side, the kingdom is **rule by two kings.** One is **more popular** than the other. The **three ribs** in the **mouth** thereof suggest **the conquering** of the first **three kingdoms,** and the episode of devouring much flesh.

The Leopard__The **Leopard suggests swiftness.** The **four wings of a fowl** denote **great speed.** The **four heads** of the beast suggests that the **kingdom will be divided** between **four different rulers** after the first king. In the speech of **symbolism,** each part must fit the explanation.

FIGURATIVE

"And if thy **right eye offend** thee, **pluck it out,** and cast if **from thee:** for it is profitable for thee that one of thy members should perish, and not *that* thy whole body should be cast into hell. [30]And if thy **right hand offend thee, cut it off,** and cast it from **thee:** for it is profitable for thee that one of thy members should perish, and not *that* thy whole body should be cast into hell." (Matt. 5:29, 30—KJV)

Figurative of speech is the art of using words of a literal speech to **teach a secondary meaning.** It is somewhat a **rhetorical** approach to the **use of words.**

In this case of scripture, the **true right eye** or **right hand,** of an individual, is more in the **rhetorical value of the right eye or hand** than in the literal meaning.

The **right eye** or **hand** is **most dearest** eye/hand than **the other**, which is considered to be the best.

Another **term** that is **often** used **is:** "And another of his disciples said unto him, Lord, suffer me first to go and bury my father. But Jesus said unto him, Follow me; and **let the dead bury their dead."** (Matt. 8:21, 22)

The **first term** dead, **hath to do with the living dead**, and the **second** term dead has to do with **dead corpses**. The father of this disciple evidently was **not yet dead** as far **as his body** was concern. The son wanted to **wait** until his farther had **deceased**, before going to preach the gospel of the kingdom. Once we **all were dead** in trespasses and sins (Eph. 2:1).

LITERAL

The literal speech of the Bible has to do with a **statement** that simply **means what it said**. In addition, it is spoken to **suggest no other point** than that **which is spoken**. For **an example: "And seeing the multitudes, he went up into a mountain**: and when he was set, his disciples came unto him:" This statement is made to show that Jesus sat up in the mountain. This does not require our thoughts to be carried away into some high elevation coinciding with Jesus' going up into a mountain. **We should not use this scripture or any other scripture to make a spiritual meaning out of that which is to be taken naturally.** Neither should we take that which was meant to be spiritual and make it literal. There is a scripture **spoken by the Apostle Peter** concerning the writing of the Apostle Paul.

"And account *that* **the longsuffering of our Lord is salvation;** even as our beloved **brother Paul** also **according to the wisdom given** unto him hath written unto you; As also in all his epistles speaking in them of these things; in which are some things **hard to be understood,** which they that are unlearned and unstable wrest, as they do also the **other scriptures**, unto their own destruction." (2 Pet. 3:15-16)

PARABLES

It is a **well-known fact** that one of **greatest method of teaching** that Jesus used, is **Parables**. The use of parables is one of the **simplest** and yet **profound** way of teaching. By this method the simplest **minded** or **unlearned** person who had not yet been **exposed to a subject**, can **immediately grasp an understanding** with parables.

The word parables can be **better understood** from the prefix **(para)**, which means to **go along side** of. From words like paragraph, which is a group of **sentences** that goes along aside each other to **support a context**. The **term** parallel, which are **two lines** that goes along side by side even though extended indefinitely.

"And he spake many things unto them in parables, saying, Behold, a **sower** went **forth to sow;** [4]And when he sowed, some *seeds* fell by the way side, and the **fowls** came and **devoured them up:** [5]Some fell upon **stony places,** where they had **not much earth:** and forthwith they **sprung up,** because they had **no deepness of earth:** [6]And when **the sun** was up, they were **scorched;** and because they **had no root,** they withered away. And some **fell among thorns;** and the **thorns sprung up,** and **choked them:** [8]But other fell into **good ground,** and brought **forth fruit,** some an **hundredfold,** some **sixty fold,** some **thirty fold.**" (Matt. 13:3-8)

All of the **elements** in this parable and **all other** parables, **pertinent** and **relevant,** and must be **considered in the explanation;** the **elements are** as follows:

1. **The Sower**——The preacher
2. **The seed**——The Word
3. **The ground**——The heart
4. **The fowls**—— The enemy
5. **The sun**——Trials
6. **The weeds**——Cares of life
7. **The fruit**——Another soul

The **effort** of the **sower** is to **cause** the **hearer** to **understand.** The **difference** in **all** of the elements can be **found** from the **contrast** of number **one** to number **seven.** Many other parables did Jesus speak; but time and space will **not allow** me to divulge upon in this **treatise.**

ALLEGORY

These Scriptures were used in such incident that **happened in history to teach** an **Allegorical lesson.** This is slightly different from a parable, which deals with **the law of a thing that does** happen. An **Allegory** deals with a **certain event that did happen.**

The scriptures states: "For it is written, that **Abraham had two sons,** the one by a **bondmaid,** the other by a **freewoman.** [23]But he *who was* of the **bondwoman was born** after **the flesh;** but he of the **freewoman** *was* by **promise.** [24]Which things are an **Allegory:** for these are the **two covenants;** the one from the **mount Sinai,** which gendereth to **bondage,** which is **Agar.**

[25]For this Agar is **mount Sinai in Arabia,** and answereth to **Jerusalem which now is,** and **is in bondage with her children.** [26]But Jerusalem, which is **above is free,** which is the **mother of us all.**" (**Gal. 4:22-26—KJV**)

This Allegory is a **well-fixed historical event** and deals with the **event that happened.** However, a parable deals with a **well-understood law,** it works the **same way each time.**

In this Allegory, **Hagar** and **Ishmael** are **slaves** or in **bondage**, while **Sarah** and **Isaac** are **free**. This allegory deals with the **rights of the freeborn**, and **no rights of** the **slave**; therefore, only the **freeborn son has the right of the Father's inheritance.**

"Wherefore she said unto Abraham, **Cast out this bondwoman and her son:** for the son of this bondwoman **shall not be heir with my son,** *even* with **Isaac.** [11]And the thing was very grievous in **Abraham's sight** because of **his son.** [12]And God said unto Abraham, Let it not be grievous in thy sight because of the lad, and because of thy **bondwoman;** in all **that Sarah** hath said unto **thee, hearken unto her voice;** for **in Isaac shall thy seed be called.**" (Gen. 21: 10-12)

The **lesson is well shown in this event**, which illustrates **the rights of the freeborn son** compared to the **slave born son.** Though Isaac is noted as being the **recipient of the promise** of the his father, Ishmael **does not**, but is rather **cast out.**

On the other hand, in the **New** Testament **Isaac is cast out.** This is done from the **same principal** of the **Old Testament reference;** where **Ishmael is cast out because** he was **a slave.** However; from this **same point, Isaac is cast out because he is a servant** and **not a freeborn son in the New Testament** setting. Only **Christ is the** ONE who has the **position of the freeborn son.** "**Now to Abraham** and **his seed were the promises made.** He saith not, and to **seeds,** as of **many;** but as **of** ONE, and to **thy seed, which is Christ.**" (Gal. 3:16)

In this scripture, **Isaac is not considered. Only Jesus Christ** can be classified in this position and **privilege.** The reason being, because **Isaac is born as a servant to sins.**

The scripture said, "**The wicked** are **estranged** from **the womb: they go astray as soon as they be born, speaking lies.**"(Ps. 58:3) Jesus **Christ was born holy** or **free from sin.** [35]"**And the angel answered and said unto her, the **Holy Ghost shall come upon** thee, and the **power of the Highest** shall **overshadow thee:** therefore also that holy thing which shall **be born of thee** shall be called the **Son of God.**" (St. Luke 1:35)

All people that are born into the world, **excepting Christ**, were **born into sin**, and is **a slave** just as much **as Ishmael.**

But more importantly, **note the following Scriptures:** "Then said Jesus to **those Jews which believed on him,** if ye **continue in my word,** *then* are ye **my disciples indeed;** [32]And ye shall **know the truth,** and the **truth shall make you free.** [33]The Jews answered him, We be Abraham's seed, and were **never in bondage to any man:** how sayest thou, Ye **shall be made free?**

Jesus answered them, verily, verily, I say unto you, whosoever **committeth sin is** the **servant of sin.** [35]And the **servant** abideth **not** in the **house forever;** *but* the **Son abideth ever.** [36]If the Son therefore shall **make you free, ye shall be free indeed.**"(St. John 8:31-38)

From the **foregoing** scriptures, **sin makes a person a servant. Ishmael** and **Hagar** were **not the focus;** but rather, they **were a lesson for allegorical reason,** so that **we** may **avoid** being in **bondage to sin.** Which will **disqualify** any **from abiding in the house forever,** or from having **everlasting life.**

"For when ye were the **servants of sin**, ye were **free from righteousness**. [21]What fruit had ye then in **those things whereof** ye are **now ashamed?** for **the end of those things is death.** [22]But now being made **free from sin**, and **become servants to God**, ye have your **fruit unto holiness**, and the **end everlasting life**. [23]For the **wages** of sin **is death;** but the gift of God is eternal life through Jesus Christ our Lord." (Rom. 6:20-23)

So, from this lesson in **Allegorical study**, the **focal point is that whosoever is born** in **sin is** the **servant** of sin, and CANNOT have everlasting life. He that **doeth righteousness is righteous,** even as he is righteous." (1 John 3:7)

The **things** that **happen** in the preceding **Allegory**, and with many others were not that God wanted to give any **ill will;** but more so, to teach **a lesson** on **election** and **grace**.

The scripture said, "What if God, **willing to shew** *his* **wrath**, and **to make** his **power known**, endured with much longsuffering the vessels of wrath fitted to **destruction:** [23]And that he might make known **the riches of his glory** on the **vessels** of **mercy**, which he had **afore prepared unto glory**, [24]Even us, **whom he hath called**, not of the **Jews only**, but also of the **Gentiles?**" (Rom. 9:22-24)

BIBLICAL CONTRASTS

To study Biblical Contrasts, is **an effort** to look at a **subliminal** message. The message that doesn't catch the **conscious eye**, or the **attended ear;** is a message to the **subconscious mind**. To see this, one would have to be **tapped** on the shoulder, and be asked to **take a second look**.

Biblical Contrasts are to be found in scripture such as this: **"Annas** and **Caiaphas** being the **high priests,** the **Word of God** came unto **John** the son of **Zacharias** in the **wilderness."** (St. Luke 3:2)

Annas and **Caiaphas** are contrasted with **John the Baptist**. The **subliminal** message is this: Inasmuch as **Annas** and **Caiaphas** are priests, the **Word of God should have been with them**. But rather, it came to **John in the wilderness**.

The scripture said, "For the **priest's lips should keep knowledge**, and they should **seek the law at his mouth:** for he is the messenger of the Lord of hosts. But ye are **departed out of the way;** ye have **caused many to stumble at the law;** ye have **corrupted** the **covenant of Levi**, saith the Lord of hosts." (Mal. 2:7-8–KJV)

This is **the reason John was sent**, and given the **Word of the Lord**, because they had **abandon the Word of God**.

"There is another that beareth **witness of me;** and I know that the **witness which he witnesseth of me is true.** [33]Ye sent unto John, and he bare witness unto the truth. [34]But I receive **not testimony from man:** but these things I say, that ye **might be saved...** [38]And ye **have not** his **Word abiding in you:** for whom he hath sent, him ye **believe not."**(St. John 5:32-38). In another place, **Biblical Contrasts** are shown as it **relates** to **both King Saul**, and **King David**, which are as follows:

NOW THERE was a man of **Benjamin**, whose name *was* **Kish**, the son of **Abiel**, the son of **Zeror**, the son of **Bechorath**, the son of Aphiah, a **Benjamite**, a **mighty man of power.** ²And he had a son, whose name *was* **Saul**, a choice young man, and a **goodly:** and *there was* not among the children of Israel a **goodlier person than he:** from his shoulders and upward *he was* **higher than any of the people**. ³And the asses of **Kish Saul's father** were lost. And Kish said to Saul his son, **Take** now **one** of the **servants with thee,** and **arise,** go seek the asses." (1 Samuel 9:1-3)

These scriptures are **contrasted** with the scriptures which **relates to David** noted as the following: ¹¹"And **Samuel** said unto **Jesse, Are here all thy children?** And he said, There remaineth **yet the youngest**, and, behold, he **keepeth the sheep.** And Samuel said unto Jesse, **Send and fetch him:** for we will not sit down till he come hither. ¹²And he sent, and brought him in. Now he *was* **ruddy,** and withal of a **beautiful countenance**, and goodly to look to. And the Lord said, Arise, **anoint him:** for this is he." (1 Samuel 16:11-12)

From the foregoing scriptures, there is a **contrast** between **Saul** and **David**. The scripture said that **Saul sought after mules** while **David tended Sheep.**

The scripture also said, "**Be** ye **not** as **the horse,** *or* as **the mule, which** have **no understanding:** whose **mouth must** be held in with **bit** and **bridle**, lest they come near unto thee." (Ps. 32:9)

The **contrast is; Saul** was **associated with mules**, and he was as **the Mule.** For he was **stubborn** and **rebellious.**

"And Samuel said, Hath the Lord *as great* delight in **burnt offerings** and **sacrifices,** as in **obeying the voice of the Lord?** Behold, **to obey is better than sacrifice,** *and* to **hearken than the fat of rams.** ²³For rebellion is as the sin of **witchcraft**, and **stubbornness** is as **iniquity** and **idolatry.** Because thou **hast rejected** the **word of the LORD**, he hath also rejected thee from *being* king." (1 Sam. 15:22, 23)

Saul had **developed a mule type mentality.** His **association** with mules demonstrated his **eventful characteristic.** He ended up being rebellious and stubborn as a mule. And therefore, God rejected him. **Saul was the people's choice.** They asked for **a king** like **other nations.** Hence, the name **Saul** means **"Asked for".** God said, "I gave thee a king **in mine anger,** and took him **away in my wrath.**" (Hos. 13:11)

The **people rejected God from being their king**, and God gave them a king whom he later rejected. (1Sam. 8:1-7, 16:1) David is **contrasted** with Saul, in the point that David is **associated with sheep.** He **tended his father's sheep** while **Saul followed** his **father's mule.** Mules have to be driven while **sheep must be led.**

David was not ask for as Saul was, **he was sent for. His family rejected** him when Samuel came to **select a king.** He had been **sent away to tend the flock** while his older brothers stayed at home **to be selected to be king.** David was **not man's choice,** but rather **God's choice.** The scripture said: And afterward they **desired a king:** and God gave unto them **Saul the son of Cis,** a man of the **tribe of Benjamin,** by the space of **forty years.** And when he had removed him, he raised up unto them **David to be their king;** to whom also he gave testimony, and said, "**I have found**

David the son of Jesse, **a man after mine own heart**, which shall **fulfill all my will**." (Acts 13:21-23)

David's **character was as a sheep**. A sheep is **very humble and meek**, and is easily led. David **walked in front** of his father's **sheep**, while **Saul had to run after his** father's **mules**. From this we can see the **lesson of contrasts** between **David** and **Saul**.

This is seen in many other passages of the scriptures. **Adam is contrasted** with **Christ** and was of the **earth earthy** while **Jesus was of the heaven**.

The **children of Israel desire for earthly** foods such as; **melons, cucumbers, garlic**, onion, **leeks**, etc. They ate this food **when they were slaves** or desired **earthly things**. These earthly things are **associated with Egypt**." (Num. 11)

But the manna, which **came from heaven**, they **did not desire** it. This was food **sent by God**, when they **were freed**. This was **angels' food** (Psalms 78:23, 24, 25).

The **carnal minded** person seeks after **the things of the world** from which he came out as Israel sought after the things of Egypt from which they came out. The law that came from **Mt. Sinai accepted by man**, which did **enslaved** them; but **the grace** from **heaven was rejected**, which **did free them** (Gal. 4).

It appears that **those things that associates with our bondage**, we **desire** them, rather than the things that **associates with our freedom**. From this you see there are many contrasts.

BIBLICAL IMPLICATION

The term Biblical Implication, is **another aspect** where the **speech of God is silently spoken**. There must be **an effort put forth beyond the common sense** to **observe** and **hear**.

The word Implication is so used in the sense that there is something said that must **be read** or **reasoned within** the statement made.

Let's consider **Genesis 2:16—KJV,** When **God made man** and **placed him in the garden, God said** unto **him:** [16]"And the **Lord God** commanded the man, saying, Of every tree of the garden thou mayest **freely eat:** [17]But of **the tree of the knowledge of good** and **evil**, thou **shalt not eat** of it: for in the day that thou eatest thereof **thou shalt surely die**."

Here is the point of **Implication:** Inasmuch as God said that man can eat of every tree of the **garden;** however, **he restricted him eating from only one tree**, which was the tree of the **knowledge of good and evil**. But **by implication**, he wanted **man to eat of the tree of life.** However, **God did not directly tell him to go quickly and take of the tree of life, and live forever!** But it is implied.

In fact, **both of these trees are placed side by side in the garden**. Both the **tree of life** and **the tree** of the **knowledge of good** and **evil** are said to be **in the midst** of the **garden** (Gen. 2:9; 3:3).

The above-mentioned trees are there to **test the obedience of man.** Just as the **law was placed before Israel:** "See, **I have set** before thee this day **life and good,** and **death and evil,**" (Deu. 30:15, 19) As **grace,** which **is placed before us,** has given us **a choice of life** (Rom. 10:1-11).

"This is also done **in the privileges given** to us in the **implications suggested in faith.** Wherein anything that **pertain to life** and **godliness** are implied in the scriptures which **said: "All things are possible to him that beliveth"** (Mark 9:23), As in the scripture **which said:** "And we know that **all things work together for good to them** that **love God,** to them **who are the called according to his purpose."** (Rom. 8:28; 2 Pet. 1:3)

To **test** the **obedience of man** and his **volunteer service** to him, God implemented this test in the garden. God wants our **obedience** and worship **to originate** from **both a willing mind** and **a willing heart.** The **scripture said: "If ye be willing and obedient,** ye shall **eat the good** of the land." **(Isa. 1:19)**

The **desire of God was that man would go quickly to the tree of life, and eat,** and live forever. But he **could not forcefully tell him that,** or else **he would not be made** in the **likeness of God.** Man **had been made in God's Image,** but **not yet in his likeness.** The **purpose of God** was to make man **in his Image** and **in his likeness.** To be in the likeness of God, **man would have to eat of the tree of life, voluntarily.**

Since **Adam** and Eve **did not willingly take of the Tree of Life,** God now forcibly **forbids them from eating thereof.**

"And the Lord God said, **Behold,** the **man is become as one of us,** to know **good** and **evil:** and now, **lest he put forth his hand, and take also of the tree of life, and eat,** and **live for ever:** [23]Therefore the Lord God sent him **forth from the garden of Eden,** to till the ground from whence he was taken." (Gen. 3:22, 23)

From the foregoing verses, **God strictly forbids man from eating of the tree of life,** because he **had eaten of the tree of death. The tree of life is pointed** rather than the rest of the trees. But by **biblical implication,** God pointedly wanted man to take of the tree of life so that he could live forever.

In contrast, the eating of the tree of the **knowledge of good** and **evil restricts** you to **only one** tree. But **man was given the privilege to eat of many trees** of the garden except **one.** This **shows that God wants us to have life and that more abundantly.** But Satan has **one thing** to offer that **is death.** Or dying ye shall die! **Life comes from a free choice** rather than **a forced obedience.** Satan **forcefully persuaded Eve** by **deception.**

Now there was a **battle stage set** before God and Satan. Satan in his **fallen state,** wanted also to **bring man down.** He rushes to Eve, and uses forceful **rhetoric** and **deception** to cause **Eve to obey his voice.** For you know, Satan **speaks loud!** and forceful; for he has **"...a mouth speaking great things,"** (Dan. 7:8)

But many times God speak with a **still small voice** (Isa. 19:11-13). As another scripture said: **"Give ear, O ye heavens, and I will speak; and hear, O earth,** the **words of my mouth. My doctrine shall drop as the rain,** my speech shall distil as the dew, as the small rain upon the tender herb, and as the showers upon **the grass: Because I will publish the name of the Lord:** ascribe ye greatness unto our God." (Deu. 32:1-3)

But his **speech can be forceful! loud! And strong!** "For ye are not come unto the mount that might be touched, and that burned with fire, nor unto blackness, and **darkness,** and tempest, and **the sound of a trumpet,** and the **voice of words;** which voice they that heard entreated that the word should not be **spoken to them any more:.** and **so terrible was the sight, that Moses said, I exceedingly fear and quake:**"(Heb. 12:19, 21)

Adam heard that **judgment voice** coming **walking** in the **garden.** ⁸ "**And they heard the voice** of the **Lord God walking** in the **garden** in the **cool of the day:** and **Adam** and his **wife hid themselves** from the **presence** of the **Lord God amongst the trees** of the **garden.** ⁹And the Lord God **called unto Adam,** and said unto him, **where art thou?** ¹⁰**And he said, I heard thy voice in the garden,** and **I was afraid,** because **I was naked;** and I hid myself." (Gen. 3:8-10—KJV)

It is true that, "**GOD, WHO at sundry times** and **in divers manners** have **spake in time pass** unto the **fathers by the prophets, Hath in these last days spoken unto us by** *his* **Son, whom he hath appointed heir of all things, by whom also he made the worlds;** (Heb. 1:1-2) But when He wants to implicate, "**He shall not cry nor lift up,** nor **cause his voice to be heard** in the **street.**" (Isa. 42:2)

Another **episode of Biblical Implication,** is found in the case of God's dealing with **Abram and Sarai.**

"**Now THE Lord had said unto Abram,** get thee **out of thy country,** and from thy kindred, and **from thy father's house,** unto **a land that I will show thee:** ²And I will make of **thee a great nation, and I will bless thee, and make thy name great;** and thou shalt be a **blessing:** ³And **I will bless them that bless thee,** and curse him that **curseth thee:** and in thee shall **all families of the earth be blessed.**" (Gen. 12:1-3)

And behold, the word of the Lord *came* **unto him, saying, this shall not be thine heir;** but he that shall come forth out of **thine own bowels shall be thine heir.**" (Gen. 15:4)

God having said all this made a promise to Abram that out of his seed shall all the families of the earth be blessed. It **is not plainly said in words** that **through Sarai** was to be the **fulfillment of the promise.**

But Sarai was barren and had never given to Abram a child. Now Sarai and Abram **thought** that God was not going to **bless the seed to come through Sarai.** "**And Sarai said unto Abram Behold now,** the Lord hath restrained me from bearing:

I pray thee, go in unto **my maid;** it may be that I may obtain children by her. And Abram **hearkened to the voice of Sarai.** And Sarai Abram's wife **took Hagar her maid the Egyptian,** after Abram had dwelt **ten years** in the land of Canaan, and **gave her to her husband Abram to be his wife.**" (Gen. 16:2-3—KJV)

From this you see **whenever God speaks**, there are always **another voice**, which **speaks contrary** to that which **God had said**. Sarah now speaks to Abram and give her **opinion**. **"This is what Satan does to Eve."**

He gives his opinion as to what God hath said. And through **Eve's weakness** she **yields** to the **voice of Satan**, than what God hath said, because **she did not understand biblical implications.**

Now in this case with Sarai and Abram, being **influenced possibly** by Satan, **did not** understand **biblical implications**. She gives Abram **a voice of consent** to take her handmaid **to be his wife.**

This was **not** the plan of God. God **intended** for **Sarai** to **have a Son**. It is **interesting** to **note God's** original plan: just as soon as Abram and Sarai's child **Ishmael** were circumcised in the **sixteenth chapter of Genesis,** God **Appeared** unto **Abram** in the **seventeenth chapter** and **changed** the **name** of **Abram** and his **wife Sarai** to the names of **Abraham** and **Sarah**. Both increased because of the **multitude** of **children** coming from them.

This was a shock to **Abraham** and **Sarah** when God told them that they were going to have a **Child by one another.**

It **is striking to note God's Blessing:** "And **God** said unto **Abraham, As** for **Sarai thy wife,** thou shalt not call her name **Sarai,** but **Sarah shall** her name be. And I will **bless her,** and **give** thee **a son** also **of her:** yea, I will bless her, and she shall be a **mother of nations;** kings of people shall be of her. Then **Abraham fell** upon **his face,** and **laughed,** and said **in his heart,** shall a child be born unto him that **is an hundred years old?** And shall Sarah, that is **ninety** years old, **bear?** (Gen. 17:15-17)

From this **we see that God had implied** that a **Child should be born to Abraham through Sarah** and not through **Hagar.**

Because **Abraham** and **Sarah did not understand Biblical Implications,** a great affliction against the true natural seed of Abraham had occurred and is continued unto this day. **When Sarah saw** the Son of **Hagar mocking her son, this was the beginning of the affliction of Israel.** And requested that Abraham cast out the son by this **bondwoman.** But when Abraham hesitated in doing that, God said to him hearken to the **voice of thy wife,** "For **in Isaac Shall thy seed be called."**

If we don't **hear the voice of God in biblical implications,** we will **suffer many** consequences that we would **not otherwise** suffer. Yet, on the other hand, **if we do** understand **biblical implications,** what **great benefits** we would reap **beyond what other have ever dreamed.**

In studying the Bible, we must **find out who is talking, to whom he is talking to,** and **what he is talking about.** There are several covenants in the Bible. That is, something **made to a specific person, nation** or **class of people.**

THY WORD IS TRUTH
QUESTIONS AND ANSWERS

1. **WHAT IS THE BIBLE?**

The Bible is the written **Word of God**. The term Bible comes from the Greek word Biblus__meaning **The Book.**

2. **HOW WAS THE BIBLE WRITTEN?**

Holy Men chosen and inspired by God wrote the Bible. "Knowing this first, that **no prophecy** of the scripture is of any **private interpretation**. For the prophecy came **not in old time by the will of man:** but **holy men of God** spake *as they were* **moved by the Holy Ghost.**" (2 Pet. 1:20, 21—KJV)

"All scripture is given by inspiration of God, and is profitable for doctrine, for reproof, for correction, for instruction **in righteousness;** That the man of God may be perfect, thoroughly furnished unto all good works." (2 Tim. 3:16)

3. **SHOULD WE USE THE OLD TESTAMENT AS WELL AS THE NEW TESTAMENT TO TEACH DOCTRINE? YES.**

"This second epistle, beloved, I now write unto you: in both which I stir up your pure minds by **way of remembrance:** That ye may be mindful of the words which were spoken before by the Holy prophets, and of the commandment of us the apostles of the Lord and Savior." (2 Pet. 3:1, 2) "For whatsoever things were **written aforetime** were written for **our learning,** that we **through patience** and **comfort of the scriptures** might have hope." Rom. 15:4; 2 Tim. 3:15-17; 1 Cor. 10:1-11)

4. **HOW SHOULD WE STUDY THE BIBLE?**

"Study to **show thyself approved unto God**, a workman that needeth not to be ashamed, **rightly dividing** the word of truth." (2 Tim. 2:15)

5. **WHAT SHOULD WE STUDY IN THE BIBLE?**

"**Seek** ye out the **book of the Lord,** and **read:** no one of these shall fail, none shall **want her mate:** for my mouth it hath commanded, and **his Spirit** it hath **gathered them.**" (Isa. 34:16) This means we must study the entire Bible.

6. **WHEN WOULD WE BE ABLE TO BEGIN UNDERSTANDING THE BIBLE?**

"Whom shall he teach knowledge? and whom shall he make to understand doctrine? Them that are **weaned from the milk, and drawn from the breasts.** For precept must be upon precept, **precept upon precept**; line upon line, **line upon line**; here a little, and **there a little:**" (Isa. 28:9, 10)

"Of whom we have many things to say, and hard to be uttered, seeing **ye are dull of hearing.** For when for the time ye **ought to be teachers**, ye have **need that one teach you again** which be the **first principles** of the **oracles of God:** and are become such as have **need of milk, and not of strong meat.** For every one that **useth milk is unskillful** in the **work of righteousness:** for he is a babe. But **strong meat belongeth to them that are of full age**, even those who **by reason of use have their senses exercised to discern** both good and evil." (Heb. 5:11-14)

7. Is God's Word True? Yes.

In St. John 18:38 "Pilate saith unto him, What is truth?..." St. John 17:17 "**Sanctify** them through thy **truth:** thy **word is truth.**" [5] "**Every Word of God is pure:** he is a **shield unto them that put their trust** in him. **Add** thou not unto **his words**, lest he **reprove thee**, and thou be **found a liar.**" (Prov. 30:5, 6)

"For what if some **did not** believe? shall their **unbelief make the faith of God** without **effect?** God **forbid:** yea, **let God be true,** but **every man a liar;** as it is written, That thou mightiest be justified in thy sayings, and mightiest overcome when thou art judged." (Rom. 3:3, 4; Num. 23:19; 1 Sam. 15:29)

THE PREACHING OF THE WORD

8. What Is Preaching?

Preaching is the expounding the **Word of God.**

9. Can Anyone Take Upon Himself To Preach? No.

"And how shall they preach, **except they be sent.**" (Rom. 10:15) "I have not sent these prophets, **yet they ran: I** have **not spoken to them**, yet they **prophesied.**" (Jer. 23:21) "To **the law** and to the **testimony:** if they **speak not according to this word**, it is because there **is no light in them.**" (Isa. 8:20)

"For **He whom God hath sent speaketh the words of God:** for God giveth not the Spirit by **measure** unto him." (St. John 3:34; Matt. 7:15; 2 Pet. 2:1, 2; Deut. 18:18-22; Jer. 23:25-31; 2 Cor. 11:13-15; Rom. 16:17, 18; 1 John 4:1-3; 2 John 8-10)

"If any man **will do his will**, he shall know of the **doctrine**, whether it be of God or whether I speak of myself." (St. John 7:17)

RIGHTLY DIVIDING THE WORD

10. IS IT POSSIBLE TO MISUNDERSTAND THE SCRIPTURES? YES.

"And Philip ran thither to him, and heard him read the prophet Isaiah, and said, Understandest thou what thou readest? And he said, How can I, except some man should guide me? And he desired **Philip** that he would come up and sit with him. And the **eunuch** answered Philip, and said, I pray thee, of whom speaketh the prophet this? of him himself, or of some other man**?"** (Acts 8:30, 31, and 34)

"Jesus answered and said unto them, Ye **do err**, not knowing **the scriptures**, nor the **power of God**." (Matt. 22:29) As also in all his epistles, speaking in them of these things; in which are some things **hard to be understood**, which they that are **unlearned** and **unstable wrest**, as they do also the other scriptures, unto their own destruction." (2 Pet. 3:16)

11. WHAT THINGS SHOULD WE AVOID IN STUDYING THE WORD OF GOD?

There are **Four** things such as:

1. Mis-interpretation
2. Mis-application
3. Mis-quotation and,
4. Dis-location.

12. WHAT SHOULD WE LEARN ABOUT ANY SCRIPTURE?

We should **learn** the following **information such as: Who is talking? Who is it talking to? And, What is it talking about**?

For instance, in **Acts 2:25-36**, we're **not talking about David**, but of **Jesus Christ**. Read, and **see another example**, which is found in **St. John 8:19**, "Then said they unto him, **Where is thy Father**? Jesus answered, Ye neither **know me**, nor **my Father:** if ye had **known me,** ye should **have known my Father also.** I said therefore unto you, that ye shall **die in your sins:** for if ye believe not that **I am he**, ye shall **die in your sins**. They understood not that he spake to them of **the Father**." (St. John 8:19, 24, 27; 10:22-30; Matt. 11:25-27; St. John 14:1-11)

BIBLE COVENANTS

The study of **Bible Covenants is very important** so that we may know who the bible is talking to or about. This would **help us to avoid mis-application** of the Word of God. There are **eight covenants**, which we would like to take under consideration in this study. The **eight** outstanding covenants are as follows:

1) Edenic (Gen. 2:16)
2) Adamic (Gen. 3:15)
3) Noahic (Gen. 9:16)
4) Abrahamic (Gen. 12:2)
5) Palestinian (Gen. 17:18; Deut. 30:1-10)
6) Mosaic (Ex. 12:5).
7) Davidic (2 Sam. 7:12).
8) The New Covenant (Jer. 31:31, Heb. 8:8).

Out of the **eight covenants**, there are three **universal** or general **covenants** and they are as follows:

1. **Edenic** - All people were represented in the fall with Adam.
2. **The Adamic** - This shows that the penalty of sin passed on to all mankind.
3. **Noahic** - God makes a promise that the waters will never become a flood to destroy all flesh again. All the **rest of the Covenants** are primarily unto **Israel** and the **Israelites,** also with far reaching blessings on the Gentiles. We shall examine each of the **eight** covenants at this time as follows:

THREE GENERAL COVENANTS

I. THE EDENIC COVENANT (Gen. 1:28; 2:15, 16—KJV)

1. Adam is to propagate the earth.
2. To subdue the earth for man.
3. To have dominion over all living things.
4. To care for the garden of Eden.
5. To abstain from eating of the tree of the knowledge of Good and Evil, with the penalty of death if he disobeyed it.

II. THE ADAMIC COVENANT (GEN. 3:14-19 - - - KJV).

1. The serpent, Satan's instrument, is cursed. (**v. 14**).
2. The promise of a Redeemer (**v. 15**).
3. The change of the state of the woman.
   a. Multiplied conception.
   b. Sorrow (pain) in motherhood.

c. The man shall rule over her.
4. He was to have sorrow in life. (vv. 17).
5. The sorrowful penalty of death. (vv. 18, 19).
6. He became burdened with the job of tilling He soil (vv. 18, 19).

III. The Noahic Covenant (Gen. 9:15, 16—KJV)

A. This covenant set up Human Government.

1. Whoso sheddeth man's blood, by man shall his blood be shed (Gen. 9:5, 6).
2. No additional curse is placed upon man at this time, neither will God destroy the earth with a flood again (Gen. 8:21).
3. While the earth remaineth, seedtime and harvest, cold and heat, summer and winter, and day and night shall not cease (Gen. 8:22).
4. Man can eat flesh in his diet (Gen. 9:3, 4).
5. Canaan, the son of Cush, will be a servant to the sons of Shem and Japheth (Gen. 9:25).

SPECIFIC UNCONDITIONAL COVENANTS

IV. Abrahamic Covenant (Gen. 12:2)

A. To Abraham and his seed:

1. The promise of a great nation "I will make thee a great nation" (Gen. 12:2).
2. Four personal promises to Abraham:
   a. A father of many nations (Gen. 17:16).
   b. I will bless thee (Gen. 13:14, 15, 17; Gen. 15:6; John 8:56).
   c. Make thy name great (Gen. 12:2).
   d. Thou shalt be a blessing (Rom. 4:1-22; Gal.3:16).
3. Promise to the Gentiles I will bless them that bless thee and curse them that curseth thee (Gen. 12:3).

V. Palestinian Covenant (Gen. 17:8; Deut. 30:1-10—KJV)

1. Through Abraham, Isaac, and Jacob.
2. The land of Palestine is promised to Israel for an everlasting possession or homeland (Gen. 13: 16).
3. There have been three dispossessions from the land. This shows that Israel has not yet possessed the land in the fullness of the unconditional covenant.

a. They left Canaan and went into Egypt for 215 years (Gen.15:13, 14).
b. They went into captivity in Babylon for seventy years (Jer.25:11; 27:22).
c. The final and worldwide disbursement in A.D. 70 (Deut. 28:63-67).
4. They will be restored, never to go out again (Amos 9:14, 15; Acts 15:16-18).

VI. Mosaic Covenant (Parenthetical Conditional Covenant)

1. Royal Law (Ex. 20:1-26)
2. Civil Law (Ex. 21:1-24)
3. Ceremonial Law (Ex. 24:12-18)

VII. Davidic Covenant (2 Sam. 7:16–KJV)

1. A house (dynasty), a kingdom, and a Throne forever (2 Sam. 7:8-17).

VIII New Covenant (Jer. 31:31; Heb. 8:8)

A. Last Unconditional Covenant

1. Better than the Mosaic Covenant (Heb. 7:19).
2. Better promises. The Mosaic Covenant said: "If you will" (Ex. 12:5).
   a. The New Covenant said: "I will" (Heb. 8:8, 10, 12).
3. It gets rid of sin and brings in everlasting righteousness and life (St. John 3:16; Heb 9:13, 14)

   things were **written aforetime were written for our learning**, that we through patience and **comfort of the scriptures might have hope**." (Rom. 15:4; 2 Tim. 3:15-17; 1 Cor. 10:1-11)

Seven Feasts Of The Lord
Compared With
The Seven Days Of Creation

CREATE- To create means to **bring into existence** something that was not in existence before. There is a difference in the words create and form. The word "**FORM**" means the **shape and structure of anything** as distinguished from the material of which it is composed; particular disposition or **arrangement of matter:** giving it individuality or distinctive character. For **example:** *The earth was without form and void.*

EARTH- The globe or planet that we inhabit is the fifth in order of size and third in order of distance from the sun. The earth on which we live is a planet. It is one of a family of nine planets, which, with many smaller heavenly bodies, travel around our sun. Our earth is a tiny speck compared with the whole universe, which consists of millions of stars. Some of these stars are millions times larger than our planet. Symbol = 4. At the poles, the earth's diameter is 7,899.74 miles. The diameter at the equator is 7,926.56 miles. The **earth rotates to bring our night**, and **revolves around the sun to bring our year**.

It travels around its orbit at a speed of nearly 67,000 miles per hour. The earth rotates on its axis about once every 24 hours. The exact time is 23 hours, 56 minutes, 4.1 seconds. It dashes along this orbit at nearly 19 miles a second and completes its trip around the sun in 365 days, 6 hours, 9 minutes, and 9.54 seconds. The earth is about 93,000,000 miles from the sun. Little is known about the earth's interior, but it must be very dense, since its density as a whole is 5.6, and also very hot, since the temperature increases regularly (as far as man has been able to penetrate), at a mean rate of about 1° F. for every 53 feet. If this rate holds steady through to the center of the earth, then the temperature is approximately 39,484.52 degrees Fahrenheit HOT! In the depth center of the earth.

HEAVEN- The heaven is the firmament above the earth. Though we must understand that there are planets above and below the earth in the same solar system. The **Bible speaks** of **three** heavens as follows:

(1) The heaven where the clouds are, or the heaven where the **fowls fly,** (Psa. 104:12).
(2) The heaven where the **stars** are, (Rev. 6:13).
(3) The heaven where the **righteous dead** goes, or the paradise of God (2 Cor. 12:2). These must be understood in a concentric surroundings/envelops, as we move to areas above the heavens. God's glory is always considered as being above the heavens. **Psalm 50:4 (KJV)**
⁴ He shall call **to the heavens from above,** and to the earth, that he may judge his people.

THE CREATION

The Bible did not start with a **philosophical argument** of the **existence of God.** It simply **said: "In the beginning God created the heaven and the earth."** The **evolutionist strives to ignore, or disprove the existence of God in their creative story.** They **theorize the existence** of **all things** by saying that things just **spontaneously sprung into existence without any direct, or indirect act of a Creator.**

They claim that **all life** came from **one species**. If that **was true**, my **argument** with them **would be this:** (In the **proof of the existence of a Creator**), where did this **ONE** species come from? There is **one fact we all must witness** to, we came from **somewhere**. Then if we came from somewhere, that thing, or **force had to have life** to **produce life**. That something would have the **ability, or wisdom to fashion its offspring's** in the **shape of which it is**, and to place it in the boundaries where **it now resides.**

This something, which brought this thing **into existence**, would be **superior** to the thing which was brought **into existence**. As **the potter is greater than the clay;** and has **power over it;** so is the something that brought the thing **into existence**. Therefore, this something would be **superior** to the thing that was brought into existence. By being in existence, it **automatically reserves the right of self-existence**. The thing that was brought into existence would automatically, without any alternative, accept the position of dependent existence. Therefore, the something that brought the thing into existence would be called the **CREATOR**, and the thing that **was brought into existence** would be called **CREATURE**. Then with this process and **relationship**, the creator would **be God over the creature** or creation.

Then some would say; "Where did **God come from?** And if He came from something; where did this something come from?" It **would be useless** to **ask questions** from this **perspective,** and **unnecessary for me to answer** them, because the something that brought the **thing into existence would be the very God** I am talking about. It would be like trying to **sail around the world:** you would always end where you started. So, we **conclude that there is a God in existence upon the evidence of the things that do appear.** (Rom. 1:19-21).

Now we shall deal with the **creative story from the book of Genesis**. The Bible said, "In the beginning God **created** the heaven and earth." (Gen. 1: 1) When the earth was created, it was **without form, or shape, and it was void**. From this, it appears to me, that the earth was a mass of matter mixed with water that could be shaped into a form, or figure. It is **evident that the earth did not have any distinct individuality**, because it was without form or a particular shape. In Psalm 95:5, the Bible **said:** "The **sea is his**, and he **made it:** and his **hands formed the dry land.**" In Isaiah 45:18 **states:** "For thus saith the Lord **that created the heavens; God himself that formed the earth and made it; he hath established it,** he created it not in vain, he **formed it to be inhabited:** I am the LORD; and **there is none else.**

In this scripture, we have the words **created** and **formed**. There is a **difference** in the word **create** and **form**. Create means to **bring into existence** things that were not in existence before. The word **form** means **to shape the matter that has been brought into existence**. As we would say, God **created** and **formed the earth**. It appears that the earth was once a hot mass of matter like lava from a volcanic eruption (Job 28:5). But as the water began to cool the matter, it began to **solidify** into the shape of God's forming.

The process of these creative acts were **revealed unto Moses** and the children of Israel. According to Psalm 103:7, "He made **known his ways unto Moses**, his acts unto the children of Israel."

It is my conviction that God made His ways and acts of creation known unto Moses and the children of Israel in the Seven Feasts Of The Lord. I shall list these feast in order and **compare them with the creative acts of each day** of creation.

Exposition On The Days Of Creation

In the book of Genesis, we have the law of the **first mentioning of things**, which is a very **good observation**. For in it is revealed a great deal of information.

For **an example:** the **first mentioning of light is in separating it from darkness**. This establishes a **divine principle that light and darkness must always be separated**. Hence, **this scripture:** "Be ye **not unequally yoked together with unbelievers:** for **what fellowship hath righteousness with unrighteousness? And what communion hath light** with **darkness?** (2 Cor. 6:14) Whatever God has separated must not be joined together.

Now, here is another **interesting** thing **in the law of the first mentioning of things:** The first time we read about **the Spirit of God**, it is **associated with water**. "And the earth was **without form**, and **void;** and **darkness was upon the face of the deep".** And the **Spirit of God moved upon the face of the waters."** (Gen. 1:2)

This within itself **establishes the fact** that the Spirit of God should be understood with or by the **metaphor** of **water**. And that sense is demonstrated throughout the scriptures. Hence, **Joel speaking** about the **Spirit of God;** "And it shall come to pass afterward, that **I will pour out my Spirit upon** all flesh;" See **Joel's reference of the outpouring of Spirit as water is poured out.**

"In **the last day**, that **great day of the feast**, Jesus stood and cried, saying, If any man **thirst**, *(a metaphor associated with water)* **let him come unto me, and drink.** *(a metaphor associated with water)*, He that believeth on me, as the scripture hath said, **out of his belly shall flow rivers of living water.** (But this spake he of the **Spirit**, which they that believe on him **should receive:** for the Holy Ghost was not yet **given;** because that **Jesus was not yet glorified**). (St. John 7: 37-39) In this the **Spirit is referred to as water.** *(A metaphor associated with The Spirit).*

Paul said; "For by One **Spirit** are we **all baptized,** *(A metaphor which alludes to water)* **into** one body, whether we be **Jews or Gentiles**, whether be **bond or free;** and have been made to drink into One Spirit."(1 Cor. 12:13)

The phenomenon goes on and on. Wherever there is **mention of Spirit, water** must be **associated**. Hence "**Born of water** and **Spirit**" (St. John 3:5). "Can any man forbid water, that these should not be baptized, which have **received** the **Holy Ghost as well as we."** (Acts 10: 47; 8: 12-17; 2:38, 39).

This is **a law embedded** in the scripture that the **translators did not know** about. This is a **Bible inside of the Bible**. A **built in protection of the guardian of the truth,** which will correct **all texts** and **contexts** that are given as **wrong interpretations.** So, it is in reference to **all scriptures,** and the scriptures **warns us against taking a scripture text out of the context, or out of the bible itself.** And to make an effort to keep it for some private interpretation or pet doctrine used to support some denominational dogma.

NUMBERS IN CREATION

The next point to **observe is to take a look at the numerical value** reiterated **after each day** of function.

The number One being the **first number mentioned,** suggests the beginning, or that which has to do with **absoluteness.** Number **one is an absolute number.** It doesn't need **any other number to exist.** It exists **alone.** All succeeding numbers need the added or multiple value of one. The number two needs two ones to exist, three needs three, five needs five ones. But one is absolute. It doesn't need any other number to exist. It exists alone. This represents the absoluteness of everything that came from God, and **cannot exist without Him.** God is **self-existence** and needs no one or nothing to exist. He is self-existent, **Omnipotent, Omniscience, Omnipresent, and Infinite.** Number **one** represents **divinity.** "For I am the Lord thy God, the Holy **One** of Israel, thy Saviour..." (Isa. 43:3). We cannot get rid of the numerical value of one. For all other numbers are equal to one. If we talk about two: Two represents one for two one thing is present at same place at the same time. Two then becomes the common denominator. (One and same group) We must also understand that where ever there is a common denominator, there is a common numerator which designates or numerates how many of the same thing is present at the same place. The term two suggests that two things shares the same place, same thing, at the same time and the same number which is one. But one is only there twice. This suggested in the numerator. If the common denominator separate in the common numerator the union becomes divided in the numerator and denominator. The division is shown in the numerator and the union is the denominator:

Both expresses the same thing.

The denominator is the divisor which determines the future reunion that will be added in the numerator. If for an example that one of the two leaves the place of the common thing, the common denominator become divided in both the denominator and the numerator and both become separate halves. (1/2, 1/2) The commonality is always seem in the denominator which denotes that the one is divided into two halves. There is no such thing as the number two: Which only suggests that one is divided into two parts. Therefore when the separated halves are added in the number

½ plus ½ and becomes 2/2: which two divided by two equals one. This shows that all numbers if considered are equal to one; for 100 means that the same thing, (0ne), has been divided into a hundred pieces, 100/100 equals 1, one thing, one group, or one person, etc.

This is a very important notation, or phenomenon to understand in solving problems, searches, and researches. For in the sense of vitamins for total health: Just suppose that vitamins ABCDE are needed for a total healthy diet, and vitamin D is left out of the diet there is a deficiency of the common denominator for the common numerator denotes that the only vitamins in the diet of the denominations ABCDE are ABCE, for D is missing. So the imperfect formula is ABCE/ABCDE but when D is added into the diet it is complete and thus; D plus ABCE/ABCDE equals ABCDE/ABCDE and when divided into one another; (*or put into another*), the result is a healthy, wholesome diet, and the patient is made well/whole.

In the area of Research one may envision that an equation is not balanced by a negative or needed disposition. Meaning that if something does not work, some search/invention is needy because of a necessity. So a common need require a common numerical solution. The common denominator is seen in the need. While the common numerator is not seen. The search is begun to find the numerable solution. Suppose the denominator equals to a quadratic equation. Purposing that the needs require a four parts solution. The answer is/must be found in the numerator which would be the components that must be counted to solve the problem. It would be useless to use only two parts for the common denominator requires four. The search must continue until a reciprocal pounding, sounding, and practical result is obtained. The relevant key to all this is found in the common denominator. We must be cognitive enough to know that a pound of Gold is not the same as a pound of Silver. For both cannot fit into the same perimeter of equal distance; though both masses weighs the same, but the quantity may vary.

The number Two. The **number of division**. For God said; "Let there be a firmament in the midst of the waters, and let it divide the waters from the waters. And God made the firmament, and divided the waters which were under the firmament from the waters which were above the firmament: and it was so. And **God called the firmament Heaven**. And the **evening and the morning were the second day**." (Gen. 1: 6-8).

This further **establishes the fact** that the **law** of the **first mentioning of things** carry **much weight**. This **is the second day**. And on this day, God did some dividing. Number two then is the **number of division**. You can take **two and divide anything**. **Two different opinions will divide any home or church**. Therefore, when two persons come together it requires an agreement to continue. Hence, the **scripture says, "Can two walk together except they be agreed?"** (Amos 3:3).

Since **two** is a number of **indifference, God has added a blessing** to them that come to **an agreement**. The scripture said; "Again I say unto you, that **if two of you** shall **agree on earth as touching anything** that they **shall ask, it shall be done for**

them of my Father which is in heaven. For **where two or three are gathered** together in **my name, there am I in the midst** of them." (Matt. 18:19, 20) This **shows fellowship** and communion.

The number Three. This is another number, which is **loaded with this law**. It is a number that is **associated with resurrection** or life. On the **third day, the earth was raised out of the water**. The vegetation **rose out of the earth and life was manifested** for the **first time** upon the earth (Gen. 1: 9-13). **Three** is a **terminus ad quo** and a **terminus ad quem**. It has to do with **completeness**. The **first two lines: three lines** are needed for an enclosure in a **geometrical figure**. A circle is a continuous spiral of equidistance until it meet at the starting point. Three determines a **length or a fullness** of a point. It is a definite point or enclosure taken out of a circle. When the lines are acute they are half or less than 90 degrees, and when they are obtuse they are more than 90 degrees but less than 180 degrees which is a straight line being one half of a circle; which is 360 degree. The 360 degrees are four time a 90 degree angle. All rectangles has four 90 degrees angles which equals a circle consisting of 360 degrees. The width or length of the lines evidently determines how large the circle is.

Three periods of the day, God appeared unto **mankind:**

- To **Abraham in the heat of the day (noon)** (Gen. 18:1—KJV).
- He came **to Adam in the cool of the day (Three o'clock)** (Gen. 3: 8).
- He **appeared** unto **Paul at High noon** (Acts 22:8).
- He **sent an angel** to **Cornelius at the ninth hour** of the Day, **Three o'clock after noon**. Etc.
- The **Psalmist** said: "**Evening**, and **morning**, and **at noon**, will I pray, and cry aloud; and he shall **hear my voice**." (Ps. 55: 17)
- **Daniel** is famed as having **prayed three times** a day (Dan. 6:10).

The number Four is another number that **bears the law**. It is **related to the Earth** as **follows:**

1. The **four winds: north, south, east, west**.
2. The **Four elements: earth, air, fire, and water**
3. The **four seasons of the year: spring, summer, fall, and winter**.

The number Five, is the number that is associated with grace. Grace and truth came by Jesus Christ, who came in the fifth thousandth year of man's history (St. John. 1:17). Jesus' name is spelled with five letters. The book of Romans in its fifth chapter, give a treatise on Grace. In the fifth day of creation life came out of water. The fifth thousandth years of man history this is the waterway, we must be born of water and Spirit.

The number Six, is the number that is **associated with Man: God is still making man.** It was on the **six day that God said let us make man.** (Gen. 1:26) Man **must labor six days before rest.** The numbers of **the man of sin are 666.** The **numbers of Goliath's amour are 666.** He had **six fingers on each hand and six toes on each foot.** It is the six day **in which God is working on man.** Though in this day there are of hindrances caused by man which have caused God to prolong this period. There are many parenthesis, and untils, afters, and whens; which causes many delays. (Hosea 7:1) The seventh thousand is considered the **millennial rest.**

The number Seven is the **last number** that **we wish to consider.** This is the **perfect and complete** number. This is demonstrated in the **completion of God's creation.** (Gen. 2:1-7) This number is **stamped on the seven spectrum of light;** the seven **spectrum of sound;** the **seven spectrum of colors;** and, the **seven days of creation.** There is a counting of the **seven weeks before Pentecost** and the **seven days** of the **week.** The notes of the **musical scale is completed after the seventh count.**

The **number eight** being the repetition of the first and beginning a new count toward seven. It is the **divine number of perfection.** It's Interesting to **Note the Seven parables** of the **kingdom of heaven,** as well as the seven **churches** of Asia; the **Seven Golden Candlesticks** or lamp stands **of the Tabernacle.** There-are seven **trumpets,** the seven **vials,** the seven **thunders,** and the seven **church Epistles** which **are: Romans, Corinthians, Galatians, Ephesians, Colossians, Philippians, and Thessalonians.** And seven messages found in Revelation chapters 2-3.

The Seven **aspects of the church,** as a **son,** as a **body,** as a **vineyard,** as a **sheepfold,** as a **building,** as a **bride,** and as a **society.** There are many other points too numerous to mention in this short treatise.

There are other **numerical values** that are suggestive, showing points of which I don't have time to **expound upon such as:** number **eight, new beginning,** number **nine confusion,** number **ten, judgment,** number eleven less than the original, number **twelve eternal perfection, thirteen** number of **rebellion,** fourteen the repeating of seven in double portion, fifteen triple of five the grace, sixteen double of eight, and etc.

AN ANALAGY OF THE REAL TIME FUFILMENT OF THE SEVEN FEASTS OF JEHOVAH

These Feasts in retrospect are embedded in the Seven Days of Creation. And in prospect they are indicative of the plan of salvation. In both respects they are paralleled in the order, and progression of the same. As the first to the last. From darkness to light. They must be understood as being in real time in creation and real time in redemption. Beginning with the Passover in as much as it the first in number.

2 Corinthians 4:6 (KJV)

⁶ For God, who commanded the light to shine out of darkness, hath shined in our hearts, to *give* the light of the knowledge of the **glory of God** in the **face of Jesus Christ**." God at the beginning is Creator, and God at the ending is Redeemer. God in the beginning is in the Spirt position, and in the ending He is God (Spirit) in the flesh position.

Note this:

2 Corinthians 5:19 (KJV)

¹⁹ *To wit, that God was in Christ, reconciling the world unto himself, not imputing their trespasses unto them; and hath committed unto us the word of reconciliation.* St. Matthew 1>21-24.

In the fulfilment of the Feast of Passover Christ becomes the Passover Lamb. **1 Corinthians 5:7-8 (KJV)**

⁷ Purge out therefore the old leaven, that ye may be a new lump, as ye are unleavened. For even Christ our Passover is sacrificed for us:
⁸ Therefore let us keep the feast, not with old leaven, neither with the leaven of malice and wickedness; but with the unleavened *bread* of sincerity and truth."

As noted in these verses Christ is associated with the first feast beginning with the feast of the Passover; this being so, Paul speaks about the Feast of unleavened bread. This second Feast was celebrated simultaneously with the first. By the mere fact that Christ's death got rid of sin, (leaven), it establishes the celebrated Feast of Unleavened Bread. (Without any sin.). The 3rd feast follows in the logical and chronological order being the Feast of First Fruits. This speaks of the Resurrection, Christ being raised from the dead on the third day. The fourth Feast being the Feast of Pentecost. Which was celebrated fifty days after the resurrection. The counting of the seven Sabbaths equal Forty-nine and the next day is the fiftieth being the day of Pentecost. Which was celebrated in real time.

1 Corinthians 15:20 (KJV)

²⁰ But now is Christ risen from the dead, *and* become the firstfruits of them that slept."

Acts 2:1-4 (KJV)

¹ *And when the day of Pentecost was fully come, they were all with one accord in one place.*

2 And suddenly there came a sound from heaven as of a rushing mighty wind, and it filled all the house where they were sitting.

3 And there appeared unto them cloven tongues like as of fire, and it sat upon each of them.

4 And they were all filled with the Holy Ghost, and began to speak with other tongues, as the Spirit gave them utterance."

After the celebration of the feast of Pentecost there is a gap between the celebrations of the remaining feasts, anticipating the feast of the blowing of the trumpets.

This Feast is also called the Feast of Harvest. This feasting is over the gatherings of the matured crops. A rapture will take place after the perfection of the church. And a regathering will take place of the nation of Israel. When the church is raptured; God turns back to Israel to bring them back in covenant relationship with Him in putting them back into their land and restoration of the Kingdom.

Note this: **Acts 15:14-18 (KJV)**

14 Simeon hath declared how God at the first did visit the Gentiles, to take out of them a people for his name.

15" And to this agree the words of the prophets; as it is written,

16 After this I will return, and will build again the tabernacle of David, which is fallen down; and I will build again the ruins thereof, and I will set it up:

17 That the residue of men might seek after the Lord, and all the Gentiles, upon whom my name is called, saith the Lord, who doeth all these things.

18 Known unto God are all his works from the beginning of the world."

1 Corinthians 15:22-23 (KJV)

22 For as in Adam all die, even so in Christ shall all be made alive.

23 But every man in his own order: Christ the firstfruits; afterward they that are Christ's at his coming."

This coming is for His saints: Note this:

1 Thessalonians 4:13-18 (KJV)

13 But I would not have you to be ignorant, brethren, concerning them which are asleep, that ye sorrow not, even as others which have no hope.

14 For if we believe that Jesus died and rose again, even so them also which sleep in Jesus will God bring with him.

15 For this we say unto you by the word of the Lord, that we which are alive and remain unto the coming of the Lord shall not prevent them which are asleep.

16 For the Lord himself shall descend from heaven with a shout, with the voice of the archangel, and with the trump of God: and the dead in Christ shall rise first:

[17] Then we which are alive and remain shall be caught up together with them in the clouds, to meet the Lord in the air: and so shall we ever be with the Lord.
[18] Wherefore comfort one another with these words."

The next order is for the gathering of the Jews. Note this:

1 Corinthians 15:24-26 (KJV)

[24] Then cometh the end, when he shall have delivered up the kingdom to God, even the Father; when he shall have put down all rule and all authority and power.
[25] For he must reign, till he hath put all enemies under his feet.
[26] The last enemy that shall be destroyed is death."

The Feast that follows the Gap is the Feast of Trumpet. This is the calling of the children of Israel to their place for the finality of the restoration. While being in the land, they will go through the tribulation period for seven years. This is the 70th week of Daniel consisting of 2520 days, or 84 months. When this Feast of Trumpet is ended then the Feast of Atonement will take affect when Christ the king sits on the throne of David.

Note this:

Revelation 11:15-18 (KJV)

[15] And the seventh angel sounded; and there were great voices in heaven, saying, The kingdoms of this world are become *the kingdoms* of our Lord, and of his Christ; and he shall reign for ever and ever.
[16] And the four and twenty elders, which sat before God on their seats, fell upon their faces, and worshipped God,
[17] Saying, We give thee thanks, O Lord God Almighty, which art, and wast, and art to come; because thou hast taken to thee thy great power, and hast reigned.
[18] And the nations were angry, and thy wrath is come, and the time of the dead, that they should be judged, and that thou shouldest give reward unto thy servants the prophets, and to the saints, and them that fear thy name, small and great; and shouldest destroy them which destroy the earth."

The Seventh feast of Tabernacle will take effect in the new earth period. At the end of the feast of Tabernacle there will be the fiftieth thousandth year celebration. The fiftieth year (thousandth) is the eight year (thousand) of the 49 Sabbaths of years; being a Sabbath too, of no ending for it is the Eternal Sabbath. From which we enter into eternity.

Note this: **Ephesians 1:7-10 (KJV)**

⁷ In whom we have redemption through his blood, the forgiveness of sins, according to the riches of his grace;

⁸ Wherein he hath abounded toward us in all wisdom and prudence;

⁹ Having made known unto us the mystery of his will, according to his good pleasure which he hath purposed in himself:

¹⁰ That in the dispensation of the fulness of times he might gather together in one all things in Christ, both which are in heaven, and which are on earth; even in him."

THE OUTLINE OF THE SEVEN FEASTS

THE FEAST OF PASSOVER - The fourteenth day of first month (Lev. 23:5-8). The feast corresponds with the first day of creation. For as God separated the children of Israel (Light), from the Egyptians (Darkness), (Ex. 12:1-30), *so* did He separate the light from darkness on the first day of creation (Gen 1:3—KJV).

THE FEAST OF UNLEAVENED BREAD - The fifteenth day of first month Lev. 23:6-8). The Feast of Unleavened Bread (flat bread), corresponds with **the second day** of God's creation. As the mass of earth matter began to cool, it began to solidify and free itself from water and took the shape of God's forming. It left a firmament, or expansion above it according to **God's command** (Gen 1: 6-8).

THE FEAST OF FIRST FRUITS - The day after the Sabbath (Lev. 23:14). The Feast of First Fruits corresponds with the third day of God's creation, inasmuch as the earth brought **forth its fruits for the first time and waved themselves before the Lord** (Gen. 1:9-13).

THE FEAST OF PENTECOST - Fifty days after first fruits offering (Lev. 23:15-22). The Feast of Pentecost corresponds with the **fourth day** of creation. For, on the day of Pentecost, the church became the light of the world (St. Matt. 5:14-16; Gen. 1:14-19—KJV).

THE FEAST OF TRUMPETS - First day of the seventh month (Lev. 23:23-25). The Feast of Trumpets corresponds with the fifth day of creation where life came out of the waters; which was the **REPTILE AGE.** Giant reptiles moved upon the face of the earth. Their great voices of sound must have been somewhat like a feast of trumpets to the Lord. (Gen. 1:20-23).

THE FEAST OF ATONEMENT - The tenth day of seventh month (Lev. 23:26-32). The Feast of Atonement corresponds with the sixth day of God's creation, which is man's day. This means that we made a-tone-ment with God. For God said: "Let us make man in our image, after our likeness:' (Gen 1:26). The Bible said God created man in His image, but did not say anything about creating him in **His likeness** yet. This lets us know that **God is still working on man;** and that we are **still** in the **sixth** day of God's creation.

Thousand years of this day have passed. Because of the laxity on man's part God has prolonged this period because many untils have not been fulfilled. Jesus came in the fifth Thousandth year of the sixth day of creation **to redeem man back unto Himself**; for man fell from the image that God created him in. They that would be brought back into the image of **God would continue to be made into the likeness of God** (Col. 3:9, I John 3:2).

Now we, along with God, **can fulfill the scripture**, which said, "Let us make man." (2 Cor. 6:2; Eph. 4:11-13; Rom. 8:29, 30). We that are saved are now waiting on the Rapture to take place and the **redemption of our bodies** (Rom. 8:17-23). The **Millennium** will be the seventh and **last thousand years of this sixth day**.

THE FEAST OF TABERNACLE - Fifteenth day of the seventh month (Lev. 23:34-44). The Feast of Tabernacle corresponds with the **day of God's rest**, which has not yet come to pass literally speaking. Yes, the Bible said that **God rested on the seventh day**, but it also said **that God:** "Declaring the **end from the beginning**, and from ancient times the things that are **not yet done**, saying, **My counsel shall stand**, and **I will do all my pleasure:"** (Isa. 46:10; Ps. 46:11; Rom. 4:17; Acts 15:18).

This feast will be going on in the **new earth period.** This will be after the **Millennium, the White Throne Judgment**, and the renovation of the earth. It would be the beginning of **the time that John saw in the book of Revelation.** John said, "And **I saw a new heaven and a new earth:** for the **first heaven and the first earth were passed away;** and there was **no more sea."** (Rev. 21:1).

This new heaven and earth is in **fulfillment of the scripture**, which saith, (that is after the first creation), "For, behold, **I create new heavens and a new earth:** and the former shall **not be remembered**, nor **come into mind.** But be ye glad and **rejoice forever in that which I create."** (Isa. 65:17-18) Just Think!! **Seven Thousand (7,000) years of resting, rejoicing,** and **feasting. Seven** thousand years is the length of each **creative day**, from my understanding. We will explain this a little later on in this course.

YEAR OF JUBILEE - Tenth day of seventh month (Lev. 25:8-17). The Year of Jubilee is the dispensation of the fullness of time, where God causes everything to go back to its rightful owner. In this Year of Jubilee, God told the children of Israel to let everything go free. Every servant could be loosed from his master and every piece of land that was sold goes back to the original owner. It is a Pentecostal Jubilee. A Jubilee of Jubilees. It is the fiftieth thousandth year of God's dealing with this earth. After this, we go into ETERNITY! ETERNITY! ETERNITY!

FIFTY THOUSAND YEARS

Not knowing what the dateless pass has been before the history of mankind, Man's history has been the period of 6-7 thousand years. Inclusive of the Paleolithic, and the Neanderthals men of the Stone, and bronze periods. It is my firm conviction that there are FIFTY THOUSAND YEARS that God has allotted to deal with the earth and us before we enter ETERNITY. The time scale can be noted in the **Seven Feasts** of the

Lord that God showed unto Israel. (Psalms 103:7) We have in some of the feasts, **seven individual days** (Lev. 23:5, 34). *Also,* we have fifty days between the **Feast of First Fruits** and **Pentecost**. This is showing us that there are **seven thousand years** to each day of **creation,** which would equal to **49,000** years. For one day is with the Lord **as a thousand** (1,000) years (2 Pet. 3:8). However there are various delays and hindrances; which has hindered God's time clock. We are in the period of desolations there is no counting until many things are fulfilled in the present and future of mankind. What about the scientific methods of carbon 14 dating? It depends upon what catalyst one may go by: For that would be a major factor of determining the date of things. For clothes put out on a line to dry outside in the winter time will dry at a different rate than clothes put outside on the line in the Summer time. (The catalyst is the variant temperatures).

Here is an interesting article: "The use of various radioisotopes allows the dating of biological and geological samples with a high degree of accuracy. However, radioisotope dating may not work so well in the future. Anything that dies after the 1940s, when **nuclear bombs,** nuclear reactors and open-air nuclear tests started changing things, will be harder to date precisely." (*Internet Source*).

LEVITICUS 25:1-17

In Leviticus 25:17, God gave unto the **children** of **Israel** a work and **rest schedule** of the land of their possession. **Six years** they were to **sow** and **reap,** but on the **seventh year,** the land was **to rest for that entire year**. They were to number **seven Sabbaths of sowing**. Then on the **fiftieth** year, which is the next year, after the 49th, would be **a year of Jubilee**. From this, I believe God is showing unto us His entire **work-rest schedule,** which He is working in time (between **Eternity** and Eternity) with this **present earth** and **heaven,** according to **His eternal purpose** (Eph. 3:11;Ps.90:1).

When we come to the year of Jubilee, which is the **dispensation of the fullness of time,** God would have covered FIFTY THOUSAND YEARS, (50,000), in His **eternal purpose**. Each day of God's creation, (if we go by the **Seven Feasts** of the Lord and the work and rest **schedule** of the **land**), would equal to **7,000 years**. At the end of each six thousand years of the days of creation, there would be **a rest on the seventh thousandth year of each period**. For example, **God worked six thousand years of the first day of creation** and on the **seventh thousandth, He rested**. Even this sixth day, which is of seven thousand years period of time in God's creation, God has been working for **6,000 years on man,** (*this also includes pauses, untils, that extends many thousands of years of working on man which extends the period of the six day, what a contrary creature*)**,** and on the seventh thousandth year, (which will be the Millennium), **God will rest**.

We are in the **sixth day of creation right now**: And, **God is still working**. Jesus said, "My father worketh hitherto, and I work." (St. John 5:17) **We are in the sixth**

thousandth year stretch of this sixth seven thousand-year period of time of creation. Jesus came to earth in the beginning of the **fifth thousandth year** of this day, which has been approximately 1973 years, give or take a little. *(This book was written in 1973 the date of this writings.)*, that means, 5, 973 years of this **sixth** day have **already passed**, which would leave us about 1,027 years to go in this day. God's Long Sufferings is the catalyst that has delayed His coming. (1Pet. 3:3-13).

The **Tribulation Period** of **seven years** and **1,000 years of peace** must come out of the **remaining years**. That **does not leave us too much time** before **the Lord comes back** for the **church**, which would be some time **before the Tribulation**.

When the seventh thousandth year of this six-day is completed, we will go into the **seventh day of creation**. God will rest on **this seventh day**. This will be the **true Sabbath** of the Lord. This is the **seven Sabbaths of creation** made into **one day** of seven thousand years. Next, we have ONE THOUSAND YEARS OF JUBILEE and from there into ETERNITY!!!

CHAPTER TWO

THE GODHEAD

1. WHAT DOES THE WORD GOD MEAN?
The Supreme Being who is to be worshipped.

2. HOW MANY GODS ARE THERE?

The Bible speaks of **ONLY ONE** God. "Fear ye not, neither be afraid: have not I told thee from that time, and have declared it? Ye are even my witness. Is there a God beside me? Yea, there is **no God:** I know not any." (Isa 44:8—KJV)

"Know therefore this day, and consider in thine heart, that the LORD he is God in heaven above, and upon the earth beneath: there is none else." (Deut. 4:39)

"Is he the God of the Jews only? Is he not also of the Gentiles? Yes, of the Gentiles also: Seeing it is **ONE GOD**, which shall justify the circumcision by faith, and uncircumcision through faith." (Rom. 3:29, 30)

"But to us there is but **ONE GOD**, the Father, of whom are all things, and we in him; and one Lord Jesus Christ, by whom are all things, and we by him." (1 Cor. 8:6)

3. IS THE FATHER GOD? YES.

"Have we **not all ONE father**? Hath not **one God created** us?..." (Mal. 2:10)

"And **call no man your father** upon the **earth:** for one is your Father, which is in heaven." (Matt. 23:9; 1 Cor. 8:6) "These words spake Jesus, and lifted up his **eyes to heaven**, and said, Father,

"...And this **is life eternal**, that they might know thee the only **true God**, and Jesus Christ, whom thou hast sent."(St. John 17:1, 3)

"At that time Jesus answered and said, **I thank thee, O Father**, Lord of heaven and earth, because thou hast **hid these things from the wise and prudent**, and **has revealed them unto babes**. [26]Even so, Father: for so it seemed good in thy sight. [27]**All things are delivered unto me of my Father:** and **no man knoweth the Son**, but **the Father;** neither knoweth any man the Father, save the Son, and *he* to **whomsoever the Son will reveal him**." (Matt. 11:25-27)

4. Is Jesus Christ God? Yes.

"In the beginning was **the Word**, and the **Word was with God**, and **the Word was God**...."And the **Word was made flesh**,..." (v. 14) "All things were **made** by **him**; and **without him was not any thing made** that was **made**." (v. 3) "**He was in the world**, and **world was made** by **him**, and the **world knew him not**." (St. John 1:1, 14, 3, 10)

"In the **beginning God created the heaven** and **the earth**." (Gen. 1:1)

"Thus saith the LORD, thy Redeemer, and he that formed thee from the womb, I am **the** LORD **that maketh all things;** that stretcheth forth the **heavens alone;** that spreadeth abroad the **earth by myself;**" (Isa. 44: 24)

5. Is It Possible Not To Know Who Jesus Is? Yes.

"And I **knew him not:** but that he should be made manifest to Israel, therefore am I come baptizing with water. [32]And John bare record, saying, I **saw the Spirit descending from heaven like a dove**, and it abode upon him. [33]And **I knew him not:** but he that sent me to baptize with water, the same said unto me, "Upon whom thou shalt see the Spirit descending, and remaining on him, **the same is he which baptizeth with the Holy Ghost**." And I saw, and bare record that **this is the Son of God**." (St. John 1:31-34)

"**All things** are delivered unto me of **my Father:** and **no man knoweth the Son, but the Father, save the Son, and** *he* **to whomsoever the Son will reveal him**." (Matt. 11:27)

6. Is Jesus And The Father The Same Person? Yes.

"Jesus saith unto him, I am the **way, the truth, and the life:** no man cometh unto the Father, but by me. [7]If ye had known me, ye should have **known my Father also:** and from henceforth ye know him, and have seen him. **Philip** saith unto him, **Lord, show us the Father,** and it sufficeth us. Jesus saith unto him, Have **I been so long time with you, and yet hast thou not known me**, Philip? He that hath seen me **hath seen the Father;** and how sayest thou then, **Show us the Father?**" (St. John 14:6-9)

"**Who is a liar** but he that **denieth** that Jesus is the Christ? He is antichrist, that denieth the Father and the Son. [23]Whosoever **denieth the Son, the same hath not the Father:** *[but] he that acknowledgeth the Son hath the Father also.*" (1 John 2:22, 23)

"And We **know** that the **Son** of God **is come**, and hath **given** us an understanding, that we may **know** him that **is true**, and we are **in** him that **is true**, even **in** his **Son Jesus Christ. This is** the **true God**, and **eternal life**." (1 John 5:20)

7. **IS JESUS CHRIST CALLED GOD IN THE SCRIPTURES? YES.**

"For unto us a child is born, unto us **a son is given:** and the government shall be **upon his shoulder:** and his name shall be called **Wonderful, Counselor**, The **mighty God**, The **everlasting Father, The Prince** of Peace." (Isa. 9:6—KJV)

"Behold, **a virgin shall** be with child, and shall **bring forth a son**, and they shall call his name Emanuel, which being interpreted is, **God with us**." (Matt. 1:23)

"And Thomas answered and said unto him, My LORD and **my God**." (St. John 20:28)

"And as they went to tell his disciples, behold, Jesus met them, saying, All hail. And they came **and held him by the feet, and worshiped him**." (Matt.28:9)

"And again, when he bringeth in **the first begotten into the world**, he saith, And **let all the angels of God worship him**." But unto the Son *he saith*, "Thy **throne, O God, is for ever and ever:** a scepter of **righteousness is the scepter** of thy **kingdom**." (Heb. 1:6, 8; Phil. 2:5-11)

Jesus is called God in fulfillment of prophecy.

"The **voice of him that crieth in the wilderness, Prepare ye the way of the LORD, make straight in the desert a highway for our God**." (Isa. 40:3) "He said, I am **the voice of one crying** in the wilderness, **Make straight the way of the Lord**, as said the prophet Isaiah...". The next day John seeth Jesus coming unto him, and saith, **Behold the Lamb of God, which taketh away the sin of the world**. This is he of whom I said, **After me cometh a man which is preferred before me:** for he was before me." (St. John 1:23, 29, 30; St. John 8:57, 58; Micah. 5:2)

THE HOLY GHOST IS GOD

8. **IS THE HOLY GHOST GOD? YES.**

"God **is a Spirit:** and they that worship him must **worship him in spirit** and in **truth**." (St. John 4:24)

"But Peter said, Ananias, why hath Satan **filled thine heart to lie to the Holy Ghost,** and to keep back part of the price of the land? "...thou has **not lied unto men, but unto God**." (Acts 5:3, 4—This shows that the **Holy Ghost is** the **God** to which he lied)

"There is ONE BODY, and ONE SPIRIT." (Eph. 4:4) "Now the **Lord is that Spirit:** and where **the Spirit of the Lord is, there is liberty**." (2 Cor. 3:17) "And he said, **Who art thou, Lord?** And the Lord said, **I am Jesus** whom **thou persecutest:**" it is hard for thee to kick against the pricks." (Acts 9:5)

"Know ye not that the LORD **he is God:...**" (Ps. 100:3a)

9. **IS JESUS AND THE HOLY GHOST THE SAME SPIRIT? YES.**

Jesus said, "And **I will pray the Father,** and he shall give you another **Comforter,** that he may abide **with you for ever;** *Even* the **Spirit of truth;** whom the world **cannot receive,** because it seeth him not, **neither knoweth him:** but **ye know him;** for **he dwelleth with you,** and **shall be in you. I will not leave you comfortless: I WILL COME TO YOU."** (St. John 14:16-18) [9]"But ye are not in the flesh, **but in the Spirit,** if so be that the **Spirit of God dwell in you.** Now **if any man have not the Spirit of Christ, he is none of his."** (Rom. 8:9—KJV)

"And because **ye are sons, God hath sent forth the spirit of his Son into your hearts,** crying, **Abba, Father."** (Gal. 4:6)

10. **IS THE HOLY GHOST AND THE HOLY SPIRIT THE SAME SPIRIT? YES.**

In Matthew 3:16 said, that the **Holy Spirit descended like a dove upon Jesus,** while in St. Luke 3:22, it is said the **Holy Ghost did it.** These **are two accounts** of the **same incident.**

UNDERSTANDING THE GODHEAD

11. **HOW HAS GOD REVEALED HIMSELF IN TIME PAST?**

"GOD, **who** at **sundry** times and in **divers** manners spake in time **past** unto the fathers by the prophets, Hath in these last days spoken unto us by *his* **Son...** (Heb. 1:1, 2)

12. **WHAT MAJOR MANIFESTATIONS HAS GOD REVEALED HIMSELF?**

There are **three** manifestations: As **Father,** As **Son,** As **Holy Ghost.**
"And **without controversy great** is the **mystery of godliness:** God was **manifest** in the **flesh, justified** in the **Spirit, seen of angels, preached** unto the **Gentiles, believed on in the world,** received up **into glory."** (1 Tim. 3:16)

13. **IS IT THE SAME LORD IN EACH MANIFESTATION? YES.**

"Now there are **diversities of gifts,** but the **same Spirit.** And there are differences of **administrations,** but the **same Lord.** And there are **diversities** of **operations,** but it is the **same God** which **worketh all in all."** (1 Cor. 12:4-6)

14. **E**XPLAIN **T**HE **P**URPOSE **O**F **G**OD **H**AVING **M**ANIFESTED **H**IMSELF **A**S **F**ATHER, **S**ON, **A**ND **H**OLY **G**HOST.

A. FATHER - The Father **ordained salvation**. "According as he hath chosen us in him before the foundation of the world, that we should be holy and without blame before him in love." (Eph. 1:4)

B. SON-As the Son, (the Father-2 Cor. 5:19) He **purchased salvation** because there was **no man found worthy to do it**. "And **he saw** that *there was* **no man**, and wondered that **there was no intercessor:** therefore **his arm brought salvation** unto **him**; and his **righteousness, it sustained him**." (Isa. 59:16) "To wit, that **God** was **in Christ, reconciling** the **world unto himself...**" (2 Cor. 5:19; Matt. 1:21-23; Heb. 2:14-18; Isa. 35:5-6)

C. HOLY **G**HOST - As the Holy Ghost, He **applies salvation to** the **heart** of the **believer**. "And **hope maketh** not **ashamed;** because the **love** of **God** is **shed** abroad **in our hearts** by the **Holy Ghost** which is given unto us." (Rom. 5:5; 13:8-10)

15. **E**XPLAIN **T**HE **I**NCIDENT **W**HERE **J**ESUS **W**AS **B**APTIZED, **A**ND **T**HE **F**ATHER **S**POKE **F**ROM **H**EAVEN, **A**ND **T**HE **H**OLY **G**HOST **D**ESCENDED **I**N **T**HE **S**HAPE **O**F **A** **D**OVE **U**PON **J**ESUS.

In this incident, the **only person that is seen is Jesus**. "Who being the brightness of *his* glory, and the express image of his person...." (Heb. 1:3) "**No man hath seen God** at **any time;** the only begotten Son, which **is in the bosom of the Father**, he hath declared him." (St. John 1:18)

"If ye had known me, ye should have **known my Father also:** and from henceforth ye know him, and have **S**EEN **H**IM. Philip saith unto him, Lord, show us the Father, and it sufficeth us. Jesus saith unto him, Have **I been so long time** with **you,** and yet hast thou **not known me, Philip?** he that hath **seen me hath seen the Father; and how sayest thou then, Show us the Father?"** [30]"I and my Father are one." (St. John 14:7-9; 10:30)

16. **A**RE **T**HERE **A**NY **S**CRIPTURES **T**O **S**HOW **T**HAT **G**OD **W**AS **I**N **T**HE **B**ODY **O**F **J**ESUS **C**HRIST **A**T **T**HAT **T**IME? **Y**ES.

For **God is omnipresent**, meaning **everywhere at the same time**. "Know therefore this day, and **consider** it in **thine heart,** that the L**ORD** **he is God** in **heaven above,** and **upon the earth beneath:** there is **none else**." (Deut.4:39; Gen. 19:24; 5:19—KJV)

St. Matt. 1:23 says, "Behold, **a virgin** shall be with child, and **shall bring forth a son**, and they shall call his name **Immanuel**, which being interpreted is, **God with us**." And St. Luke 2:11 states: "For unto you is born **this day** in the **city of David** a **Savior**, which is **Christ the Lord**." Jesus said in St. John 14:11; 5:17, "**Believe me** that **I am** in the Father, and the **Father in me:** or else **believe** me for **the very works' sake**."

17. Was Jesus Christ (In Spirit) In Heaven And In Earth At The Same Time? Yes.

"And **no man hath ascended up to heaven**, but he that came down from heaven, *even* the **Son of man which is in heaven**." (St. John 3:13; **Prov. 30:4**)

18. Was The Holy Ghost In The Body Of Jesus At That Time? Yes.

Colossians 2:9 says, "For **in him dwelleth all the fullness** of the **Godhead bodily**." Colossians 1:19 tells us that, For **it pleased** the **Father** that **in him** should **all fullness dwell;**" Hence, the words of St. Matthew 3:17, "And lo **a voice from heaven,** saying, **This is my beloved Son, In Whom I Am** well pleased."

More importantly, note the Spirit: that the **Spirit of Christ** and the **Holy Ghost** is the **same Spirit**. And, that the **Spirit** of Christ is **Jesus in Spirit**, which is the **Holy Ghost in us**.

"But ye are **not in the flesh**, but in the **Spirit,** if so he that the **Spirit** of God **dwell in you.** Now **if** any **man** have **not** the **Spirit of Christ,** he is **none of his.** [10]And **if Christ** *be* **in you**, the body is **dead because of sin;** but the **Spirit is life** because of **righteousness.**" (Rom. 8:9-11)

19. Why Did This Holy Incident Happen?

This happened for **a sign to John the Baptist** that this was the **very One** that was to come. "And **I knew him not:** but he that sent me to baptize with water, the same said unto me, Upon whom thou shalt see the Spirit descending, and remaining on him, the **same is he which baptizeth with the Holy Ghost**. And **I saw, and bare record** that **this is** the **Son of God**." (St. John 1:33, 34)

"And we know that the **Son of God is come**, and hath **given us** an **understanding**, that we **may know him** that is true, and **we are in him** that is true, even in his Son **Jesus Christ. This Is The True God, And Eternal Life.** Little children, keep yourselves from idols. Amen." (I John 5:20, 21)

20. Explain The Incident Where Jesus Prayed To The Father. If He Is The Father, Why Did He Pray To The Father?

Jesus Christ, **as a Son, prayed** unto the **Father:** It was **not the Father** praying to God, but **Jesus Christ** as **the Son of God**, prayed unto **the Father**. The **Son** of God is **not the Spirit**. Neither **was it God**, but **rather** it was the **flesh in Whom the Eternal Spirit** (God the Father) **dwelt**. "...Joseph, thou **son of David, fear not** to take unto thee **Mary thy wife:** for that which is **conceived in her is of the Holy Ghost.**" (Matt.1:20)

In St. Luke 1:35 says: "And **the angel** answered and said unto her, The **Holy Ghost shall come** upon **thee,** and the **power of the Highest shall overshadow thee:** therefore also that holy thing which **shall be born of thee** shall **be call** the **Son Of God**."

Galatians 4:4 states: "But when the **fullness of time** was **come, God sent forth his Son, made** of a **woman, made under the law...,**" Philippians 2:5-7 says: "**Let** this **mind be in you**, which was also **in Christ Jesus:** Who, **being** in the **form of God,** thought it not robbery **to be equal** with **God:** 7But made himself of no reputation, and took upon him the **form of a servant**, and was **made** in the **likeness of men:**"

In St. Matthew 11:25-27, "At **that time Jesus answered** and said, **I thank thee, O Father, Lord** of **heaven and earth,** because thou **hast hid these things from** the **wise** and **prudent,** and hast **revealed them unto babes.** 26Even so, Father: for so it seemed good in they sight. 27All things are **delivered unto me of my Father:** and **no man knoweth** the Son, but **the Father;** neither knoweth **any man the Father, save the Son,** and he to **whomsoever the Son will reveal** *him.*" (Matt.16:13-17; St. John 1:33, 34; 14:7-9)

21. WHO WAS GOD TALKING TO WHEN HE SAID IN GENESIS 1:26, "LET US MAKE MAN IN OUR IMAGE, AFTER OUR LIKENESS:..?"

When God said this, He was speaking this after the counsel of His own will. "Having made **known** unto **us the mystery of his will,** according to his **good pleasure** which he hath purposed in HIMSELF:... **In whom** also **we have obtained** an **inheritance,** being **predestinated** according to the **purpose of him** who worketh **all things after the counsel of his own will:**" (Eph. 1:9, 11–KJV)

When God said "LET US", it is **evident** that God was talking **in reference** to the ATTRIBUTES **of His personality,** instead of as some say, **three distinct** persons. For the next verse says: "So God created man in his *own* image, in the **image of God created he him; male** and **female** created **he them.**" (Gen. 1:27) "**Have we not all** ONE **father? Hath not** ONE GOD CREATED US?...**" (Mal. 2:10)

When God said, "OUR IMAGE", this means **His Attributes,** such as **Knowledge, Love, Wisdom, Understanding, Sensibility, Will,** Etc. It is **striking to** note this Scripture: "**Lie not one to another, seeing** that ye **have put off** the **old man** with **his deeds; And have put on the new man,** which is RENEWED IN KNOWLEDGE AFTER THE IMAGE OF HIM THAT CREATED HIM:" (COL. 3:9, 10)

The one that did **the creation was Jesus Christ** in whose **image we were created.** "For **whom he did foreknow,** he also did **predestinate** to be **conformed** to the **image of his Son,** that **he** might be the **firstborn among many brethren.**" (Rom. 8:29)

"In the beginning was the **Word,** and the **Word was with God,** and **the Word was God**...He was **in the world,** and the **world was made by him,** and **the world knew him not.**" (St. John 1:1, 10)

"**In whom we have redemption through his blood,** *even* the forgiveness of sins: 15Who is the image of the **invisible God,** the **first-born of every creature:** 16For by him were **all things created,** that are in heaven, and that **are in earth, visible** and **invisible,** whether *they be* **thrones, or dominions, or principalities,** or **powers:** all things were **created by him,** and **for him:** 17And he is **before all things,** and **by him all things consist.**" (Col. 1:14-17)

"And immediately **I was in the Spirit:** and, behold, **a throne was set in heaven,** and *one* sat on the throne.... [10]The **four** and **twenty elders** fall **down** before him that **sat on the throne**, and worship him that **liveth for ever and ever, and cast** their **crowns before the throne,** saying, [11]Thou art worthy, **O Lord, to receive glory** and **honor** and **power:** for thou hast **created all things,** and for thy pleasure **they are** and **were created."** (Rev. 4:2, 10, 11—KJV)

"Thus saith the LORD, **(JEHOVAH)** "thy Redeemer, and he that formed thee from the **womb,** I am the LORD that **maketh all things;** that **stretcheth forth the heavens alone;** that **spreadeth** abroad the **earth BY MYSELF;"** (Isa. 44:24)

This is my explanation of the **"LET US MAKE MAN",** and I believe it to be God's as well.

22. WHAT IS THE MEANING OF THE QUOTATION, "JESUS ON THE RIGHT HAND OF GOD." (1 Pet. 3:22)

To understand the quotation, "Jesus on the **Right Hand of God",** we must understand the **meaning of** that **term, "RIGHT HAND".**

First of all, it means a **place of acceptance** and **favor** or **blessing.** Note these verses, in particular, **concerning Jesus Christ.** Psalms 16:8-11 says: "I **have set the LORD always before me:** because he is at my **right hand,** I **shall not be moved.** [9]Therefore, my heart is glad, and my glory **rejoiceth:** my flesh also shall **rest in hope.** [10]For thou wilt not **leave my soul in hell;** neither wilt thou suffer thine **Holy One to see corruption.** Thou wilt show me the path **of life: in thy presence is fullness of joy;** at thy **right hand** *there are* **pleasures for evermore."** (Acts 2:25-36)

When Rachel bore Benjamin, she named him **Ben-o-ni,** meaning **Son of my sorrow,** Jacob renamed him **Benjamin,** meaning **son of my Right Hand** (Gen. 35:16-18). Now the reason why Christ is said to be sitting on God's Right Hand is, because **He, as the son of man, is man's representative. Nowhere** in the **scriptures** do **we see that Jesus is said to be on the right hand of God before His resurrection** and **ascension. Before** Jesus came **to earth** to become **a man,** He was in the **form of God** (Phil. 2:6). "But made himself of no reputation, and took upon him **the form of a servant,** and was **made in the likeness of men:"** (Phil. 2:7)

So then, we **see Christ descended** from a **high position** to a **low position** of a man. [9]"But we **see Jesus, who was made a little lower than the angels** for the suffering of death, **crowned with glory and honor;** that he by he grace of God should **taste death** for **every** man...[14]Forasmuch then as **the children** are **partakers** of **flesh** and **blood,** he also **himself** likewise **took part** of the **same;** that **through death** he might **destroy him that** had the **power of death,** that is, **the devil;** [15]And **deliver them who through fear of death** were all their lifetime subject to bondage. For verily **he took not** on him *the nature* of angels; but he **took** on him the **seed of Abraham."** (Heb. 2:9, 14-16)

Now Christ came down to **represent** the **human family.** "For it is not possible that the **blood** of **bulls** and of **goats** should **take away sins.** [5]Wherefore when he cometh into the world, he saith, "**Sacrifice** and **offering thou wouldest not**, but a Body hast thou **prepared me:** ⁶In burnt offerings and *sacrifices* for sin thou hast had no pleasure." (Heb. 10:4-6)

When **Jesus Christ got into a body**, He began to **represent** the **human family**. What He does in God's sight is in the **behalf of man**. When Christ **Jesus died** on **the cross, it was man that died. All the world** became **dead to God** in the **death of Christ.** "For the **love** of Christ **constraineth us;** because we thus judge, that if one died for **all**, then were all **dead: And that he died for all**, that they which live should not henceforth **live** unto **themselves**, but unto him **which died for** them, and **rose again.**" (2 Cor. 5:14, 15)

So Christ became a **part of the human family** to bring **us back to God**, So as Christ **died** and **rose again**, so are they that believe in **His death, burial**, and **resurrection.** "**I am crucified with Christ:** nevertheless **I live:** yet **not I,** but Christ **liveth in me:** and the life which **I now live** in the **flesh** I live by the **faith of the Son of** God, who **loved me,** and **gave himself for me.**" (Gal. 2:20)

So **when Christ arose** and **ascended on high**, it was Jesus **as Man** who received **the position** at the **Right Hand** of God. **He was man's representative at the place of favor** and **acceptance in the presence** of God. First Timothy 2:5, 6 **states:** "For there is ONE God, and ONE mediator between **God** and **men,** the man Christ **Jesus;** Who gave himself a **ransom for all**, to be testified in **due time.**"

St. Luke tells us in Acts 2:33-35, "Therefore being by the **right hand of God exalted**, and having **received** of the **Father the promise** of the **Holy Ghost,** he hath shed forth this, which ye now **see** and **hear.** ³⁴For **David** is not ascended into **the heavens:** but he saith himself, The LORD said unto **My LORD**, Sit thou on my **right hand**, until I make thy **foes thy footstool.**" (also Matt. 22:41-46)

23. LET US NOTE THIS VERSE THAT WE HAVE JUST QUOTED FROM PSALM (110:1 - - - KJV).

In this verse, **one** is called **the LORD** and the **other** is called **my Lord**. The LORD is the **Father in Spirit**, and My Lord is **the same Father in flesh**, or we can **say** the **Son of God**, or Jesus **in a body as a Man**. This is a **prophecy of David** which saw that that was happening in **God's process of salvation**.

The LORD is suppose to make **the enemy** of my Lord, **My Lord's footstool.** When **Christ** took upon Himself the **form of man**, He also **took on** Himself the **enemies** of **man.** But that is what the Lord wanted to do. He wanted to **destroy the enemy.** Now the Enemy is the **Devil** and **Death.**

"Forasmuch then as the children are partakers of **flesh** and **blood**, he also himself likewise **took part of the same;** that through death he might destroy him that had the **power** of death, that is, **the devil;** And deliver them who through fear of death were all their **lifetime subject** to bondage." (Heb. 2:14, 15; 1 John 3:8; Hos. 13:4, 14)

"But now is Christ risen from the dead, and become the first fruits of them that slept. For since by MAN came death, by MAN came also the resurrection of the dead. For as **in Adam all die**, even so **in Christ shall all be made alive**. But every man in his **own order:** Christ the **first fruits:** afterward they the are **Christ's at his coming.** Then *cometh* **the end**, when he shall have **delivered up the kingdom** to God, even the **Father;** when he shall have **put down all rule** and all **authority** and **power**. For he **must reign**, till he hath **put all enemies under his feet**. The last enemy *that* shall be **destroyed is death."** (1 Cor. 15:20-26)

"**To wit, that God was in Christ, reconciling the world unto himself** (2 Cor. 5:19).

To show that THE LORD and MY LORD are the same one in both positions. The Lord is supposed to **make the enemy** of **My Lord**, My Lord's **footstool**. But we see in 1 Cor. 15:25, 26, that Jesus **as the Son of God**, making the **enemies to become** a footstool. Yet, in 2 Corinthians 5:19 said: that God was in Christ. Read 1 Timothy 3:16.

On this subject ON THE RIGHT HAND OF GOD, I conclude in saying that all that are saved are in heavenly places in Christ Jesus (Eph. 1:3). So the place by the Right Hand of God is **not a seat**, but a **blessed state** that man has **obtained** with **God through Jesus Christ.**

NAME'S OF GOD

24. HAS GOD REVEALED HIMSELF THROUGH ONLY ONE NAME? No.

God has revealed Himself through **various** names. Note His Deity: "And God spake unto Moses, and said unto him, **I am the LORD:** And I appeared unto Abraham, unto Isaac, and unto Jacob, by *the name of* God Almighty, but by my name JEHOVAH was I not known to them." (Ex. 6:2-3)

25. WHY DO SOME SAY THAT GOD'S NAME SHOULD BE CALLED JEHOVAH, SOME YAHWEH, SOME YASHUAH, AND SOME JESUS?

THE REVELATION OF GOD
THROUGH HIS NAMES

What is a name?

A name is an appellative by which **a person is known**. Hence, the **term** known is taken from the Greek word O-known-ma, and the Latin O-know-en. This is where the word O-Known-ma originated from. It is a designation **by which a person is**

known. Though in Biblical treatise it **goes beyond the** title, and lay **heavier** on the **characteristics** of a person, place or thing named or famed.

In other words, when Jacob was fleeing from his brother **Esau,** he lit upon a place previously name **Luz**. But when he had a **vision of God**, he **changed** the **name** of that place to **Bethel**, which means the **house of God**. And Because it was in that place, Gen. 28:19-22–KJV).

Where **Uzza** reached forth his hand to **stabilize the Art** of the Lord **unwittingly** when the **oxen stumbled**, the Lord **smote him that he died**. That place was named **Pera-Uzza**. Which mean **breaking** or **breaching forth**. Signifying the coming **forth of the hand of the Lord** because of Uzza's mistake.

When **Naomi** was returning home from her sojourning in the **land of Moab**, her acquaintances said, "Here comes Naomi. Naomi replied and said;" Don't call me Naomi, but **call me Marrah**, for the Lord had done very **bitter toward me**. Hence Naomi means **pleasant,** while Marrah **means bitter**. In reference to her bitter experiences in **losing her family in Moab**.

Other persons were named in the bible such as **Abram**, which simply **means** father. And later his name was changed to Abraham, which means a father of a multitude. Sarai was changed to **Sarah**, to mean **a mother of nations** (Gen. 17:15).

When **Isaac was born** he was name Isaac simply because his name mean laughing. According to Genesis 17:17–KJV, For when God told Abraham that he was going to bless him with a child through Sarah, he felled on his face and laughed. Sarah also laughed in Genesis 18:15 and Genesis 21:6 as well.

When Jacob and Esau were born their name became characteristically as it relates to **their actions. Jacob** means **sup-planter,** while **Esau** means **hairy** for he was **hairy all over**. Being indicative of his **wilderness** involvement in hunting. Though **both** these **boys** name are later changed to suggest another characteristic. **Esau** being changed to **Edom**. Meaning redness concerning the **red bean lentil** he ate selling his birthright. **Jacob** name is **changed** after he prevailed in a wrestle with an Angel. He later called the place Peniel, which means face of God. His name was changed to **Israel**, which means Prince of God.

The name **Isaiah,** which mean salvation of Jehovah, Daniel means God is Judge. Elijah means my **God is Jehovah**. The name of Elisha means **My God is** savior. The names of the Hebrew boys are significant in their meanings. Hananiah means My God Is Gracious. **Mishael** means, **there is none like my God**. Azariah God is my helper.

Unfortunately, **time** will not **permit** me to labor in presenting **any other names** other than **our particular** study. This should **suffice** to show how that names were significant concerning person, place or thing in biblical days.

Now for our presentation of the revelation of God through his names. God does work according to the meaning of his names. **God's names were not primarily** a word or given by a **specific sound** with a meaning. But more so in reference to his characteristics and various **functioning**. His names **Jehovah, Eloah, Elohim, Adonai,**

Adon, Yah, Nissi, Gmolah, are not sounding words but rather various **functions** and **relationships**.

No one will gather the main or **whole intent** of the names unless he study them from this approach. God is progressive in his action and revelations. Just to get a verbal sound of the names of God, is not the intent of this book. But to **observe God** in his **various functions** even unto **our day**. God can be one thing to one and something else to another. For an example, He is **Adon to others**, while He is Adonai to his **Own**. He is **Elshaddai unto Abraham, Isaac, Jacob** and Jehovah unto Israel. Hence He said; "I appeared unto Abraham, Isaac, and Jacob, by **the name of God Almighty,** but by my name **Jehovah** was I not known unto them." (Exd. 6:4)

Some say that God's name should be called Jehovah instead of **the term** LORD, as is primarily used in the **King James** Translation. The Old Hebrew only used **consonants** and **no vowels**. Hence, if you used the **consonants** in the name Jehovah, they would be "YHVH". If you used the consonants in the name Yahweh, they would be "YHWH". In ancient Hebrew there was no J in the name Jehovah, but there was a "Y" of Yahweh. Yet, on the other hand, there was no "W" of the name Yahweh, but a "V" was used instead of a "W". Therefore, the letters would be "YHVH" instead of "YHWH". There were no vowels between the letter of either name.

So, in the Hebrew, the Ancient writing would be "YHVH" (7!7). At this point, we shall **study the origin** of the alphabet contained in the name of YEHOVAH.

The original **Hebrew** Alphabet contained **twenty-two** characters called **consonants**. None of those letters have a vowel sound. Whoever spoke any words that were made up of those characters should have learned through **tradition** the correct sound of the word those letters made up. For **an example**, we know the **term** CAN'T, we understand it to mean CANNOT. So likewise the pronouncing of **terms** in Ancient Hebrew before the Massoretes put the **Vowel System** to the Hebrew language.

Let's examine the letters that are used in the name "YHVH". We will compare these letters and terms in five different ancient languages:

1. Egyptian
2. Semites
3. Phoenicians
4. Greek
5. Latin. We shall first deal with the letter "Y".

YHVH
EGYPTIAN (WAW)

In the **Egyptian** language, the letter is made this way, **v., which was pronounced** with this **sort of sound, "WAW"**. It began with the **Egyptian language about 3000**

B.C. **The Semites** and **Phoenicians** used the same form of the letter and the **sound** from about **1,000 B.C. See diagram.**

Y

EGYPTIAN -if- **3,000 B.C (WAW). Meaning Hook. PHOENICIANS & SEMITES -Y - 1,000 B.C. Meaning Hook. GREEKS -= - 600 B.C. Sound (Upsilon) ROMANS -by- A.D. 114.**

A

EGYPTIANS - Meaning Ox's Head - 3,000 B.C.

SEMITES - Sound ALEPH - Meaning Ox - 1,500 B.C.

PHOENICIANS - Sounds - ALEPH - Meaning Ox - 1,000 B.C.

GRECIAN - Sound - ALPHA - 600 B.C.

(A) ROMANS - A.D. 114

V, W

EGYPTIANS - Sound - "WAW" 3,000 B. C.

SEMITES - Sound - "WAW" 1,000 B.C.

(Y) PHOENICIANS - Sound "WAW" 1,000 B.C.

(r) GRECIAN - Sound "UPSILON" 600 B.C.

(V) ROMANS - 114 B.C.

(W) Medieval Scribes V V, 1,000 A.D.

Also written UU, became known as double U.

E,

EGYPTIANS - Sound - "HE" - Meaning Joy - 3,000 B.C. SEMITES - Sound - "HE" - Meaning Joy - 1,500 B.C. PHOENICIANS - Sound - "HE" - Meaning Joy - 1,000 B.C. **GRECIANS** - Sound "EPSILON" 600 B.C. ROMANS - 144 A.D.

H,

EGYPTIANS - Sound "CHETH" - 3,000 B.C. SEMITES - Sound "CHETH" 1,500 B.C. **PHOENICIAN** - Sound "CHETH" 1,000 B.C. GRECIAN - Sound "ETA" 600 B.C. **ROMANS** - 144 A.D.

Y A H V E H ~(SEMITES)

WAW- -ALEPH- -WAW- -HE--CHECH ~(EGYPTIAN)

UPSILON-ALPHA- UPS ILON-EPSILON-ETA
(GRECIAN)
YEHOVAH- Yeh-ho-vaw

YEHOWSHUWA - Yeh-ho-shoo-ah
IESOUS- Ee-ay-sooce *(GREEK)*

THE MASSORETES

The **Massoretes, so called from the Talmudic word Mass rah or** Massoreth, signifying tradition, was a body of **Jewish scholars** who succeeded the **talmudists,** and who during the period from the **sixth** to the **eleventh century** worked out the **Massoretic** System. Their objective, like that of the **Talmudists** was to provide means for the inviolate preservation of the **traditional reading** and understanding of the **Old Testament Text**, but what was still left to oral transmission by their **predecessors** was now reduced to writing and incorporated into the text by means of a most **elaborate** and **ingenious** system of annotations and conventional signs.

The **Massoretes** drew up **Rules for the Guidance** of copyists, made **exhaustive** statistics of **verses, words,** and **letters** contained in the **sacred books**, noted **peculiar forms**, etc., but the most important part of their great work was the elaboration of the **Vowel System**, whereby all **ambiguity** was henceforth **practically** removed, at least so far as the **traditional reading** was concerned.

26. **DOES GOD RECOGNIZE OTHER LANGUAGES OR TRANSLATIONS OF THE BIBLE? YES.**

For, the Bible that was mostly used in **Jesus' day** was from the **Greek** translation called the "**Septuagint**," made in the 3rd century B.C. Greek was the language in general use throughout the Roman world. The **Old Latin** translation, made in the **2nd century**. The Old Testament part was **translated** from the Septuagint instead of **the Hebrew**.

The **Vulgate**, which was a **revision** of the **Old Latin**, by **Jerome, A.D. 382404**, its Old Testament, **except the Psalms**, was direct from the Hebrew. It became the **Bible of the Western world** for a thousand years.

In the **4th century**, we have the **Ethiopia** and **Gothic** translations. The 5th Century, Armenian. The **9th Century**, **Arabic** and **Slavic**. With the growth of the Papacy, the **Bible fell into general disuse** being supplanted by the decrees and **dogmas** of councils and **Popes**. With the **protestant Reformation**, a renewed **interes**t in the **Bible arose**, until **now the Bible**, or **parts of it, is translated** into more than a thousand languages and **dialects**. It is **believed that nine-tenths** of the **whole world's population**, at the **present time**, may **read** or **hear** the Bible in their own **language**.

27. **DO NAMES SOMETIMES HAVE DIFFERENT SOUNDS IN OTHER LANGUAGES? YES.**

For example, **St. John 1:38-42** reads **as thus:** "Then Jesus turned, and saw them following, and saith unto them, **What seek ye?** They said unto him, RABBI, (which is to say, being interpreted, **Master,**) where **dwelleth thou?** ...One of the **two** which **heard John speak**, and **followed him, was Andrew, Simon Peter's brother.** He first **findeth his own brother Simon**, and saith unto him, **We have found the** MESSIAH, **which is, being interpreted, the** CHRIST. And he brought him to Jesus. And when Jesus beheld him, he said, Thou **art Simon the Son of Jonah:** thou shalt be called **Cephas** which is by interpretation, **A stone."** Jesus' name was **written** in three languages at **His crucifixion.** It was written in **Hebrew, Latin**, and **Greek. It is also interesting to** _Note the following:

A. **HEBREW** - The Vernacular language.
B. **LATIN**———The official language_ St. John 19:19-22.
C. **GREEK**———The speech generally understood by all strangers.

THE SUPERSCRIPTION WRITTEN OVER JESUS AT HIS CRUCIFIXION

(LATIN)
IESVS OF NAZARETH THE KING OF THE JEWS

(GREEK)
(HEBREW)

This let's us to know that the **name of Jesus** could be written in **three languages** (St. Matt. 27:37; St. Luke 23:38; St. John 19:19, 20)

HEBREW- YEHOWSHUWA

GREEK - INOOUS

LATIN - IESUS

ENGLISH - JESUS

"And a **superscription** also was **written** over him in letters of **Greek**, and **Latin,** and **Hebrew, This Is The King Of The Jews.**" (St. Luke 23:38)

"And Pilate wrote a Title, and put it on the cross. And the writing was, Jesus Of Nazareth The King Of The Jews. This title then **read many of the Jews:** for the place where Jesus was **crucified** was nigh to the **city:** and it was written in Hebrew, And Greek And Latin." St. John 19:19, 20)

A Comparative List Of Hebrew Names With Greek Or English

Hebrew	Greek	English	Scripture
Messiah	Christ	Christ	St. John 1:38
Cephas	Peter	Peter	St. John 1:42
Tabitha	Dorcas	Tabitha	Acts 9:36
Saul	Paul	Paul	Acts 13:9
Yashua	Inoous		Heb. 4:8
YaHveh	Theos	God	

The Revelation Of God Thru His Names

Elohim	God The Creator	Gen. 1:1
Elshaddai	God Almighty	Gen. 17:1
Jehovah Ji-Reth	God Will Provide	Gen. 22:14
Yahveh	God Of The Covenant	Ex. 6:3

EH-YEH-ASHER-EH-YEH	I WILL BE, THAT I WILL BE	Ex. 3:14
JEHOVAH ROPHEAKA	GOD THAT HEALS	Ex. 15:26
JEHOVAH NISSI	GOD MY BANNER	Ex. 17:15
JEHOVAH SHALOM	GOD OF PEACE	Judges 6:24
JEHOVAH SHAMMAH	GOD IS THERE	Ezek. 48:35
JEHOVAH MEDKADISKIM	GOD THAT SANCTIFY	Ex. 31:13
JEHOVAH TSIDKENU	GOD OUR RIGHTEOUSNESS	Jer. 23:6
JEHOVAH TSAIOT	GOD OF HOSTS	Isa. 6:3
JEHOVAH ROI	THE LORD MY SHEPHERD	Psa. 23:1
JEHOVAH ELYON	GOD MOST HIGH	Psa. 7:17
JEHOVAH GMOLAH	GOD OF RECOMPENSE	Jer. 51:56
JEHOVAH MAKKEH	GOD THAT SMITES	Ezek. 7:9
JEHOSHUA	JESUS SAVES	Matt. 1:21

PROPHECY

Prophecy is a word meaning to **predict** or **foresee** things to come. The secondary meaning of the word is to **speak with divine inspiration,** or **to preach.**

I consider the **first prophecy of** the Bible to be when **God said** unto **Adam,** "Of every tree of the garden thou mayest **freely eat;** But of the tree of the **knowledge** of **good** and **evil,** thou shalt **not eat of it:** for **in the day that thou eatest thereof** thou **shalt surely die."** (Gen. 2:16, 17—KJV)

The next **prophecy** was in reference **to life,** when the **seed of the woman** would **bruise the serpent's head** (Gen. 3:15).

The **first man** to prophecy **in the Bible was Enoch** (Jude 14, 15). The **second** prophet was **Noah** (2 Peter 2:5). The prophet was first called a **Seer** meaning a man that Sees (1 Sam. 9:9; Isa. 30:10). The **Prophet** was and **is a spokesman for God;** he goes to **God** in the **behalf of** the people (St. John 3:34).

The Prophet was commissioned by a **direct experience with God.** As the case of **Samuel** (1 Samuel 3:1-10), As the case of **Isaiah** (Isaiah 6:1-10), As it was with **Jeremiah** (Jeremiah 1:4-10), As the case with **Amos** (Amos 7:10-16), and also the case of **Moses** (Exd. 3:1-12).

"We have also a more **sure word of prophecy;** whereunto ye do well that ye take heed, as unto **a light that shineth** in a dark place, until the day dawn, and the **day star** arise in your **hearts:** Knowing this **first,** that **no prophecy** of the scripture **is** of any **private** interpretation. For the prophecy **came not in old time** by the **will of man:** but holy men of God spake as *they were* **moved** by the **Holy Ghost."** (2 Pet. 1:19-21)

Moses was a **great prophet** but he was **only a type** of the **real prophet** that was to **come.** For God **said: "I will raise** them up a **prophet** from among their **brethren,** like unto thee, and **will put my words** in **his mouth:** and he shall **speak** unto them all that **I shall command him."** (Deu. 18:18)

"God, **who at sundry times** and in **divers manners spake** in time **past** unto the **fathers** by the prophets Hath in these **last days** spoken unto **us by his Son,** whom he hath appointed heir of all things by whom also he made the worlds;" (Heb. 1:1, 2)

There are **many divisions** in prophecy, such as: prophesy concerning the **coming of the Messiah,** the prophecy about the scattering and **regathering of Israel** and there are **political** prophecies dealing with the **kingdoms** of the **world.** We **shall deal** now with the **Political Prophecies,** primarily from the books of **Daniel** and **Revelation.**

POLITICAL PROPHECIES

In this study we shall deal with the **kingdom of this world** and the **kingdom of God.** The **term** kingdom means, "The **King's Domain,"** or a place where the King rules. We shall endeavor to **show** that the whole **right to rule** in heaven and earth belongs **to God.** But, we **must keep in mind,** that there is an **opposing force** trying to take the **right** to rule **from God.** This opposing force is **"Satan",** or whom Isaiah called **Lucifer:** Saying, **"How art** thou **fallen** from **heaven, O Lucifer, the son of the morning!** *how* art thou **cut down** to the **ground,** which didst **weaken** the **nations!** For thou hast said in **thine heart, I will** ascend into **heaven, I will** exalt my throne **above the stars of God: I will** sit also upon the **mount of the congregation,** in the sides of **the north: I will** ascend above the **heights** of the **clouds; I will** be like the **most High."** (Isa. 14:12-14—KJV)

Ezekiel refers to him as the **anointed cherub,** saying, **"Thou art the anointed cherub** that **covereth;** and I have set **thee so:** thou wast upon the holy mountain of God; thou hast walked up and down in the midst of the stones of fire. Thou was perfect in thy ways from the **day** that thou wast **created,** till **iniquity** was **found** in thee.

By the **multitude** of thy **merchandise** they have filled the **midst** of thee with **violence, and thou has sinned:** Therefore **I will** cast thee as **profane** out of **the mountain** of God: and **I will destroy thee,** O covering **cherub,** from the midst of stones of fire, **Thine heart was lifted up because of thy beauty,** thou hast **corrupted** thy **wisdom** by reason of **thy brightness: I will cast thee to the ground, I will lay** thee **before kings,** that they may **behold thee.** Thou hast **defiled** thy **sanctuaries** by the multitude of **thine iniquities,** by the iniquity of **thy traffic; therefore will I bring forth** a fire from **the midst** of thee, **it shall devour thee, and I will bring thee to ashes upon the earth in the sight of all them** that behold thee." (Ezk. 28:14-18)

Let's **note** these **opposing words of God** and **Satan** from the above-mentioned Scriptures. **Both passages of Scripture said: I WILL,** etc. **Isaiah** presents the **words of Satan,** but **Ezekiel** presents the **Word of God.** Satan said, **I will** five times. God said, **I will six times.** It's interesting to **Note the Wills as follows:**

SATAN'S

1. **I will ascend** into heaven.
2. **I will exalt** my throne above the start of God;
3. **I will sit** also upon the mount of the congregation...
4. **I will ascend** above the heights of the clouds;
5. **I will be like** the **Most High** (Isaiah 14:13,14).

GOD'S

1. **I will cast thee** as profane out of the mountain of God.
2. **I will destroy** thee.
3. **I will cast** thee to the ground.
4. **I will lay** thee before kings.
5. Therefore **will I bring forth a fire** from the **midst of thee, it shall devour thee.**
6. **I will bring thee to ashes** (Ezek. 28:16-18).

We **see that Satan** has set himself in **Battle array against God**. But, God has declared with **Great Foreknowledge** and Confident saying, "Declaring **the end** from the **beginning**, and from **ancient times** the things that **are not yet done**, saying, **My counsel shall stand, and I will do all my pleasure:** Calling **a ravenous bird** from the **east**, the man that executeth my counsel from a **far country:** yea, **I have spoken it, I will also bring it to pass;** I have purposed it, **I will also do it."** (Isaiah 46:10, 11)

Satan **began challenging God**, as far as man is concerned, **in the garden** when he told the woman (Eve) that **Big Lie**; Saying, "Ye shall **not surely die:** For God doth know that in the day ye eat thereof, then **your eyes shall be opened**, and ye shall be as **gods**, knowing good and evil." (Gen. 3:4, 5–KJV)

Satan was **the instigator of the violence** and **great wickedness** of the **ante-diluvian Age** (Gen. chapter 6). Satan **inspired Nimrod** to begin the kingdom of **rebellion** against God (**Genesis chapters 10-11**). The **beginning** of the kingdom of **Nimrod was Babel,** which became Babylon, and also **Assyria**. These are **two** of the **Great Kingdoms** of **antiquity**. These kingdoms were **erected against God** and were **the bed** of **Idolatry** and **Witchcraft**. **Satan** was behind all of these functions. We shall **show in our next** section how **Satan will try to take over the Kingdom of God**. We will now show the **opposition Satan will give God** in the books of **Daniel** and **Revelation.**

DANIEL

The meaning of the name Daniel is – "God Is My Judge."

There are **three** other **characters** famous in the book of Daniel are; Hananiah, Mishael, And Azariah (Dan. 1:6).

The prince of the **Eunuchs changed their Hebrew names**, which represented **their God;** to the **Chaldean** names, which represented the gods of the **Babylonians.** Hence, their Hebrew **names are as follows:**

HEBREW	CHALDEA
1. Daniel - God is my Judge	1. Belteshazzar - O Bel protect his life
2. Hananiah - God is Gracious	2. Shadrach - Command of Aku
3. Mishael - Who is like God	3. Meshach - Who is as Aku
4. Azariah - God is my helper	4. Abednego - A servant of Nego

Through the changing of those names, **Satan is trying to blot out** that which **pertains to God.**

Now, we will consider the **Dream that Nebuchadnezzar** had concerning the **political kingdoms** and the interpretations.

In Daniel 2:1 says, "And in the **second year** of the reign of **Nebuchadnezzar,** Nebuchadnezzar **dreamed** dreams, wherewith his spirit was troubled, and his **sleep brake** from him."

Note, in **particular,** Daniel 2:28, God used dreams to attract Nebuchadnezzar's attention to show him the things which shall **come to pass in the latter days** upon the earth.

None of the **wise men** were **able to interpret** or ever to **tell** what the king had dreamed (Daniel 2:2-13).

Daniel asked **permission** of the **king to pray** unto God to receive the **Dreams** and **interpretation there of** (Dan. 2:14-23).

Daniel, **after prayer,** received the **Dream** and **the interpretation** from **God** and required **an opportunity** to be **brought before the King** (Dan. 2:24, 25)

Daniel informed the king that God was the one who gave him the **interpretation.** Hence, none of the gods of the **Babylonians** were able to give the interpretation (Dan. 2: 26-30).

The Vision

Daniel 2:31-34__ "Thou, O king, sawest, and behold a **great image.** This great image, whose brightness was excellent, stood before thee; and the form thereof was terrible. [32]This image's **head** was of **fine gold**, his **breast** and **his arms** of **silver**, his **belly** and his **thighs** of **brass**, **His legs** of **iron, his feet** part of **iron** and **part of clay.** Thou sawest till that **a stone was cut out without hands,** which **smote the image** upon **his feet** that were of **iron** and **clay,** and **brake them to pieces."**

THE INTERPRETATION

"This is the dream; and we will tell the interpretation thereof before the king." (Dan. 2:36) The interpretation is given in vv 37-45. **It's important to Note** the **summary** of the interpretation.

THE HEAD OF GOLD 606 B.C. 538 B.C.

The **Head of Gold** represented the **Babylonian Empire** of which **Nebuchadnezzar** was the **first king.** It is classed as **Gold** because it **is excellent** in **quality of government.** It was a kingdom that was an ABSOLUTE MONARCHY, which means to be **ruled by one.**

The **city of Babylon** is considered to be one of the SEVEN WONDERS OF THE WORLD, with its **Hanging Gardens,** and with its **fortified protection in its walls** that was so thick that **6-8 chariots** could **ride** on top of it **at the same time.** It had the river of **Euphrates** to **run** down **through the center** of that city. It had its beautiful **gates of Bronze,** which could be closed to **ward off any attack by its enemies.** It was secure within itself and could be shut up for months or **years** without the need of **outside help** or source of supply.

But, **God decreed that Cyrus would conquer that city. Cyrus was the king of Persia,** who according to history, made a dam to turn the water of the **Euphrates** River so that he and his army might go through the **first Gates** of the city. .

But, they couldn't have **conquered the city,** because there were **secondary gates** that protected the **innermost city.** But God decreed in **Isaiah 44:27,** "That saith to the deep, **Be dry, and I will dry up thy rivers:** That saith of Cyrus, He is my **shepherd,** and shall perform all of my **pleasure:** even saying to Jerusalem, **Thou shalt be built;** and to the temple, **Thy foundation shall be laid."**

Thus saith the LORD to his **anointed,** to **Cyrus,** whose right hand I have holden, to **subdue** nations before him; and **I will loose the loins of kings,** to open before him the **two leaved gates;** and **the gates shall not be shut;** (Isa. 45:1)

The Kingdom of Babylon was **subdued** by Cyrus the **Persian,** and **Darius** the Median. "And **Darius** the **Median** took the **kingdom,** being about **threescore** and **two years old."** (Dan. 6:28)

538 B.C. - 331 B.C.

The **next kingdom** that was to **rise** after Babylon was **the Breast and Arms of Silver Kingdom, which was the Media Persia Empire. Cyrus** and **Darius** were the **co-kings** or **rulers** of that **kingdom**. It is classified **as Silver because the quality of** government **is less than Babylon,** which represented the **Head of Gold.** As silver is **inferior in quality to gold,** so were **Media Persians inferior in** government to Babylon. **Babylon was an absolute monarchy,** which means **ruled** by **one.** Media Persia was **duumvirate** ruled by **two, Cyrus** and **Darius.** The kingdom was brought **to its end** approximately 331 B.C. **by Greece.**

331 B.C. -161 B.C.

The **next kingdom** was the **Kingdom of Belly and Thighs of Brass,** which was the **Kingdom of Greece.** As **brass is inferior** to **silver,** so was this kingdom to **Media Persia. Alexander the Great was its first king.** The form of government after **his death** became a **Qua-umvirate,** that is, **rule by four**.

161 B.C. - 476 A.D.

The **next kingdom** was the **Legs of Iron,** representing the **Kingdom of Rome.** As **iron is inferior to brass** and the **other metals,** so was this kingdom in its governmental function. Its form of government was a **Democracy,** meaning rule **by the people.** It was the kingdom that was **in power** during **the birth of Christ,** the **birth of the church,** and also during the persecution of the **Martyrs** of the Saints.

It existed in **its original form** from **161 B.C.** to about **476 A. D.** and it became **divided** into the **ten Toes of the image,** meaning **ten nations** that came up in its place and have continued unto this day, **waiting** for the forming of a **Confederacy under the Anti-Christ System** with the **Anti-Christ** being the **ruler.**

The **next kingdom** that would be established is the **Stone Kingdom.** It's **interesting** to **Note that** this **kingdom is not made of the same substance** that the other kingdoms were made of. This **stone** was **cut out** of the mountain **without** hands, signifying that it would **not be set up by man.** That is, it is **not of the world.** It is the **Kingdom of Heaven.** The Kingdom that will be **set up by God,** which will not be left to another.

The **Image** that we have considered represents **the four Great Gentile World Powers.** It also represents the **times of the Gentiles,** which **includes** the time from **606 B.C. to the end,** when the **Stone Kingdom** would be set up, which will be the **second coming of the Lord Jesus Christ.**

This **Gentile kingdom** must come down, because it is **top heavy.** That is to say, **Gold is heavier** than **Silver.** Silver is **heavier** than **Brass,** which is **heavier** than **Iron.**

This is true chemically. So, the Image being in that state, **its equilibrium** could easily be **noted off balance**. For anything to be **top** heavy **is subject to fall**.

The next portion from the book of Daniel we will deal with the Seventh Chapter of Daniel. This chapter brings out other **aspects of the Gentile** world that Daniel brought out.

In Daniel, **chapter two**, is how man **sees himself** as beautiful as Gold, Silver, Brass, and Iron. But, in Daniel chapter **seven**, is the way **God sees man as a ravening Beast** of the Jungle, **devouring one another**. These are the Visions of Daniel.

DANIEL CHAPTER 7:1-3 - - - - KJV

"In the first year of **Belshazzar** king of Babylon, Daniel had a **dream** and **visions** of his head upon his **bed:** then he wrote the dream and told the sum of the matters. Daniel spake and said, I saw in my vision by night, and, behold, the **four winds** of the heaven **strove** upon the **great sea**. And **four great beasts** came up from the **sea,** diverse one from another."

It's important to **Note** the **King:** Daniel had his dream evidently, when Nebuchadnezzar was **dead**, and his son or grandson, **Belshazzar,** was on the **throne.**

The **four winds** that **strove** upon the **Great Sea,** represent **wars, commotion**, and **strife** between the four **Great Universal Empires** upon the face of the earth. The **Sea** represents **great masses of people** (Rev. 17:15).

Daniel 7:4—KJV "The first was like **a lion**, and had **eagle's wings**: I beheld till the wings thereof were **plucked**, and it was lifted up from the earth, and made **stand upon the feet as a man**, and a **man's heart** was given to it."

It is **interesting to note** this first Beast was like **a lion**. This **lion** represents the **Babylonian Kingdom** of the **Head of Gold** of the **Metallic Image**. As **Gold** is supreme in metals, so is **a lion superior** in the **beasts of the field**.

The **Two Eagle Wings** also **denote superiority**, as an eagle is **superior to** other **birds**. But, when two wings were plucked, and lifted up from the earth, it made stand **upon the feet as a Man**. This evidently shows **Nebuchadnezzar's pride** and being brought down **by God** when **he was driven into the wilderness and ate grass like an ox** until **seven years** passed.

Daniel 7:5 "And behold another beast, a second, like to a bear, and it raised up itself on one side, and it had three ribs in the mouth of it between the teeth of it: and they said thus unto it, **Arise, devour much flesh**."

This Beast represents the **Media-Persia Empire**. For as a bear is **inferior to a lion**, so was **Media-Persia to Babylon**, which corresponds to **Breast** and **Arms** of **Silver of the Images** in Chapter two. "**It raised up itself on one side**" signifies that **one King** shall be greater than the other. Out of this Confederacy of two nations, Media and **Persia**, the **Persian side became greater**, Cyrus being its King.

Daniel 7:6–KJV "After this I beheld, and lo another, like a leopard, which had upon the Back of it four wings of a fowl; the beast had also four heads; and dominion was given to it."

This Beast represents the **Kingdom of Greece**, being the same as **the belly** and **thigh of Brass** of the **Image of Daniel** in Chapter two. The **four wings of a fowl**, show that this kingdom became **divided into four parts** (Dan. 8:8).

Daniel 7:7 "After this I saw in the night visions, and behold a **fourth beast, dreadful** and **terrible**, and **strong exceedingly; and it had great iron teeth: it devoured and brake in pieces,** and stamped the **residue with the feet of it:** and it was diverse **from all the beasts that were before it; and it had ten horns**."

This **fourth beast is Rome**, being the same as the **legs of iron on the Image** of Chapter two. It being different from **all beasts** before, shows **its form of government** is **downward to the people**, while this **government is ruled by the people to the top**. That is, this government received **its orders from the people**. Anything that is ruled by the people has broken down in **quality** of government. This beast **is last** of the **Great World** Empires. It continues to the end in its divided state, and shall be reunited into a **European Confederacy**. This beast had **Ten Horns**.

Daniel 7:8 "I considered the horns, and behold, there came up among them another **little horn**, before whom there were **three of the first horns plucked up** by **the roots:** and, behold, in this horn were **eyes like the eyes of man, and a mouth speaking great things**."

These **ten horns** correspond to the **ten toes of the Image** of Chapter two. They are the **kingdoms** that **Rome** was **divided** into and will continue until the **stone cut out without hands, smite the Image at his feet**. The division of the ten toes took place about **476 A.D.**, when **Ancient Rome fell**. It's interesting to **Note the ancient divisions** and modern **names** thereof.

Daniel 7:9 "I beheld till the **thrones were cast down**, and the **Ancient of days did sit**, whose garment was **white as snow**, and the **hair of his head like the pure wool:** his throne was *like* the **fiery flame**, and his **wheels as burning fire**." This verse corresponds with the **Stone Kingdom of Daniel, Chapter 2**, which supplanted all the rest of the kingdoms. **Revelation, Chapter 19** also corresponds with **Daniel, Chapter 2,** representing the **Second Coming of Christ**. Let's **note Revelation, Chapter 19** and verse **eleven.**

"And **I saw heaven opened**, and behold **a white horse;** and he that sat upon him was called **Faithful and True**, and in **righteousness he doth judge** and **make war**. His **eyes** were as a **flame** of **fire**, and on his **head** were **many crowns;** and he had a **name written, that no man knew**, but he himself. And he was **clothed with a vesture** dipped in **blood:** and his name is called **The Word of God.**

And the **armies** *which were* in **heaven followed** him **upon white horses**, clothed in **fine linen**, white and **clean**. And out of his **mouth** goeth **a sharp sword**, that with it he should **smite the nations:** and he shall **rule** them with **a rod of iron:** and he treadeth the **winepress of the fierceness** and **wrath of Almighty God**. And he hath on *his* **vesture** and on **his thigh** a name written, KING OF KINGS, AND LORD OF LORDS.

And I saw the **beast**, and the **kings of the earth**, and their armies, gathered together to **make war against** him that sat on the horse, and **against** his army. And the beast was taken, and with him the **false prophet** that **wrought miracles** before him, with which **he deceived them** that had **received the mark of the beast**, and them that **worshiped his image**. These **both were cast alive into a lake of fire burning with brimstone."**

Daniel 7:11 "I beheld then because of the voice of the great words which the horn spake: I beheld even till **the beast was slain,** and **his body destroyed**, and given to **the burning flame."** (Also Rev. 19:20)

Daniel 7:12 "As concerning the rest of the beasts, they had their dominion taken **away:** yet their lives were **prolonged for a season** and time." (Also Matt. 24:31-34)

Daniel 7:13, 14 "I saw in the **night visions**, and, behold, one like the Son of man came with the clouds of heaven, and came to the Ancient of days, and they brought him near before him. And there was given him dominion, and glory, and a kingdom, that all people, nations, and languages, should serve him: his dominion is an everlasting dominion, which shall not pass away, and his kingdom that which shall not be destroyed."

In these two verses, we have **a point we would like to clarify**. That is, concerning **who is the Ancient of Days**, and **one like the Son of man receiving** a **kingdom**.

The **Ancient of Days** is **God Almighty** in the person of the Lord **Jesus Christ**. The **one like** the **Son of man** is the **saints of God** who **shall reign with him for 1,000** years **(The Israelite Saints)**.

It's important to **Note the interpretation** given in **Daniel 7:15-27—KJV**.

Daniel 7: 21 "I beheld, and the same horn made **war with the saints,** and **prevailed** against them;"

These are **not the church saints**. For Jesus said in St. **Matthew 16:18,** "And I say also unto thee, **That thou Peter, and upon this rock I will build my church;** and the **gates of hell shall not prevail against it."**

These are the **Israelites** that shall be in the **Great Tribulation** Period where **Christ** will return and **restore Israel** as the head of **nations**. Of course, the **church** shall **return with him** and shall **reign** with **Christ** for **1,000 years** (Rev. 20:4; Acts 15:16, 17—KJV).

In Ezekiel 21:26, 27 "Thus saith the LORD GOD; Remove **the diadem**, and take off the **crown:** this shall **not be the same:** exalt *him that is* low, and abase *him that* is high. I will overturn, overturn, **overturn, it:** and it shall be no more, until he come whose **right it is;** and I will give it him."

Daniel 7:27 "And the kingdom and dominion, and the greatness of the kingdom under the whole heaven, shall be given to the people of the saints of the **most High,** whose kingdom is an everlasting kingdom, and all dominions shall serve and obey him."

The Ram And Goat Of

Chapter 4

Daniel 8:3–KJV "Then I lifted up mine eyes, and saw, and, behold, there stood before the river **a ram** which had **two horns:** and the two horns were **high;** but one was **higher** than the other, and the **higher came up last.**"

This **Ram** represents the Kingdom of **Media-Persia.** For even the emblem of that nation was a **Ram.** The **two** horns represent the kings of **Media** and Persia **(v 2).** The **one** being **taller** than the other shows that **one king shall be greater** than **the other;** that is, **Cyrus the Persian,** which became **more famous** than **Darius** the **Median.**

Daniel 8:5, 6, "And as I was considering, behold, an he goat came from the west on the face of the whole earth, and touched not the **ground:** and the goat *had* a notable horn between his eyes. And he came to the ram that had *two* horns, which I had seen standing before the river, and ran unto him in the fury of his power."

This **He Goat** is the kingdom **of Greece,** which brought down the **Media Persia Empire.**

Daniel 8:8–KJV, "Therefore the **he goat waxed very great:** and when he was strong, the **great horn was broken;** and for it came up four notable ones toward the four winds of heaven."

The **Notable** between the **eyes of the He Goat** was broken. The **Notable horn** was the **first King Alexander the Great.** This horn was **broken in four parts,** and for it stood up **four little ones.** That is, **four kings stood up in the place of Alexander the Great.** They were **Alexander's Four Generals** in his army. When he **died at the age of 33 years,** the **Kingdom** was divided **toward the four winds** of **direction as follows:**

1. **Lysimachus** of Thrace to **the North**
2. **Ptolemy** of Egypt to **the South**
3. **Cassander** of Macedonia to **the West**
4. **Seleucus** of Babylonia to **the East**

These kings **fought one against the other** until especially in the **North, Seleucus** subdued **Lysimachus** to the **North** and **Cassander** to the **West,** and became known as the King of the North. He made war with the **King of the South, Ptolemy,** which is demonstrated in the **Eleventh Chapter** of Daniel.

Daniel 8:9-11, "And out of one of them came forth a **little horn;** which waxed exceeding great, toward **the south,** and toward **the east,** and toward the pleasant land. And it **waxed great,** even to the **host of heaven;** and it cast down some of the host and of the stars to the ground, and stamped upon them. Yea, he **magnified** himself even to the prince of the host, and by him the **daily sacrifice** was taken away, and the place of his sanctuary was cast down."

This is the **little horn of Daniel 8:9**, which ultimately ended up being the same character of **Daniel 7:8.** Both of these horns are shown to be coming up **against** the **most High**, which gives **us to understand** that it would be **finalized in the End**. This **little horn** is the **Beast of Revelation 13:1-10.**

The **Little Horn of Daniel 7:8**—KJV, and **the Little Horn** of **Daniel 8:9**, ended up as being **the same**, for they **both** have the **same characteristics**. The **Little Horn** of Daniel **7:8**, "...**in this horn were eyes** like the **eyes of man**, and a **mouth speaking great things.**"

Daniel 7:25 "And he shall speak *great* **words against** the **most High**, and shall **wear out** the saints of the **most High**, and think **to change times and laws:** and they shall be given into his **hand** until a time and times and the dividing of time." This little horn **is the Anti-Christ** in the **last days**, which **corresponds with the beast** of **Revelation 13.**

Revelation 13:2, "And the beast which I saw was like unto **a leopard**, and his feet were as the **feet of a bear**, and his mouth as the **mouth of a lion:** and the **dragon gave him his power,** and his seat, and **great authority.**"

Revelation 13:5 "And there was given unto him a **mouth speaking** great things **and blasphemies;** and power was given unto him to continue **forty** and **two months.**"

These are like **comparisons** between this **little horn** and **the beast:**

1. They both have a mouth speaking great things (Dan. 7:8, 25; Rev.13:2, 5).
2. Both are **given power to continue** a time and times and the dividing of time. This time is **3 1/2 years**, or **42 mon**ths, or **1260 days**.
3. Both are in the **time of the End** (Dan. 7:26; Rev. 1:1).

The Little Horn of Daniel 8:9 in the first beginning is different, but the ending is the same as the **little horn of Daniel 7:8**, and the **Beast of Revelation 13**. The first part of this **little horn** deals with **episodes of the King of the North**, of the **Four horns** that came up out of **Alexander's Empire.**

This **King of the North** was known as **Antioch Epiphanies** who fought against **Israel** and the **King of the South** for many years. But, he especially fought against **Israel** for approx. **3 1/2 years**, where at one time he offered up a Sow on the altar of Israel. This brought about the **Maccabeean Revolt**, when the Maccabees rose in defiance of such abomination.

But Daniel 8:11 gives the **last half of the action of this little horn** which **said:** "Yea, he **magnified** *himself* even to the prince of the host, and by him the daily *sacrifice* was taken away, and the place of his sanctuary was cast down... ²³And in the latter time of their kingdom, when the transgressors are come to the full, a king of fierce countenance, and understanding dark sentences, shall stand up. ²⁴And his power shall be mighty, but not by his **own power:** and he shall destroy wonderfully, and shall prosper, and practice, and shall destroy the **mighty** and **holy** people. And through **his policy** also he shall cause craft to **prosper in his hand;** and he shall magnify *himself* in his heart, and **by peace** shall **destroy many:** he shall also stand up against the Prince of **princes;** but he shall be broken without hand." (**Dan. 8:11, 2325**)

This Little Horn activity is also recorded in the **eleventh** chapter, (vv. 21-45) and (vv. 36-38) **reads as follows:** "And the king shall do according to **his will;** and he shall exalt himself, and **magnify himself above** every god, and shall speak marvelous things against the God of gods, and shall prosper till the indignation be **accomplished:** for that that is determined shall be done. Neither shall he regard the God of his fathers, nor the **desire of women,** nor regard **any god:** for he shall magnify himself above all. But in **his estate** shall he honor the **God of forces:** and a god whom his fathers knew not shall he honor with gold, and silver, and with precious stones, and pleasant things."

The **willful King,** as he is **called** in verse 36, is also called the **Son of Perdition** and that **Man of Sin** in **2 Thessalonians 2:3-12.** "**Let no man deceive you by any means:** for *that day shall not come,* **except there come a falling away first,** and that man of **sin be revealed,** the **son of perdition;** [4]Who opposeth and **exalteth** himself **above all that is** called **God,** or **that is worshiped;** so that he as God sitteth in the **temple of God,** showing himself that **he is God.**" (vv. 3, 4) From the above-mentioned scriptures, **we see how Satan is going to put within this Man** of Sin, his power and authority. This is the **Anti-Christ** which is **prophesied** that would come in to **the world.** This brings us down to the **time of the End.**

It's interesting to note Daniel 12:1, "AND AT that time shall **Michael** stand up, the great prince which standeth for the children of **thy people:** and there shall be a **time of trouble,** such **as never was since there was a nation** *even* to that **same time:** and **at that time** thy people shall **be delivered,** every one that shall be **found** written in the **book.**"

Daniel 12:4, "But thou, **O Daniel,** shut up the words, and **seal the book,** even to the time of the **end:** many shall **run to and fro,** and **knowledge** shall be **increased.**"

Daniel 12:9, "And he said, Go thy way, **Daniel:** for the words are closed up and sealed till the time of **the end.**"

Our next study in prophecy shall be taken up in the **Book of Revelation,** which is the book that deals with the **time of the END** (Rev. 1:1-7; 10:5-7).

THE BOOK OF REVELATION

The book of Revelation is so called because it is the **unfolding** and **revealing** of things **hidden, prophesied,** or **spoken** in times **past** by **Daniel** and many of the other prophets. The **opening words** of this book use the word "**Revelation**". It is **not called** the Revelation of **Saint John the Divine,** as some would call it, but the **Revelation of Jesus Christ.**

The **Greek** use the **term Apocalypse**, (meaning uncovered), It is the **last book** in **God's whole plan** and revelation of **His word**. The **Old Testament** is considered the **Preparation**, the Gospels the **Manifestation**, Acts the **Proclamation**, the Epistles the **Explanation**, the **Revelation the Consummation**. I also consider it to be **God's last letter or message to the Church: Wherein are seven messages to the church.**

The **Book of Revelation** is considered by many to be the **book** of **Sevens**. Hence, The **Seven Churches**, The Seven **Stars**, The Seven **Spirits of God**, The Book of **Seven Seals,** The Seven **Trumpets,** The Seven **Vials,** The Seven **Personages,** The Seven **New Things,** The Seven **Heads on the Beast and Dragon**, The Seven **Thunders**. This book was to be sent to the **Seven Churches of Asia Minor**, which **are as follows: Ephesus, Smyrna, Pergamus, Thyatira, Sardis, Philadelphia**, and **Laodicea**. The Chapters are as follows:

Chapter One is the introduction and **purpose** of the Book. That is, **to show** God's **servants** what must **shortly come to pass.**

Chapter Two and **Three** show the Church as being yet **on the earth. Chapter Four** shows the **Church rapture** from the earth up **into heaven. Chapter Five** introduces the Book of **Seven Seals**, and shows the **necessity** of a **Kinsman Redeemer. Chapter Six** demonstrates the **beginning** of the **opening of the** Book of **Seven Seals,** which the first **Six Seals** are **opened** in this **particular chapter**. The **Seventh Chapter** deals with the sealing of the **one hundred forty-four thousand Jews** and another number which **no man could number**.

Chapter Eight deals with the **Opening of the Seventh Seal**, and introduces Seven **Angels** with Seven **Trumpets of which Four Trumpets** are **sounded. Chapter Nine** the **fifth** and **sixth Trumpets** are **sounded. Chapter Ten** through **Chapter Eleven** verse **fourteen** are the other events associated with the **sounding** of this trumpet. **Chapter 11:15**, the **Seventh Trumpet is sounded.**

Chapter Twelve introduces the **last half** of the **Tribulation Period**. The characters of this chapter are **the woman, the dragon, the man-child, and Michael the angel. Chapter Thirteen** introduces other characters **such as:** The **Beast**, The **Lamb** or the **False prophet**, the Image and mark of the **Beast 666. Chapter Fourteen**, the **144,000** are **in heaven**, the messages of warning from angels, and harvest of the earth.

Chapter Fifteen, Seven **Angels are introduced** and given **seven vials** with the **seven last plagues of God. Chapter Sixteen**, the **pouring out of the vials** upon the earth. **Chapter Seventeen** deals with **false religious systems – "Mystery Babylon".**

Chapter Eighteen, the **City of Babylon** is judged and brought down. **Chapter Nineteen,** the **marriage** of the **Lamb** and the **Church takes place**, and the **second coming of Christ to the earth. Chapter Twenty**, the **Millennial kingdom** is set up. **Satan** is bound for a **thousand years. The White Throne Judgment.**

Chapter twenty-one includes the **New Heaven** and **New Earth**, the New **Jerusalem**, and other **New** things. **Chapter twenty-two** is a **summary** of what had been said, and that **Christ shall come quickly.**

REVELATION EXPLAINED

We shall **begin** at this time **to explain**, by the grace of God, the book of REVELATION. The first portion of this book, especially from **chapters one** through **three**, we will deal with the **History of the Christian Church. Chapter One** introduces us with **John the Apostle on the isle called Patmos.** He was there because of **persecution directed against the Church.** Tradition says, that he was first put in a **kettle of hot oil** to be destroyed, but **God delivered him.** While on this Isle, **he saw** the **vision contained** in the Book of **Revelation.** Jesus appeared unto him **in glory saying:** "I am **Alpha and Omega,** the **beginning** and **the ending,** saith the Lord, which is, and which **was,** and which **is to come, the Almighty.**" Jesus here identifies Himself as the beginning and ending (Rev. 1:8).

In **verse eleven** Jesus tells John, in so many words, the **purpose of the vision** that will be shown in this **book:** It was to be sent to the **Seven churches of Asia,** which **are as follows: Ephesus, Smyrna, Pergamus, Thyatira, Sardis, Philadelphia,** and **Laodicea.** Christ is shown **walking in the midst** of them. This is to show that **He is** beholding their state and **works.**

A **mystery is unfolded** in this particular chapter. The **Seven stars** are revealed to be the Seven Angels of **messengers** of the **Churches.** The **Seven candlesticks** are the **seven Churches** (Rev. 1:20).

SEVEN STAGES OF CHURCH HISTORY

It is a well-known practice that **church history** is usually divided into **Seven Periods** or **stages;** beginning with the Church of **Ephesus** and ending with the Church of **Laodicea.** In other words, beginning with the **Apostolic** Age and ending with the **Modern** Age. The dates are given such as:

Ephesians' Age	A.D. 30 - A.D. 100
Smyrnians' Age	A.D. 100 - A.D. 313
Pergamians' Age	A.D. 313 - A.D. 476
Thyatirains' Age	A.D. 476 - A.D. 1453
Sardians' Age	A.D. 1453 - A.D. 1648
Philadelphians' Age	A.D. 1648 - A.D. 1901
Laodicians' Age	A.D. 1901 - to the Rapture

THE EPHESIAN AGE

(APOSTOLIC)
A.D. 30 - A.D. 100

When Bible students consider the subject of **Church History**, they must start with **the establishment** or **founding of the Church by Jesus Christ on the day of Pentecost** about **A.D. 30 or 33**, as some may give the date.

In St. Matthew 16:16, 17, after Peter made the great **declaration**: "Thou art the **Christ**, the **Son of the living God**", Jesus made mention of **the building of His church by saying**: "...Blessed art thou, **Simon Barjona**: for **flesh and blood** hath not revealed it unto thee, but **my Father** which is in heaven. [18]And I say also unto thee, That thou art Peter, (petrol, a stone), and upon this rock (Petra, a massive rock) I will build **my church;** and the gates of hell shall not prevail against it."

The word church comes from a **Greek term, ecclesia**, meaning call out. The church is composed of **Jew and Gentile** infused into ONE body. It is a nation made out of nations. It is a group made up of all races, languages, various cultural backgrounds, learned and the unlearned, rich and poor, etc., brought into ONE body and brotherhood of **baptized believers in Christ**.

It is **evident** that the church is **yet in existence** today, because Jesus said that the gates of hell shall not prevail against it. Though it has gone through much **persecution** and **hard tribulation**, to near extinction of the true believers, God has never left Himself **without a witness** throughout each stage of **Church History**. I am confident that this very Church, with all of **its first doctrine**, is yet in existence today. We need **not substitute** the original doctrine for some **man-made modernistic opinions** and **interpretations** of the Bible, in order to satisfy the **desires** and pleasures **of man**. But, as JUDE **3 stated:** [3]"Beloved, when I gave all diligence to write unto you of the **common salvation**, it was needful for me to write unto you, and exhort *you*, that ye should earnestly **contend for the faith** which was **once delivered** unto the **saints**."

The Church of Jesus Christ arose out of Judaism because **Israel rejected Christ as** a **nation,** God turned to individuals of **all nations**. (St. John 1:11-**13**; Acts 15: 14-18). Paul said that this was a **mystery hidden in time past**, but now revealed unto the Apostles and prophets by **the Spirit**; "[6]That the Gentiles should be fellow heirs, and of the same body, and partakers of his promise in Christ by the **Gospel:"** (Eph. 3:5, 6) Now for the topic under **consideration;** that is, the **Ephesians'** Church Age. This is the **Apostolic** Age, for it reaches from the **beginning of the Church** to the death of the **last Apostle**, who was **St. John**, in approximately **A.D. 100**. The word **Ephesus** means to let go or **relax.**

In this Age, the Church was kept under the **watchful care of the Apostles**. We will examine **the doctrine** of this Age, and what constituted the **way of salvation**. This will be done under the heading "**Contents In This Age**".

CONTENTS IN THIS AGE

BELIEF - **Mark 16:15-17.** They taught that an individual should believe in the **death, burial, and resurrection of Jesus Christ** (Acts 10:34-43; 8:36, 37).

REPENTANCE - They believed and taught **repentance** (Acts 2:38; 3:19; 17:30).

BAPTISM - They taught that Baptism in Jesus' Name was part of the method to receive the remission of Sins (Acts 2:37, **38;** 8:12-17; 10:44-48; 19:1-6; 22:16; I Pet. 3:21) They understood the command of Jesus in **Matthew 28:19, 20,** which saith: "Go ye therefore, and **teach all nations**, baptizing them in the name of the Father, and of the Son, and of the Holy Ghost: ²⁰Teaching them to observe all things whatsoever I have commanded you:" to mean that they should **baptize in the name of Jesus**. That name being the **name of the Father** (St. John 5:43), **the Son** (Matt. 1:21, 23), **Holy Ghost,** (St. John 14:26). Jesus **clarified this fact in St. Luke 24:47, by saying:** "And that **repentance** and **remission of sins** should be preached in HIS NAME, among all nations beginning at Jerusalem." **(Acts 4:10-12)**

Baptism OF THE HOLY GHOST - They believed and taught that a person should be baptized or **filled with the Holy Ghost**. They taught that the reception of the Holy Ghost was **a separate** and **distinct act** performed upon the believer AFTER and **not WHEN** he believed in the **death, burial, and resurrection** of the Lord **Jesus Christ**.

Note such an important Question: ³⁷"Now when they heard *this*, they were pricked in their heart, and said unto **Peter** and to the rest of the **apostles**, Men and brethren, **what shall we do?**

³⁸Then Peter said unto them, **Repent**, and **be baptized** every one of you in the **name** of **Jesus Christ** for the remission of sins, and ye **shall receive the gift** of the Holy Ghost." (Acts 2:37, 38) ¹²"But when they BELIEVED Philip preaching the things concerning the Kingdom of God, and the name of Jesus Christ, they were BAPTIZED, both men and women." (Acts 8:12) Now at this point there is a separation of their **Believing** and **Receiving** the Holy Ghost. They now **have already believed** and are baptized but **have not as yet received the Gift** of the Holy Ghost.

Let's **Note that important point:** "Now when the **apostles which were at Jerusalem** heard that **Samaria had received the Word of God**, they sent unto them **Peter and John:** ¹⁵Who, when they were come down, **prayed for them**, that they might **receive the Holy Ghost:** ¹⁶(For as yet he was fallen upon **none of them:** only **they were baptized in the name** of the Lord Jesus.)" (Acts 8:14 -16)

Let's note another very vehement **incident with the apostle Paul** in his conversion, when he was on the **road to Damascus**. "And suddenly there shined round about him **a light from heaven:** and **he fell to the earth,** and **heard a voice** saying unto him, **Saul, Saul, why persecutest thou me?** ⁵And he said, **Who art thou, Lord?** And the Lord said, **I am Jesus whom thou persecutest**: it is hard for thee to kick against the pricks. [6]And he trembling and astonished said, **Lord, what wilt thou have me to do?**" Right here Paul **became a believer in Jesus Christ** and **repented** or surrendered himself unto Him **by saying: "Lord, what wilt thou have me to do?** (Acts 9:6) At this point, he had **not been filled with the Holy Ghost**, neither had his **sins been remitted**.

"And the Lord said unto him, **Arise,** and **go into** the **city**, and **it shall be told** thee **what thou MUST DO**…[10]And there was a certain **disciple at Damascus**, named **Ananias;** and to him said the Lord **in a vision**, Ananias. And he said, Behold, I am *here*, Lord. [11]And the Lord said unto him, **Arise,** and go into the street which is called **Straight,** and **inquire in the house of Judas** for *one* called **Saul,** of **Tarsus:** for, behold, he prayeth.

[17]And Ananias went his way, and entered into the **house;** and putting his hands on him said, Brother Saul, the Lord, *even* Jesus, that appeared unto thee in the way as thou camest, hath sent me, that thou mightest **receive thy sight**, and **be filled with the Holy Ghost.**" Note this following point, Paul **had not yet been filled with the Holy Ghost**. It is evident that there **must be some sort of sign that God uses to show** when a person **has been filled with the Holy Spirit**. Up to **this point, his sin had not been remitted**. To **prove this point or fact**, turn with me to **Acts 22:12-16**.

"And **one Ananias**, a **devout man** according to the Law, having a **good report** of **all the Jews** which dwelt *there*, [13]Came unto me, and stood, and said unto me, Brother Saul, **receive thy sight**. And the **same hour I looked up upon** him. [14]And he said, The **God of our fathers hath chosen** thee, that thou shouldest **know his will**, and see that Just **One**, and shouldest **hear the voice of his mouth**. For thou shalt be his **witness unto all men** of what thou **hast seen and heard**. AND NOW WHY TARRIEST THOU? ARISE, AND BE BAPTIZED, AND WASH AWAY THY SINS, calling on **the name of the Lord**." (Acts 9:3-6, 10-11, 17-20; 22:12-16)

It is evident that Paul **had not received the remission of sins until** his subsequent **baptism** in **the name of the Lord Jesus**.

Let's **note another point on this subject**, that when the disciples of **Ephesus** received the **Holy Ghost it was a distinct act**. "And it came to pass, that, while Apollos was at Corinth, Paul having passed through the upper coasts came to **Ephesus:** and finding certain disciples, [2]He said unto them, **Have ye received the Holy Ghost SINCE** ye believed? And they said unto him, **We have not so much as heard** whether there be **any Holy Ghost**. [3]And he said unto them, Unto **what** then were **ye baptized?** And they said, Unto **John's baptism**. [4]Then said Paul, John verily baptized with the **baptism of repentance**, saying unto the people, that they should believe on him which should come after him, that is, on Christ Jesus. [5]When they heard this, **they were baptized in the name of the Lord Jesus**."

We will **pause here** and **note the fact** that these people or disciples **believed** the **gospel that Paul preached to them**, and were **baptized**, but the Holy Ghost **had not come into them**.

⁶"And **When** Paul had **laid his hands** upon them, the Holy Ghost **came on them; and they spake with tongues, and prophesied.**" (Acts 19:1-6)

In Ephesians 1:13, Paul gives an outline of **what happened to these disciples** of **Ephesus**. "In whom ye also *trusted*, after that ye heard the **word of truth**, the gospel of your **salvation:** in whom also **After** that ye **Believed,** ye were **Sealed** with that Holy Spirit of promise,"

The Godhead - They believed that *there* was but **One** God (I Cor. 8:6). (And that He was manifested in the **body of Jesus Christ.** (I Tim. 3:16) And that Jesus Christ was that God (St. John 1:1, 2, 10, and 14)

Holiness - They believed in holy living on the part of the one that was saved (Rom. 6:1, 22; I Pet. 1:15, 16; Ja. 5:19, 20).

The Apostles felt that their doctrine was complete and needed no additions or sub-tractions to or from it. Let's note some of these points.

"I marvel that ye are **so soon removed from him that called you into the grace** of **Christ** unto **another gospel:** ⁷Which is **not another;** but there be some that trouble you, and would **pervert the gospel of Christ.** ⁸But though we, or an **angel** from heaven, **preach any other gospel** unto you than that which **we have preached** unto **you,** let him **be accursed.**" (Gal. 1:6-8) "**This Second** epistle, beloved, I now write unto **you;** in *both* which **I stir up your pure minds by way of remembrance:** ²That ye may be mindful of the words which were spoken before by the holy prophets, and of the commandment of **us the apostles** of the Lord and Saviour:" (2 Peter 3:1, 2)

"Beloved, when I gave all diligence to write unto you of **the common salvation,** it was needful for me to write unto you, and **exhort you** that ye should **earnestly contend** for **the faith** which was **once delivered** unto the saints." (Jude 3) (2 Tim. 3:10-17; 1 Tim. 6:3-5; 1 Tim. 1:3; 2 Tim. 2:2; Rev. 22:18)

Apostolic Warnings

The Apostles knew that "**Some shall depart from the faith,** giving heed to **seducing** spirits and **doctrines of Devils.**" Therefore, for that reason, they **warned** the church **of this fact.**

Paul said unto the **elders of Ephesus:** "For I have **not shunned to declare** unto you all the **counsel of God.** ²⁸Take heed therefore unto yourselves, and **all the flock,** over the which the **Holy Ghost hath made you overseers,** to feed the church of God, which he **hath purchased with his own blood.** ²⁹For I know this, that after my **departing shall grievous wolves enter in among you, not sparing the flock.** ³⁰Also of your own selves shall **men arise,** speaking **perverse things,** to **draw away disciples** after them." (Acts 20:27-30)

The Apostle Peter said: "**But There** were false prophets also among the people, even as there shall be **false teachers** among you, who privily shall bring in damnable **heresies**, even denying the Lord that bought them, and bring upon themselves swift destruction. ²And many shall follow their **pernicious ways;** by reason of whom the way of truth shall be **evil spoken** of." (2 Peter 2:1, 2)

The Apostle John said: "**Beloved, Believe** not every spirit, but try the spirits whether they **are of God:** because **many false prophets** are gone out into the world." (1 John 4:1). "They went out **from us,** but **they were not of us;** for if they had been of us, they would *no doubt* **have continued with us:** but *they went out*, that they might be made manifest that they were **not all of us.**" (1 John 2:19)

Jude said, "For there are **certain men crept in unawares**, who were before of old **ordained to this condemnation, ungodly** men, turning the grace of our God into lasciviousness, and **denying the only Lord God**, and our Lord Jesus Christ." Jude 4.

Above all, Jesus warned us saying, "For there shall arise **false Christs**, and false **prophets**, and shall show great signs and **wonders;** insomuch **that, if it were possible,** they shall **deceive the very elect.**" (Matt. 24:24)

From the Apostolic Warning, we see that many **false preachers** and **churches** would arise. I must say they have arrived and have **deceived** many. But, we that have the truth, **must stand firmly** on the **Word of God** and **refute every false** church and **doctrine**. The best way to do this is from the written **Word of God**. For the scripture said, "To **the law** and **to the testimony:** if they speak not according to **this word**, it is because **there is no light in them.**" (Isa. 8:20)

To **refute every false doctrine**, we must do it under the light of the **Word** God. of The Apostle Paul said to Pastor Timothy, "If **any man** teach otherwise, and consent not to wholesome words, even the words of our Lord Jesus Christ, and to the doctrine which as according to **godliness;** ...from such withdraw thyself." (1 Tim. 6:3, 5d)

"Therefore we ought to give the more **earnest heed** to the things which we have heard, lest at any time we should **let them slip**. ²For if the word spoken by angels was **steadfast,** and every transgression and **disobedience received** a just recompense of **reward;** ³How shall **we escape, if we neglect so great salvation;** which at the first began to be **spoken by the Lord**, and was confirmed **unto us** by **them that heard him;**" (Heb. 2:1, 2)

The Apostle Peter said, "**This Second** epistle, beloved, **I now write unto you;** in *both* which **I stir up your pure minds** by **way of remembrance:** That ye may be mindful of the words which were spoken before by the **holy prophets**, and of the commandment **of us the apostles of the Lord and Savior:**" (2 Peter 3:1, 2)

The Apostle John said, ⁷"For many **deceivers** are entered into the world, who **confess not** that **Jesus Christ is come in the flesh. This is a deceiver** and **an anti-Christ.** ⁸Look to yourselves, that **we lose not those things which we have** wrought, but that we receive a full reward. ⁹Whosoever **transgresseth**, and **abideth not** in the **doctrine of Christ, hath not God**. He that abideth in the doctrine of Christ, he hath **both** the **Father** and the **Son**. ¹⁰If there come any unto you, and **bring not this** doctrine, **receive him not** into your house, neither **bid him God speed:** [11]For he that **biddeth** him **God speed is partaker of his evil deeds.** (2 John 7-11) **We,** therefore, **see from these scriptures**, that the Apostles knew that they **had received the full truth of God's plan of salvation,** and that the church that was established in their day was the church that would remain **until the rapture**.

We will see, as we continue this study throughout History, that a lot of other churches would be established by men contrary to the doctrine that was **once delivered** unto the **saints.** We find this coming to pass in the last part of the Ephesian or Apostolic Stage. They had **lost** their **first love.** They had become **relaxed.** There were some there, which practiced the deeds of the **Nicolatans**. The admonishment was that they should repent or else he would remove the candlestick from among them.

The Smyrnian Age

(Persecuted Period)
A.D. 100 - 313

Smyrna was about fifty miles north of Ephesus. The meaning of the term Ephesus is **bitter, which signifies its suffering.** In this particular age, we find the church in the **midst of a great persecution inflicted by the Roman Empire.** All the **Apostles are now dead** and **the church is now under their disciples.** This is the period where the **Apostles warned that** men shall **arise after their departure.**

Some of the **outstanding men** of that age were: **Polycarp,** (a disciple of the **Apostle John**), **Justin Martyr, Origen, Montanus, Tertullian, Eusebius, Arius, Saballeus,** and **Athanasius.** Some of these men began to **teach doctrines contrary** to what the **Apostles had taught.**

Polycarp is referred to **quite often by historians** that when he **was asked** by his **persecutors to recant Christ,** he said, "For **Eighty-Six years have I been a servant** of **Christ** and he had done me nothing but **good,** and **I will not renounce** him now." He **sealed his testimony** with his **blood** and **died a martyr** for **Jesus Christ.**

Justin Martyr, A.D. 156, is **the first** to have **mentioned** the **Trinitarian Formula of Baptism,** that is, in the **name of the Father and of the Son, and of the Holy Ghost.** This had begun to be used instead of the formula **in the name of Jesus Christ,** which is considered by **almost all historians as being the one practiced** by the **Apostles and the early Church.**

From the **Encyclopedia Britannica,** the **Eleventh Edition Vol. 3**, Page 365, section 5, on the **Baptism formula,** it is said: "The **Trinitarian** formula and Triune Immersion were **not** uniformly used **from the beginning,** nor did they always go together. **The teaching of the Apostles indeed prescribes baptism in the name of Father, Son,**

and Holy Ghost, but on the next page **speaks of** the **name of the Lord,** the normal formula of the **New Testament**. In the **third century** baptism in **the Name** of **Christ was still so widespread that Pope Stephen**, in Opposition to Cyprian of Carthage, **declared it to be Valid**. From **Pope Zachariah** we learn that the **Celtic** Missionaries in baptizing omitted one or more persons of the Trinity, and this was one of the reasons why the Church of **Rome** anathematized them."

From the foregoing reading, **we see** that a **conflict had** begun over **the formula** of **baptism**. There is a difference between **Pope Stephen** and **Pope Zachariah**.

Pope Stephen was **Bishop of the Church of Rome** from **A.D. 253-257**. Baptism **in Jesus' name was still practiced**. But Pope Zachariah, who was Pope over the **Roman** Church from A.D. 741-752, **rejected those that baptized in the Name of Jesus only**. We see, then, that between **A.D. 253-741**, there had been a **drastic change** from the **formula of baptism in the Name of Jesus Christ**, to the formula in the name of **the Father, Son, And Holy Ghost**.

This **influence came** chiefly from the **Nicene Council**, where they **officially adopted the Trinity of God** in **three distinct Persons.**

ORIGEN is considered to be, one of the **well-known**, and **outstanding Bible expositors of that time**. He had somewhat of a **Biblical Library** established.

MONTANUS is well noted for **his speaking in other tongues by the power of** the **Holy Ghost.** He began teaching a distinction between the Holy Ghost, saying the dispensation of the Holy Spirit was soon to come. By that teaching, **he established a difference in the Father, Son, and Holy Ghost. This is the beginning of the idea** of the **Trinity in the second Century A.D.**

Many **denounced this teaching** as the **work of demons**. But, when his pupil, **Tertullian took up the doctrine**, it began to **win popularity**. For **this man** was considered **by many** to be **a Great Theologian.**

TERTULLIAN is the first one to have coined the word **Trinity**. This was a strange and **foreign word to Christianity**. For that word Trinity, **is nowhere found in the Bible.** These **doctrines began to bring a great confusion** in the doctrine of **the Godhead.** Many **former heathens had become associated** with the church. They were used to the doctrine of a **Trinity from their heathen worship,** or **religion**.

It is said that Tertullian **advocated** baptism should be **done by dipping the candidate, once in the name of the Father, once in the name of the Son, and once in the name of the Holy Ghost.**

These **methods and new doctrines brought about a great confusion** on the **Godhead.** The subject came up as to whether **Jesus Christ was God**, and **what part** the **Holy Ghost had in the Godhead.**

ARIUS began to teach that Jesus Christ was not God.

ATHANASIUS taught that Jesus was God.

Sabalieus taught that there was **but one God who manifested Himself as Father, Son,** and **Holy Ghost**.

This controversy continued throughout the period until **Constantine called a Council** at **Nicea in 325 A.D.**, of which we will take up under the Pergamians' period.

The Pergamian Age

A.D. 313-476
(Imperial)

PERGAMUS means **married to the world**. It was located fifty miles north of Smyrna. This name **signifies its association with the world through the edict** of **toleration by the Emperor Constantine**. In A.D. 313, **Christianity became a State** or **National religion**.

Some of the **things** that are **listed** in **this period** are: **Satan's seat in the Church**. We can see that Constantine was **an influential force** in the **Council of Nicea**.

They had the **Doctrine of the Nicolaitans** who taught there was nothing evil and therefore you could enjoy life without restrictions.

When **Constantine gave** the **edict of toleration**, he came **to the knowledge** of the **Church being in great confusion and uproar over the doctrine of the Godhead**. And if nothing could be done about it, the **church would be ripped apart** by **internal strife**. Upon this point, he **convened a Council at Nicea in A.D. 325 to settle** this **question on the Godhead**.

The Council Of Nicea

A.D. 325

This Council was **attended by a great number of Bishops** throughout the **Roman world**. Of course there was **one prominent absentee** in the person of the Bishop of Rome. Because of **age and ill health**, he **sent a representative in his stead**.

In this particular Council, Arius presented his **Doctrine** on the **Godhead. His doctrine** was that **Jesus** was **not God**, and that **He was only** the **Son of God. Being the first of God's creation, his doctrine is known in church history as Arianism.**

Another Doctrine was set forth known as the **Doctrine of Saballeus**. He taught that there was but **one God,** who was **manifested in the positions of the Father, Son,** and **Holy Ghost. Just like a man can be father, husband, and trustee,** that is, one person occupying three positions, such as, water can be solid (ice), liquid and gas (steam).

They were all ready to accept this form. But, when Arius was willing to accept this form, they suspected that he was willing to do so because he could see where he could use this form and maneuver his doctrine into theology. They rejected this teaching of Saballeus for that reason and sought for another form.

After which, Athanasius presented the Trinitarian form. He endeavored to present a distinction between the Father, Son, and Holy Ghost as each separately being God, but yet one in substance (Homo-ousion), which means to say there are three persons who are God, but they are one in substance. They knew that the terms "one in Substance" and "three in person" were not found in the scripture.

The predicament that they were in was that they were trying to prove that Jesus was God, which was denied by Arius. They wanted to retain the fact that Jesus was God, but they ended up with three distinct persons in the Godhead.

I do support the conclusion of the Council of Nicea on the fact that Jesus is God, but not on the point of their adopting a non-scriptural term, (Homo-ousion) to support their doctrine of the three distinct Persons in the Godhead. Any type of doctrine that is brought into theology that cannot be supported by the scripture is a doctrine of Hearsy. It is not to be followed by those who love the truth.

The word "Homo-Ousion" is the Unscriptural word which the Council of Nicea adopted to explain the belief of some, that there were three distinct persons in the Godhead. By doing this, they ended up with a generation of three distinct Gods.

The Bible never taught such doctrine. The Bible teaches that there is but one personal God. God said, "I am the Lord, and there is none else." Isa. 45:5. The pronoun "I" is a personal pronoun. God is saying, that He is a personal God and there is no other personal God beside Him.

So, when we look at the Father, the Son, and the Holy Ghost, we see that same God in different manifestations. The Son of God was actually the flesh that God begot to manifest Himself. Jesus said, "He that hath seen Me, hath seen the Father;" St. John 14:9. Paul said, "And without controversy great is the mystery of Godliness: God was manifested in the flesh, justified in the Spirit, seen of angels, preached unto the Gentiles, believed on in the world, received up into glory." (1 Tim. 3:16)

The next day after the Council adopted the Athanasius Creed, most of them changed their mind about the new doctrine they had just instituted the day before, as being a doctrine of error. The Athanasian's Creed was not fly fixed until the Council of Constantinople in A.D. 381.

Augustine, the mighty saint of God, did not go along with that Trinitarian doctrine. He said that God was as the Fountain, Stream, and Pond in which the water entered.

The doctrine of the Godhead has been an issue throughout church history. Even to this day, there is a continual debate as to who constitutes the Godhead.

Many **refuse to be baptized only in the name of Jesus:** For fear they would be leaving out the Father and Holy Ghost in that formula. The Trinitarians formula of baptism in the name of the Father, Son, and Holy Ghost was **not used in the beginning.** It began to be used more so **after the Council of Nicea.**

These are **the things**, which **happened in the Pergamians' Period.** This period continued until approximately **A.D. 476, at the end or fall of the Roman Empire.** The **strange doctrine**s are listed in the Bible **as being in this period.** "The **Doctrine of Balaam"__Balaam** taught **Balak how to cast a stumbling block** in the way of **the Children of Israel.** After **he saw that God had blessed Israel**, and that **nobody could curse** what **God had blessed, he counseled Balak to invite the Children** of Israel to a **feast of Baal-Peor.** This was **an Idolatrous feast** included much **sensuality, and sexual pleasure.** Then **the Children of Israel went to that feast,** they **saw the ungodly attires** and **unchaste behavior** of **those that were in the feast. They fell into spiritual whoredom and natural fornications and adultery.** When **Israel fell into that state, God destroyed many thousands** of them.

Therefore, the **doctrine of Balaam in the church of Pergamus** stated that it was **all right to allow the church to mix with the world. Constantine** and the **Roman Empire** became a part of the **Church unconverted.** Hence, the word **Pergamus** means **married to the world.**

The doctrines of the **Nicolaitans** were there. In the church of Ephesus, it is mentioned about the **deeds of the __Nicolaitans.** Now, **these deeds have become a doctrine.**

THE THYATIRIAN AGE

A.D. 476-1453
(CATHOLIC)

The name THYATIRA means a **continual sacrifice.** This church is classified in church history as the **Medieval or Dark Age** Church. It was located between **Pergamus** and **Sardis.** The **sins of this church were that they allowed Jezebel,** who called herself **a prophetess,** to **teach** the church to **commit fornication.** This woman **represents the spirit of the Jezebel** who brought the **worship of Baal into Israel.**

It was in this **church age** that **images** were introduced for **worship** in the church.

When **Rome fell politically in 476 A.D.,** she strove to continue her conquering **ecclesiastical**ly by taking over the **leadership** of the church.

Pope Gregory in A.D. 590 began the **Catholic** Church. What I mean by that is, he began to **organize churches,** (who were independently ruled in local congregations), **to submit to the church of Rome** and **to accept that the Bishop** of the **Roman Church should be head over all other Bishops** and **Churches.**

This period is one of the **darkest hours of Church History**. The privilege to **read the Bible was taken away from the laity**. Therefore, **biblical Knowledge began** to be on a **stand-still** for the average person.

The **political aspect of the time** was **ravished by savages invading the Roman Empire**. Rome was **divided into approximately Ten Different Kingdoms**. The **schools of learning** were **ultimately demolished**. The result was the **Dark Ages**.

In approximately the years 610-632 A.D., a **powerful religious system** was **established**, known as **Islam** or **Mohammedism**. They taught that **there was no God**, but **Allah**. They spread their doctrine **with the use of the Sword of war**. This religious system emerged **from the Arabs**, who were **descendants from Abraham** through **Ishmael.**

The **reason for their teaching** was, because, of Christianity adopting the **Nicean Creed**, which actually means **three Gods in one Substance. They took over the land** of **Palestine** and **Jerusalem** and **established a foothold in the Holy Land**.

Because of this, there were **many expeditions administered by what is called the Crusaders.** They **fought to recover the** birthplace of Christianity and take it out of the hands of the Turks who were a **powerful Arm** of the **Mohammedan's** political religion. The Turks held onto that land **until the outbreak of the World War One, in 1914.**

In the meantime, the **Catholic Church was establishing new doctrines** and **ordinances** that were **foreign to the original** church. They **began to worship Saints who had died.** They established the **Priesthood to offer the Communion Service**, or the Lord's Supper, as a sacrifice of the **body of Jesus Christ** every time it was given.

In 593 they established the doctrine of Purgatory. They say, *"It is of faith that there is a place we call Purgatory, where petty faults, or temporal punishment due to sin, are expiated."*

The **Bible does not speak** anywhere of a **Purgatory.** "Jesus said unto him, (the thief on the cross), Verily I say unto thee, **Today shalt thou be with me in paradise."** (Luke 23:43). **Abraham** said to the **rich man**, "Between us and you there is a **great gulf fixed:** so that they which would pass from hence to **you cannot; neither can they** pass **to us, that** *would come* from thence." (Luke 16:26; Heb. 9:27; Rom. 8:1; 2 Cor. 5:19)

In **858 A.D.** there was a **forged document circulated** that was **called the "Donation of Constantine."** (The "Donation" is a **spurious document** of Emperor Constantine **the Great**, addressed to the **Pope Sylvester I (314-335) purporting privileges and possessions such as:**

(1) The Bishop of **Rome as successor of St. Peter**, is to have the **primacy** over the **four Bishops of Antioch, Alexandria, Constantinople, and Jerusalem**, also over **all the Bishops in the World.**

(2) The **Lateran basilica at Rome**, built by **Constantine,** shall surpass all churches as their head.

(3) The **Bishop of Rome** shall enjoy the same **honorary rights as the emperor**. Among them, **the right to wear an imperial crown, a purple cloak, tunic**, and in general all **imperial insignia** or signs of distinction. Etc.

Today, many understand that this was a "**Forged document of Emperor Constantine the Great**, by which large privileges and rich possessions were conferred on the pope and the Roman Church." (**Catholic Encyclopedia V "Donation of Constantine" P. 118**)

Even **if this document was not forged, Constantine had no power given by the scripture** to do so. When the Apostle Paul left the churches, he said unto them, "**I commend you to God, and to the word of his grace, which is able to build you up, and to give you an inheritance among all them which are sanctified.**" (Acts 29:32). Peter called himself an elder (or bishop) along with other elders even though he was an apostle (1 Pet. 5:1, 2).

All local churches and Bishops (pastors) **are responsible directly to God for their tending His flock.** (Heb. 13:17). Of course, at all times, we must **strive** for the **unity of the church and doctrine**.

In A.D. 1075, the greatest mass Divorce in History was forced upon the Clergy by **Pope Gregory VII**. Gregory VII, declared **all clerical marriages invalid**.

"**Our Judgment upon marriages** contracted by persons of this kind (the clergy) is that they must be broken." (**First Lateran Council, 1123, Cannon VI**).

The Bible said, "**Marriage is honorable in all**." (Heb. 13:4) ("All" **includes** the **clergy**).

The Bible gives information that **Peter** was married. "But **Simon's wife's** mother lay sick of a fever, and **anon they tell him of her**." (Mark 1:30)

The Apostle said, "Have we not **power** to lead about **a sister, a wife**, as well as other apostles, and as the brethren of the Lord, and as Cephas?" (1 Cor. 9:5) The Bible said, "What therefore **God hath joined** together, let **not man** put asunder." (Mark 10:9).

In 1213 A.D., the Pope established "The inquisition" together with the **death penalty for heresy. The inquisition was instituted with the torture of trials** of those who did **not accept all the teaching** of the Pope.

The only thing the Bible tells us **to do with a Heretic** was to **reject** and **withdraw ourselves** from him (Titus 3:10; 2 Thess. 3:6; I Tim. 6:3).

In 1190 A.D., various kinds of "Indulgences, (By a plenary indulgence is meant the remission of the entire temporal punishment due to sin so that no further explanation **is required in Purgatory**). "**A partial indulgence** commutes only a certain portion of the penalty." (**Catholic Enc. VII, "Indulgences" P. 783**)

Jesus **Christ is the only One** that can **take away our sins** (St. John 1:29; 1 John 1:7, 9; 2:2-4; Ps. 49:7, 8).

In 1545 the Council of Trent, Rome finally turned from **the authority of God's Word** to the **authority of tradition. Traditions were made equal in authority to the Bible**. Justification by faith **condemned**. But the Bible warns us through the Apostles, saying, "But though we, or an angel from heaven, preach any other gospel unto you than that which we have preached unto you, let him be accursed." (Ga. l: 8, 9; Cor. 2:8, 9)

THE ANTE NICENE FATHERS

The **Ante Nicene Fathers were men who were** (some of them) **disciples of the Apostles.** They wrote **many epistles** and **books** of their Day. Some of them that wrote **were: Polycarp (A.D. 69-156), Student of Apostle John, and Bishop of Antioch. Papias, (about A.D. 70-155)** another **student of John Bishop of Herapolis;** about 100 miles east of Ephesus. **Justin Martyr (A.D. 100-167).** Born at Neapolis; ancient Shechem; **about the time John died. Iranaeus (A.D. 130-200)** Brought up in **Smyrna, Student of Polycarp, and Papias. Origen (185-254), one of the most learned men of the ancient church of his day. Two-Thirds of the New Testament** was quoted in his writings.

Tertullian (160-220), of Carthage, **"The father of Latin Christianity, a Roman Lawyer, a pagan before his conversion. Eusebius (264-340), "Father of Church history" Bishop of Caesarea at the time of Constantine and had great influence to win** him. He wrote an **"Ecclesiastical History"** from **Christ to the Council of Nicea.**

POST NICENE

John Chrysostom (345-407), "The Golden Mouthed" a matchless orator, greatest preacher of his day, born at Antioch. Jerome (340-420) most learned of **the Latin Fathers, educated at Rome, lived many years at Bethlehem, translated the Bible into the Latin language; called the Latin Vulgate. Augustine, (354-430) Bishop of Hipo, North Africa.** He was **the great Theologian** of the **church** in **his day.**

During the time of the **Thyatirian Church Period, the Catholic Church took the Bible out of the hand of the laity. Only the pope, Bishop, and priest were given the privilege to read and interpret it for the people.** As time began to draw toward **the Reformation Period,** some of the men began to **translate the Bible into the language of the people.**

MANUSCRIPTS

The **original manuscripts or writing of the Apostles of all the New Testament books,** as far as is known, **have been lost.**

COPY

Copies of these writings **began to be made from the very first** for other **churches;** and copies, time after time, as the older ones wore out.

They were **made on Papyrus, made of slices of the plant that grew in Egypt.** Two slices, **one vertical, the other horizontal,** were **pressed together and polished** ink was **made of charcoal, gum and water.**

Shorter sheets were fastened, side, to side to form rolls. A roll was usually approximate **30 feet long** and **9 or 10 inches high.**

In the **second century A.D., the New Testament books began to be made up in the "Codex"** form, our modern book form.

In the **4th century A.D., Papyrus was superseded by Vellum** as the main writing material. **Vellum was parchment taken from skins** much more durable, and **made up in book form.** With the invention of the printing press, **by John Gutenberg A.D. 1454, the making of manuscript Bibles ceased.**

There are **now in existence about 4,000 known manuscripts of the Bible;** or parts of the Bible, **made between the 2nd and 15th** centuries. This seems **few to us,** but **it is far more than the manuscripts of any other ancient writings.** There is not a **complete known copy of Homer earlier than A.D. 1300;** nor of **Herodotus earlier than A.D. 1000.**

The **Vellum Manuscripts,** now known **as the Uncials,** were written in large capital letters. There are about **160 of them, made between the 4th and 10th** centuries. The **Cursives were written in small running letters linked together,** and were **made between the 10th and 15th** centuries. The **Uncials, being more ancient,** are far more valuable.

BIBLE TRANSLATIONS

The **Old Testament was written in Hebrew.** The **New Testament** was written **in Greek. A Greek translation of the Old Testament called "The Septuagint" made in** the **3rd century B.C., by order of Alexander the Great,** was in common use in **Jesus' Day. Greek** was the **language** in general used **throughout the Roman world.**

VARIOUS TRANSLATIONS

1. **The Old Syriac. 200 A.D. No complete manuscripts extant.**
2. **The Peshito Syriac. 400 A.D. Source - Old Syriac.**
3. **The Old Latin - Made in 2nd century A.D. from Septuagint.**
4. **The Vulgate A.D. 388-404 by Jerome from Hebrew.**
5. **The Coptic (Egyptian) A.D. 200.**

6. **Ethiopic and Gothic 300-400 A.D.**
7. **Armenian 400-500 A.D.**
8. **Arabic and Slavic 900 A.D.**

The Bible was **suppressed by the Roman Papacy**, and **decrees and dogmas of councils and Popes were instituted instead. The Reformation Period** constituted a **renewed interest in the Bible. Many translations** have been **made in various Languages** around the **world.**

THE ENGLISH TRANSLATIONS

1. **Caedmon A.D. 676.**
2. **Bede 672-735 A.D**
3. **Alfred the Great 849-901. They translated short parts of the Bible into Anglo Saxon.**
4. **John Wycliff - First whole English Bible 1382 A.D. from Latin Vulgate.**
5. **John Tyndale 1525 A.D. from Original Greek.**
6. **Coverdale's Bible 1535 A.D. from Dutch and Latin Sources.**
7. **Roger's Bible - 1537 from Tyndale.**
8. **The Great Bible - 1 539, from Tyndale, Roger, and Coverdale.**
9. **Geneva Bible - 1560. A group of Protestant Scholars from Tyndale followed by the Bishop's Bible 1568 A.D. Authored for Methodist church of England.**
10. **King James Version, 1611 A.D. ordered by King James for the sake of uniform service in Presbyterian Scotland and Episcopal England, a revision of Versions based on Tyndale.**
11. **Anglo-American Revision 1881-1885, the work of 51 English and 32 American scholars. It became necessary because of changes in the meaning of some English words, and clearer text.**
12. **The Revised Standard Version, 1952 A.D.**

Italics in our Bibles **indicate that the word is lacking in the original text;** therefore, it was **filled in to complete the sense.**

There were **no chapters and verses in the original text**. They **were added by Cardinal Caro A.D. 1236, and Robert Stephens A.D. 1551**.

THE SARDIAN AGE

A.D. 1453- 1750
(REFORMATION)

This Church is **classified in church history as the Reformation Church**. The word **Sardis** means "The Escaping One," which signifies **coming out of the Dark Ages and from the Papal authority.** It had **a name that it lived but was dead**. This is to **signify** that the **reformers,** who made an effort to come out of the **Catholic Church, fell short of their purpose. Many denominations were formed** bearing the **very names and purposes of the reformers.** Their efforts were to go back to the **original teaching** of the church. But instead, **they ended up** being **Mini-Catholic Churches or daughter churches with many ways and doctrines like their mothers.**

Many of them **today have not developed** any closer to the original church than when they came out of the **Catholic to reform** the church. But **be confident that God has always had His church around** and someone to **lead His people back to the place where the church first began in Acts Chapter 2.**

THE REFORMERS

Martin Luther - In A.D. 1517, began the **Lutheran Church**, which bears his name unto this day.

John Calvin began the **Reform Church 1528.**
John Knox began the **Presbyterian Church 1547.**

When the **Catholics saw that many were leaving their church, they made war against the Protestants.** This war lasted **Thirty years and was won by the Protestants in A.D. 1648.**

John Smyth began **the Baptist Church in 1609.** They were called Baptist because of the **strong belief in immersion as the mode of baptism.** Many others had held this **same conviction throughout the period of church history**.

THE PHILADELPHIAN AGE

A.D. 1648-1901
(WESLEYAN)

This church is listed in **church history as the Wesleyan Age** or the beginning of the **holiness movement**. It is dated from **1648-1900**. This church was the praise of the Lord. The meaning of the word **Philadelphia** is "Brotherly Love."

Some of the men of this day were **John and Charles Wesley, D.L. Moody, Charles G. Finney, William Carry, and Livingston**.

This church was **famous in the missionary and evangelistic endeavors**. We must also emphasize that many denominations **continued to be established** such as:

1. **Church of England - 1534 by Henry the VIII.**
2. **Congregational - 1600 by Robert Brown.**
3. **Methodist - 1740 by John and Charles Wesley.**
4. **Quakers - 1648 by George Fox.**
5. **Spiritualist - 1848 by the Fox sisters.**
6. **Church of Christ - 1809 by Alex Campbell.**
7. **Seven Day Adventist - 1816 by Williams Miller.**
8. **Mormons - 1830 by Joseph Smith and Brigham Young.**
9. **Church of God - 1830 by John Wilmebremes.**
10. **Christian Science - 1866 by Mary Eddy Baker.**
11. **Jehovah Witness - 1872 by Charles T. Russell.**
12. **Salvation Army - 1865 by Williams Booth.**
13. **Church of the Living God - 1889 by William Christian.**
14. **Church of God in Christ - 1897 by C.E. Mason.**

All of these denominations are yet in existence today. We must **remember** the words of the **Apostle Paul** when he **warned the Elders** of the, **"Take heed therefore unto yourselves, and to all the flock, over the which the Holy Ghost hath made you overseers, to feed the church of God,** which He **hath purchased with his own blood.** For I know this, **that after my departing** shall **grievous wolves enter in among you**, not **sparing the flock**. Also of your own selves **shall men arise**, speaking **perverse things**, to draw **away disciples** after them." (Acts 20:28-30) See also subject entitled **"Apostolic Warnings"**.

THE LAODICIAN AGE

A.D. 1901-END
(MODERN CHURCH)

This church period is **classified in church history as the Modern Church Age**. The meaning of the name **Laodician** is "**Judging the People**". It is a **selfish, lukewarm, and worldly church. Jesus is on the outside of the door knocking.**

The **world supports this church** or religion. At the end, the religion controls the world after the **true church is taken out**. It will be **destroyed by the ten nations.**

In this particular time, God has a **group of people who continue** to march back to **the faith** which was **once delivered** to the saints. Jude 3.

In this time, **a great Pentecostal Revival** ensued in **1901 in Topeka, Kansas** with **C. F. Parham** and his students as they sought for the understanding as to how the disciples and **early saints were filled with the Holy Ghost** in the days of the Apostles.

They found that **in many places in the book of Acts**, whenever an individual **received the Holy Ghost, the evidence that they had received the Holy Ghost was speaking in other tongues.** After checking this out to the fullest extent: On **December 31, 1900, they began an all-night seeking service for the Holy Ghost. Early that morning, January 1, 1901**, the first one that was filled with the Holy Ghost **was one of the students named Agnes N. Ozman** who began to speak in other **tongues as the Spirit gave utterance.**

This date and **incident began the great Revival** of the Baptism of the Holy Ghost as it was in the **days of the Apostles.**

The news media began to **publish stories concerning this in incident and phenomena.**

Soon **Parham closed his school in Topeka, Kansas and began to travel** to various places **preaching and teaching this Pentecostal experience.** He held several **revivals in Texas. His most famous one was in Houston, Texas.** There, **a Black man** by the **name of William J. Seymour** who was converted to this Pentecostal way.

One other that **received the Holy Ghost at Parham school**, in Texas was a **visitor from Los Angeles, California**, by the name of **Sister Neely Terry.** Upon returning to California, she told her friends about her **having received the Holy Ghost.** She was a member of a small Nazarene Mission. After hearing her **testimony,** they sent for **Brother Seymour**, to come and visit their church, and **preach** to them. Brother Seymour **arrived** in Los Angeles in **April of 1906. His first sermon was preached from Acts 2:4**. He told them that whenever **an individual receives the Holy Ghost, he will speak in other tongues.**

It is said that **the members accepted this enthusiastically; But, the pastor rejected it** and therefore she **padlocked the door** of the mission **to keep Brother Seymour** from **coming back** the **next night.**

This left Brother Seymour with **no place to go and with no friends in a strange town.** However, a man by the name of **Richard Asbury** invited him to stay in his home, although he **did not accept** the **message** of **Brother Seymour,** he did allow him to **preach** in the **living room** of his home, which was located at **210 Bonnie Brae Street.**

Many came to this house and **received the Holy Ghost.** Soon this living room was **too small.** After diligently searching for **larger quarters,** they found an abandoned **Methodist Church building at 312 Azusa Street.** There **he continued** his **revivals for three years more.** Many **men** and **women were filled with the Holy Ghost,** who later became **great leaders of various Pentecostal Bodies.**

It is said that **Bishop Mason of the Church of God in Christ** came to this mission and **received the baptism of the Holy Ghost;** and also, the founder of the **Assemblies of God** and many **others throughout the world and were filled.** One of the **oldest of the Pentecostal bodies** is considered by **many** to be the **Pentecostal Assemblies of the World, comely called the P.A.W. Founded in 1906 and incorporated in 1919.**

BAPTISM IN JESUS' NAME

In 1913, it was revealed to some that the formula of baptism during the days of the **Apostles,** was in the **name of the "Lord Jesus Christ."** It is said that Frank Ewart, who boldly broke the **ice** of this **"New Issue" by baptizing Glenn Cook and himself in the Name of Jesus Christ,** as they did in the **book of Acts.**

This brought about a **great division in the Pentecostal Movement.** Some warned to hold onto the **Triune or Trinitarian Formula for baptism.**

The **die had been cast** and many churches **baptized their members over again in the name of Jesus Christ,** which is the **New Testament formula for Baptism.**

The Assemblies of God broke away from the **other Pentecostal fellowships** and began the **Assemblies of God in 1914.**

In **1918, Elder R.C. Lawson began the Church of Our Lord Jesus Christ.** The **reason: (1) women preachers, (2) head covering; and (3)** the **marriage** and **divorce** questions.

The **PAW** has always been an **integrated organization.** In **1924** another organization, for **racial** reasons, **was formed.** In **1925, the P.A.W. established** the **office of Bishops of which Bishop G.T. Haywood was elected** as the **first Bishop of that position.**

Bishop G.T. Haywood, a black man, was **one of the greatest men of this day.** His **knowledge of the scriptures** was seemly **unlimited.** He was **famous in the songs** he wrote. He **designed** and **taught from his own charts.** Being **an artist by trade, he painted pictures of God's Word on a canvass.**

He was pastor of Christ Temple Church of Indianapolis, Indiana. He was saved in 1908, and one year later **became pastor of Christ Temple** until his **death.** He traveled extensively all over the world. His **books** and **songs are** read and **loved** by many throughout the world. A **great man of God.** He **died in April 1931.**

In 1932, there was a merging of the P.A.W. with the P.C.J. to form the Pentecostal Assemblies of Jesus Christ. When the **Blacks were denied** some privileges given to the **White brothers,** this brought **a mass exodus from that newly organized body,** and went back and **reorganized the P.A.W.**

The remaining group **later organized the United Pentecostal in 1945.** It has grown to be **one of the largest predominately white oneness groups in the world.**

Many other organizations have been organized since those days.

Now, there is a **great effort to gather all the oneness organizations** into a **"fellowship group through the effort of the Apostolic World Christian Fellowship,** which began in **1971, led by Bishop W.G. Rowe."**

THE CHURCH CAME BACK TO PENTECOST. THE WAITING END...

By: Bishop W.J. Duncan

WD/ad

TESTS FOR GENERAL BIBLE KNOWLEDGE
THROUGH CHURCH HISTORY

EXAMINATIONS

1. Name the two main divisions of the Bible.

    _____

2. Name the divisions of the Old and New Testaments.

    _____

    _____

3. Name the books of the Bible.

    _____

    _____

    _____

    _____

    _____

4. Name the Dispensations of the Bible.

    _____

    _____

5. Name about two Characters of each Dispensation.

    _____

    _____

6. How many Ages are there in time?____Name Them

    _____

    _____

7. What is an Age?

    _____

    _____

8. What is a Dispensation?

_____

8b. Name the function of each Dispensation, and with what judgment it ends with.

    1. _____   2. _____

    3. _____   4. _____

    5. _____   6. _____

    7. _____

9. The Old Testament is what of the New Testament? The New Testament is what of the Old Testament? Give at least three in sequence._____

10. What three things must we avoid doing in studying the Bible?

    1. _____

    2. _____

    3. _____

11. What does the word Bible mean?_____

12. The Bible was written by how many different writers?_____

13. From What date to what date was it written?_____

14. Name the seven speeches of the Bible_____

_____

15. Give a brief summary of each speech_____

EXAMINATION ON BIBLE COVENANTS

Name the Covenants of the Bible.

_____

_____

_____

1. A covenant is an

_____

2. Name the (3) General Covenants

    1. _____

    2. _____

    3. _____

3. The Covenant shows that all people were represented in the fall of Adam.

4. The Covenant, the sin nature was passed to all mankind.

5. The _____Covenant promised that the waters will never flood and destroy all flesh again.

6. The five other covenants are:

_____

_____

Number 7-15, list the primary scriptures for each Covenant. Place the name in the blank before the scriptures.

7. _____ Gen. 17:8

8. _____ Deuteronomy 30:1-10.

9. _____ Gen. 12:2

10. _____ 1 Samuel 7:16.

11. _____ Jer. 31:31: Hebrews 8:8.

12. _____ Gen. 1:28; Gen. 2:15-16

13. _____ Gen. 3:14-19

14. _____ Gen. 9:15-16.

15. _____ Exodus 20:1-6;21:1-24;24:12-18.

Listed below are laws that led to a specific Covenant or promise that was given in a specific covenant. Place the name of the Covenant in the blank before the Law or Promise.

16. _____ It gets rid of sin and brings in everlasting life. It said, "I will."

17. _____ The promise that "I will make thee the father of many nations."

18. _____ Promise to the Gentiles: "I will bless

19. _____ The Land of Palestine is promise to Israel for an everlasting possession or homeland.

20. _____ The royal Law, Civil law, and the Ceremonial law.

21. _____ A house, a Dynasty, A Kingdom and a Throne forever.

22. _____ Man can eat flesh in his diet.

23. _____ No additional curse is placed upon man at this time; neither will God destroy the earth with a flood again.

24. _____ The promise of a redeemer.

25. _____ To abstain from eating of the tree of the knowledge of good and evil with the penalty of death if disobeyed.

THE MYSTERY OF THE GODHEAD
(Examination)

1. What is the meaning of the term Godhead?

_____

_____

_____

2. What does God's Character consist of?

_____

3. Name at least three of God's Attributes in both Classifications.

_____

_____

4. What name of God is used in Genesis 1:1?

5. Who was God talking to when he said, "Let Us Make Man?"

_____

_____

6. Give at least one scripture to show that there is but one God, and one to show that Jesus is this one God.

7. Is Jesus Christ called God in the Scriptures? Give Scriptures.

_____

_____

8. What brought about the necessity of the Terms; Father, Son, and HolyGhost?

_____

_____

9. Are there scriptures to show that the Holy Ghost is God.___Name some.

_____

10. Are the Father, Jesus, and the Holy Ghost the same Spirit? Prove by scriptures

_____

_____

11. If there is but One God, what was the reason for the incident where the Holy Ghost descended as a dove upon Jesus and the Father speaking form heaven.?

_____

_____

12. Why did Jesus pray to the Father, if he is God?_____

13. Explain Psalms 110:1

_____

_____

14. Explain the point concerning Jesus sitting on the right-hand of God.

_____

_____

THE NAMES OF GOD
(Examination)

1. Quote at least ten Names of God. Give their meanings and scripture reference.

   _____

   _____

2. Write the name Yahveh in ancient Hebrew characters.

   _____

   _____

3. What scripture is it to show that God have revealed Himself in various names

   _____

   _____

4. Who were the Massoretes?

   _____

   _____

5. Does God recognize other languages?

   _____

   _____

6. How many languages was the name of Jesus written in, and what are they.

   _____

   _____

7. Do names sometimes have different sounds in other languages? Give Example.

   _____

   _____

8. What name is God using today?

   _____

9. How does this name relate the name Jehovah of the Old Testament?

   _____

   _____

10. Research the various names of God as they are used in the twenty- third Psalm.

    _____

    _____

PROPHECY
(Examination)

1. Define the word Prophecy

_____

2. Who was the first man to prophecy in the Bible?

_____

3. What are the first and second words of prophecy in the Bible?

_____

_____

4. What is the main scripture that predict the future in the Bible?

_____

_____

_____

5. Who are the two main challenging forces in bible prophecy?

_____

_____

_____

6. How many I Wills do Satan have and how many does God have?

_____

_____

_____

7. What is meant by the political prophecies?

_____

8. What is the meaning of the name of Daniel?

_____

9. Give the names of Daniel and the Hebrew Boys both in the Hebrew and Chaldean names.

_____

_____

10. Who dream about the metallic image?

_____

11. Name the four metals and what kingdoms they represent, and when did they begin.

Metals   Meanings   Dates

_____

_____

_____

_____

_____

12. Name the six Beasts that Daniel's dream of and what they represent.

Beast   Represent

_____

_____

_____

_____

_____

13. What does the little horn Daniel 7:8 represent? _____

14. What do the horns one being taller than the other represent?

_____

15. What does the notable horn between the goat represent? _____

_____

16. Who do the four little horns represent which came up out of the notable horn of the he Goat when it was broken.

_____

_____

_____

17. How does the Anti-Christ arise out of the kingdoms of this prophecy?

_____

_____

18. Give Four scriptures to show the actions of the Anti-Christ in his coming forth.

_____

_____

_____

19. What does the Dragon in Revelation twelve represent?

_____

20. What is the beast of Revelation 13:1?

_____

_____

21. What do the ten horns represent? _____The Seven Heads?

_____

22. What does the woman riding the beast of Revelation 17 mean?

_____

_____

23. When does the Seventy Weeks of Daniel Begin and how does it end.

_____

_____

CHURCH HISTORY

1. Name the Greek Term for the Book of Revelation, and its meaning.

   _____

2. Where was John when he wrote Revelation?

   _____

3. What do the Seven Golden Candlesticks represent?

   _____

4. Name the Seven Churches of Asia in order.

   _____

5. What are the accusations or praises of each church?

   _____
   _____
   _____

6. What is the meaning of each Church's name?

   _____
   _____
   _____

7. Name the Dates of each Church Period and their Historical Name.

   _____
   _____

8. Name the Contents in the Apostolic Age.

   _____

9. Name at least three Apostolic Warnings.

   _____

10. Name at least three men or events in each of the remaining Church periods.

_____

_____

11. Name the three views on the Godhead.

_____

_____

12. What council was convened to settle the issues on the Godhead?

_____

13. What doctrine was adopted in this Council?

_____

14. When did Constantine Give the Edict of toleration for Christianity?

_____

15. Name about three Major Bible translations.

_____

16. Who began the reformation period, and what date?

_____

17. What purpose was the Thirty Year War?

_____

18. Who began the Catholic Church?_____The Baptist? _____

The Reform? _____ The Jehovah Witnesses?_____

19. Name the three types of Church Government.

_____

20. Who began the Pentecostal Revivals?

_____

21. Who was the first in the states to baptize in Jesus Name?

_____

22. Which and when was the first Pentecostal Organization?

_____

23. Where did the World Wide Pentecostal Revival spread from?

_____

24. Name the seven different things Christ were to each Church.

_____

25. Name the rewards for overcoming in each Church.

_____

26. Who was C.F. Parham?

_____

27. Who was Agnes N. Ozman?

_____
_____

28. Who was W.J. Seymour?

_____

29. Who was G.T. Haywood?

_____

30. What is the A.W.C.F.?

_____

VOLUME II

CONTENT

CONTENTS

PREFACE

I am delighted to present this book to you on the subject of "Typology." Because the Bible said, **"For whatsoever things were written aforetime were written for our learning, that we through patience and comfort of the scriptures might have hope."** (Rom. 15:4—Kjv)

Typology **always speaks** in the **aforetime** pointing **toward its fulfillment**.

I have shown Typology from various perspectives. I trust this book will be a guide to the students of "Typology."

Special thanks unto Sister Ann Derouin, a beloved diligent person in the Lord for her typing and proof reading of this book.

Thanks also is given to Sis. Deloris Mimms for the final draft.

I am grateful to my wife for her understanding heart and patience with me while I devoted my time in writing this book.

DR. WILLIE J. DUNCAN

INTRODUCTION

The word **type** means a **replica of the real thing** under discussion or a **foreshadowing** of a thing that is to be **presented**. In other words, that which is presented first **as a shadow** later becomes **the actual** body.

Typology is a method that uses a familiar thing and it's characteristics to portray an unfamiliar object or point. Typology is the study of that method. The Bible uses various languages and **figures of speech** to portray **a truth**. Typology is one of those methods. The main Two FIELDS of Typology in the bible are the OLD TESTAMENT (Shadow), and the NEW TESTAMENT (Body). The **two main characters** of Typology **are: Adam** and **Christ** and their associates, **Eve** and **the Church**.

Two main events: the coming of **the Flood in Noah's Day**, and **The Coming** of the **End of Jesus' Day**. **Two typical** groups **of people are:** the **Israelites**, and **The Church**. **Two typical places:** the **land of Promise of Israel's day** and a place called **Heaven** in **the Churches' day**. So goes the rest of Typology.

God has determined to show first of all; many things in typical form in order to make His purpose **plain** and **understandable**. We will cover these various **areas** under the general theme **"God's Equation."**

GOD'S EQUATION

"The **law** of the Lord is **perfect** converting the soul: the **testimony** of the Lord is **sure**, making **wise** the simple." (Ps. 19:7–KJV)

What is done on **one side of an equation** must be done on the **other side** or the equation **is wrong**. The law of **Equity** and **Justice** requires **reciprocal value** of the same thing on **both sides**.

Whatever is done to cause a thing to go into the **negative** must be done in the **same** amount and degree in the **positive** to equate or set **right with the thing** that's done.

"Who hath **measured** the **waters** in the hollow of **His hand**, and **meted** out heaven with **the span**, and comprehended **the dust** of the earth **in a measure**, and **weighed** the mountains in **scales**, and the **hills** in a **balance?"** (Isa. 40:12)

If you **borrow five** dollars, you are five dollars into the **negative.** You must **earn five** dollars in the **positive** to pay that bill in order to **bring yourself back** to the place you were before you borrowed the five dollars. If you borrow the five dollars to pay your bill, you would **still be five** dollars in the **negative.**

The **point** I am trying to convey **is that the equation has two sides**, the **positive** side and the **negative.** The **center** of the equation **is** absolute **zero** as far as debt is concern.

In **God's Equation**, we have the **positive** and the **negative** the **Body** and The **Shadow. The** OLD TESTAMENT Being The **Shadow** And The NEW TESTAMENT being the **Body.** For in Hebrews we read, **"FOR THE** law having a **shadow** of good things **to come,** *and* **not** the very image of the things, can never with those sacrifices which they offered year by year continually make the **comers** thereunto **perfect."** (Heb. 10:1)

There are many things in the **Old Testament** so written that we may learn and profit thereby (Rom. 15:4; 1 Cor. 10:11; Rom. 9: 22-24).

SPIRITUAL CHARACTERISTICS TYPES
ADAM A TYPE OF CHRIST

"Nevertheless **death reigned** from Adam to Moses, even over them that had not sinned after the similitude of **Adam's transgression,** who is the figure of him to come." (Rom. 5:14—**KJV**)

Adam in Typology is the Type of **Christ.** Christ being the Anti-Type. I consider **Adam** as being the **Shadow** of the Body of Christ. **Jesus Christ** is the **"Coming One."** He is coming from the **sun** rising. As he **walks toward the Sun,** His **body** casts **a shadow in front** of Him. The **sun strikes His back** and makes an **image of Him** in the shadow. **Adam** is the **Image of Christ** in Typology. Adam was made in the Image of Christ. "For whom he did **foreknow,** He also did **predestinate** to be conformed to the **image** of his Son, that he might be the **firstborn** among many **brethren."** (Rom. 8:29)

Jesus Christ **as a man** was **predestinated** before **Adam.** As a **body must appear before a shadow** is formed, even so **Christ** was **determined to come in flesh** as the **Son of God,** before **Adam was made.** The shadow of a **person who walks before** the **sun appears before the body does.** The one who is **waiting** for the **body will see the shadow first.** Now that which is **first,** comes **last,** and that which is last, appears **first.** Now that which **appears first is not the real thing** or the **body** of the **shadow.**

So then, that which appears **first,** is **last** and that which appears **last** is **first.** Adam is **last** and **Christ is first.** So **when Christ comes, He fulfills the Type** (Matt. 5:17)

From this we **understand** the scripture in **Colossians** 1:15-17 which **says: "Who is the image** of the **invisible God,** the **firstborn** of every **creature:** [16]For by him were **all** things, **created,** that are in **Heaven,** and that are in **earth, visible** and **invisible,** whether *they* be thrones or **dominions,** or **principalities,** or **powers: all** things were **created by him,** and **for him:** [17]And he is **before all things,** and **by him all things consist."**

Jesus existed in **Spirit** before **all things,** and it is when **He was Spirit** that **He created all** these things. But Jesus was projected in **the flesh** only in the **mind of God before** He became **Son,** that is **when he was made of a woman** (Luke 1:35; Gal. 4:4; Phil. 2:5-9—**KJV**).

In the beginning, **He was God invisible**. When He **came in the flesh** He was the **image** of the **invisible God**. Adam **was made** in the world **without a wife**. He was put to **sleep,** and the woman was taken **out of him** (Gen. 2:20-25).

Likewise, **Christ** was in the **world with a wife**. He was **put to sleep** and out of him came **the woman** {Wife, **the Church**}, [30]For we are members of **His body**, of his **flesh,** and of **His bones** (Eph. 5:25-33).

TYPE: By the sin of ONE man (**Adam**), all **are sinners** that are born of him.

ANTI-TYPE: By the **righteousness** of ONE PERSON (**Christ**), shall **all** be **made righteous** that are born of Him (Rom. 5:14-21).

Adam gave up **paradise** and **life,** and committed **sin** to be **with his wife,** Eve. Christ gave up **paradise** and chose **death** and practiced **righteousness to redeem** his **wife, the church**. Adam was from the **earth,** Christ from the **heaven** (I Cor. 15:47).

Adam was **made of the dust** Gen. 2:7; Christ was **made of a woman**, as pertaining to **his flesh (**Gal. 4:4).

Adam was **son of God**, (**created** son) (Luke 3:38).

Christ was **son of God**, (only **begotten** son) (Luke 1:35).

And so goes the Type on and on.

EVE AND THE CHURCH

The woman was taken out of **the man Adam;** Even as the **church was taken** out of **the man (Christ)** (I Cor. 11:8; Eph. 5:30; Gen. 2:21-24).

As the man is to **rule over** his wife, so **must Christ rule over His Church** (Gen. 3:16; Eph. 5: 22-25).

As the **woman is to submit** or **subject** herself **to the man,** even so **must the Church submit** and **subject** herself **to Christ** (Eph. 5: 22-33).

The **position of the woman** in the church is to be **under subjection,** for she is the **image** of the church. She is not to have **authority over the man** but rather to be in **subjection**. The **man** is the one that is **to rule according to the divine order** (I Tim. 2:12-15).

However, many times **God has used a woman to do a man's job** when there was **no man willing** and able **to do it** (Isa. 3:12). **Enoch** is a type of the **translation** of the Saints (Gen. 5: 21-24; Heb. 11:5–KJV).

Enoch, who was translated **before the judgment of the flood** (Mark 9:1; Matt.16:28; I Thess. 4:16, 17; I Cor. 15: 51, 52; I Thess. 5:10).

Noah and his family is a **type of the church** being saved **by water** from the destruction of the **flood,** Even so, the **Church is saved by water** (I Peter 3: 21).

There was **one family** and **name** in **Noah's day** (Gen. 6:18).

All that went into the Ark were **Noahites**. Even as there is but ONE FAMILY and ONE name in Jesus' day (I Cor. 12:12; Eph. 3:12-15).

There was **ONE Ark built by Noah** and his **family. Even so, there is ONE Church built by Jesus Christ** (Matt. 16:18; Eph. 2: 9-22).

There was **ONE DOOR** into the Ark, even as there is but **ONE DOOR** into the Church (Gen. 6:16; St. John 1:1, 9; 3:5).

ONE window at the top typifying **ONE source of inspiration** (2 Peter 2:20, 21).

ABRAHAM and ISAAC

Abraham is a type of the **Father**. He **offered his only son** to God (Gen. 22:1; St. John 3:16).

Isaac is a type of Christ. He bore **wood for the sacrifice**, and **Christ** bore the **cross to be crucified** on (Gen. 22:6; St. John 19:17).

As **Isaac humbled himself** to allow his father to bind him **to be sacrificed,** even so, **Christ humbled Himself** to be crucified (Gen. 22:9; Isa. 53:7; St. John 19:16, 17; St. Matt. 27:2).

As **Isaac is not seen anymore** until he went into the **field at eventide to meet his bride**, even so, **Christ, after His ascension**, will **not be seen until He comes** into the **mid** air **to meet His bride** (Church) (Gen. 24:63; I Thess. 4:13-17–**KJV**).

ABRAHAM, ELIEZER AND REBECCA

As **Eliezer** was sent by **Abraham to obtain a bride** for his son **Isaac, Genesis 24,** even so, **the Father sent forth the Holy Ghost** into the world to get **a bride for His Son** (St. John 14:5-26; Acts 2:1-40).

As **Eliezer** presented **jewels** and **raiment to Rebecca,** even so, the **Holy Ghost** gives **gifts unto the Church** (Gen. 24:53; I Cor. 12).

As **Rebecca was willing to go with the servant** even so must the church, (the bride of Christ), **be willing to submit Herself to the Holy Spirit** (Gen. 24:58; Rev. 11:17; Eph. 4:30).

As **Rebecca rode the rough camel to follow Eliezer to go to Isaac**, even so, must the **church follow the Holy Spirit through trials and suffering to go** to the Lord (Rom. 8:14; I Pet. 4:1).

As **Isaac came part way into the field to meet his bride at eventide,** even so, **Christ will come part** of the **way into the mid air at eventide to catch away His bride** (Gen. 24:62, 63; I Thess. 4: 13-18) **AMEN.**

JOSEPH AND HIS BRETHREN

Joseph is a type of Christ. And as Joseph was **betrayed and hated** of his brethren because of his **dreams** and **favoritism of his father**, even so, **Christ** was **hated by**

his brethren (Israel), for his doctrine. One of his **brethren betrayed** him. (Gen. 37: 4-1; St. John 13:21—Kjv).

As **Joseph was sold into Egypt for twenty pieces of silver;** even so, **Christ was** sold for **thirty pieces of silver** (Gen. 37: 26-28; St. Matt. 26:14-16).

As **Joseph's brethren meant evil to him**, but God meant it **for good;** even so, they who **killed Jesus meant it for evil**, but **God meant it for good** (Gen. 50:15-20; I Cor. 2;8; St. John 3;16, 17).

As **Joseph made himself known to his brethren;** even so, **Christ made** Himself **known** unto, **first**, His **Disciples.** After, He will **make himself known** unto **Israel** (Gen. 45:1-8; Zech. 12:10; I Tim. 6:14-16). **AMEN**

As **David was king over Israel;** even so, **Christ will be King over all** (II Sam. 5:1-5; St. Luke 1: 31-33).

As Aaron was **High Priest over Israel;** even so, **Christ is High Priest over** the **Church** (Heb. 8).

THE TABERNACLE

The **Tabernacle** is God's **typical method** of showing **the way of salvation**. It **shows in a panoramic** or **systematic way, the view of salvation**.

The **whole theme** of it is **how to obtain access to God**. In other words, the **method of approaching** unto **God**. One **should not be confused** about the way of salvation if he goes by **the plan/pattern** given in the **Tabernacle**.

It is interesting to note the **arrangement** of the Tabernacle: The **Tabernacle is constructed** from **within** to an **outward** direction. That is, from the **Holiest of Holies,** where **God dwells,** to the **outer court**. This signifies **our approach unto God**. We will **compare** the different **furniture** and **items** with **Christ**. For **all** these things **pertain** to the **works of Christ,** in **His Divinity** and **Humanity**.

The **material** and its **meaning** are taken from the book entitled, "**The Tabernacle."** written by Bishop G. T. Haywood.

1. **Gold**-Representing the **Divine nature** or **glory**, especially **of Christ** as revealed particularly in His **risen life**.
2. **Silver**-The **price paid** for the **sinner's redemption,** or **Christ's work** as Redeemer.
3. **Brass**- Sin bearing and **sin atoning power** of Christ through **his life** and **death** and **resurrection.**
4. **Wood**- Common **humanity** consecrated to **God's service**.
5. **Blue**- The **infinite grace of heaven** as it **unveils itself in Christ**, like the **blue sky** seen through a rent dark cloud.
6. **Scarlet**- **Royal dignity** and **majesty** as **revealed** through the **life of Christ**, or **royal** blood.

7. **Purple-** (blue and scarlet blended), **Divine Grace** and **royal majesty**, in the God man, **Christ on earth**.
8. **Fine Linen -Righteousness of Christ** and **His saints**.
9. **Goat Hair-** The **reproach upon Christ** in taking our **sins away**. (Heb. 13:12 Rom. 15:3) and upon the **saints** for partaking of this holiness.
10. **Ram's Skin Dyed Red** - Sorrow and **suffering of Christ** and **his church** here on earth.
11. **Badger Skin** - The **concealment of the divine glory** under humiliation.
12. **Shittin Wood-** The **sinless Humanity** of Christ.
13. **Oil for the Lights- Illuminating power of the Holy Ghost** in **Christ** and the **saints.**
14. **Spices for Anointing** -Divine **fragrance** of the **fruit of the Spirit** in **Christ** and the saints.
15. **Spices for incense-** The **intercessory work of Christ** and **His people** as regarded **acceptance** by the **Father in Heaven**.

THE TABERNACLE CONTENTS

The Tabernacle consisted of an **outer court with a linen fence around it**. The length of the fence was 100 cubits. The width was 50 cubits. The height was 5 cubits.

The **entrance was from the east with a twenty-cubit gate**. The **outer court** was where the **sacrifices** were brought in and **offered on the Brazen Altar**.

THE BRAZEN ALTAR
(Exd. 27:1-8--KJV)

Everything in the **outer court** was **covered with brass**. They all were used for **cleansing from sins**.

The **Brazen Altar** itself **signified the cross** where **Jesus** was **crucified**. It is **the point** where the **blood is shed**. For where there is **no shedding of blood**, there is no **remission of sins**. (Heb. 9:22).

No activity could go on in the rest of the Tabernacle without getting blood from **this point**. This **signifies that no one can approach unto God without penalty of sin** being **paid**. For the **wages of sin is death** (Rom. 6:23).

Before **the Priest** could **offer up prayers** and **walk in the light** of the golden **candlesticks** or eat of the **Table of Shewbread**, he must **consecrate** and **sanctify** himself with **the blood** of the **sacrifice**.

There were **five types of offerings** offered on the **Brazen Altar,** they are:

1. Burnt Offering	Lev. 1:3
2. Trespass Offering	Lev. 5:1
3. Meal Offering	Lev. 2:1
4. Sin Offering	Lev. 4:1
5. Peace Offering	Lev. 3:1

They **all represented Christ** in a **special way.** (Heb. 10:1-18).

THE BRAZEN LAVER
(Exd. 30:17-21–KJV)

The next step toward God was the **Brazen Laver**. The priests had to stop by there and **wash before** continuing into the Tabernacle.

This **signifies baptism**, which Jesus said except a man be born of the water and the Spirit, he cannot enter into the Kingdom of God (St. John 3:5). **Baptism is a necessary step toward salvation.** For He said: "He that believeth and **is baptized** shall **be saved**." (Mark 16:16; Acts 2:38; 8:12; 10:44-48; 19:1-6).

THE HOLY PLACE
(Exd. 26: 31-33)

The Tabernacle was **30 cubits** long, **10 cubits** wide, and **10 cubits high**. The **Holy Place** was **20 cubits** long **10 cubits** wide, and **10 cubits** high,. The **Holiest of Holies** was **10x10x10**.

The **Holy Place** signifies the **body of Christ**, while the **Holiest of Holies** signifies **Heaven** itself.

Everything **inside** the Tabernacle was **overlaid with gold**. Gold represents **Divinity**. The holy Place is **the church** or the **body of Christ**. We must become partakers of **Divine Nature to enter therein**. In other words, we must be **filled with the Spirit** of God. "For by ONE Spirit are we **all** baptized into ONE body, whether we be **Jews** or **Gentiles**, whether we be **bond or free**; and have been **all made to drink** into ONE Spirit." (I Cor. 12:13).

The **Wood** represents Christ's **Humanity**, and The **Gold** His **Divinity**. He is **Human** and **Divine**. The **God-man**, or God man-i-fested in **flesh**. It is Humanity and Divinity **infused** and not confused.

The **Seven** Golden **Candlesticks** represent the **Holy Ghost in the Church**, which opened up or **illuminates our knowledge** in the **Word of God**.

It **shines** on the **Table of Shewbread**, which **signifies** giving **understanding** in the **Word of God**.

It **shines** also on the **Altar of Incense**, which signifies giving **intercession in prayer** (St. John 14:26).

The **Holy Place** represents the **entire Church Age**. (Rom. 8:26, 27; Rev. 5:8).

THE HOLIEST OF HOLIES
(Exd. 26:33-34—KJV)

This is the area of **God's presence**. This is the **throne** room. This is the place where **God dwells**.

The only person who had **access to God** in this place was the **High Priest** once **every year** but **not without blood** (Heb. 9:7).

The reason he was **allowed to enter once** was because the **penalty for sins** needs to be **paid for only once**. Then after which, we all could come into the **Holiest of all**, even into **heaven itself** (Heb. 9:24).

THE ARK OF THE COVENANT
(Exd. 25:10-22—KJV)

This Ark is a type of Christ (Heb. 9:1-11).

CONTENTS

Pot of Manna	Bread
Covenant	Law
Aaron's Rod	Priesthood
Mercy Seat	Grace
Two Cherubim	Glory

A TREASURE CHEST

The **Ark is a Treasure Chest** consisting of various **valuables**. For **in Christ** is hidden "**All** the **treasures** of **wisdom** and **knowledge**." (Col. 2:3).

Everything we need **is in Him**. If we want wisdom, **it's in Him**. "For in Him dwelleth **all the fullness** of the **Godhead** bodily. And **ye are complete in Him** which **is** the head of **all principality** and **power**:" (Col. 2:9, 10).

"God **is made** unto us **wisdom** and **righteousness**, and **sanctification**, and **redemption**:" (I Cor. 1:30).

(THE ARK OF THE COVENANT)
IN HIM

God had determined: "That in the dispensation of **the fullness of times** He might gather together in one **all things in Christ**, both which are **in heaven**, and which are **on earth;** even in **Him:**" (Eph. 1:10–Kjv).

If we **want to know anything** about God, we must **go to Christ** (I John 2:22, 23; 5:20).

"At that time Jesus answered and said, I thank thee, O Father, **Lord of heaven** and **earth** because thou hast **hid these things from the wise and prudent**, and hast revealed them unto babes. [26]Even so, **Father:** for so it seemed good in thy sight. [27]All things are **delivered unto me of my Father:** and **no man** knoweth the **Son**, but the Father; neither knoweth **any man the Father**, save **the Son**, and **he to whomsoever** the **Son** will reveal Him." **(**Matt. 11:25-27)

"And we know that the **Son of God is come**, and hath **given us** an **understanding**, that we may know **Him that is true**, and we **are in Him that is true**, even in **his Son Jesus Christ**. This **is the True God** and Eternal Life. Little children keep yourselves from idols. Amen." (I John 5:20, 21; St. John 14:1-10).

"According as he hath **chosen us in him before the foundation** of the world, that we should **be holy** and **without blame** before him **in love:** Eph. 1:4. **We see** in **Christ** a Treasure Chest.

POT OF MANNA

The Manna is a Type Of Christ. Jesus said, "I Am That Bread Of Life." Your fathers **did eat manna in the wilderness**, and are **dead**. This is the bread which cometh down **from heaven** that a man may eat thereof, and **not die. I am the** Living Bread which came down **from heaven:** if any man eat of this bread, **he shall live forever:** and the bread that I will give **is my flesh,** which I will give for the **life** of the world.**"** (St. John 6:48-51).

So Manna is **a type** of the Life Giving Substance of Christ, which we may eat by **faith** and **live**.

THE COVENANT

The covenant is a representation of **God and man's agreement** saying **what God will** do **if man will.**

The **Covenant** is the type of Christ's **willingness to do the will of God**. "Think not that I am come to **destroy** the **law**, or the **prophets:** I am **not** come to destroy, but to **fulfill.**" (St. Matt. 5:17–Kjv)

Hebrews 10:5-7 says: "Wherefore when he come into the world, he saith, **Sacrifice** and **offering** thou wouldest **not**, but **a body has thou prepared me:** [6]In **burnt offerings** and *sacrifices* for sin thou hast had **no pleasure**. [7]Then said I, Lo, I come (in the **volume of the book** it is written of me,) **to do thy will, O God**."

Man was **not able to keep the law**, but Jesus came **as a man** and was "...**made** of a **woman, made under the law,** to redeem them that were **under the law**, that we might **receive** the **adoption of sons**." (Gal. 4:4-6)

Christ **became** a man to **keep man's part of the covenant** that he may **give Himself** as a perfect **Sacrifice** for the **redemption of man**, from the **penalty** of the **law** that man **transgressed**.

"And you, being **dead in your sins** and the uncircumcision of your flesh, hath he quickened together with him, **having forgiven you all trespasses;** [14]**Blotting** out the **handwriting of ordinances** that was **against us**, which was **contrary** to us, and **took it out** of the way, **nailing it to his cross;** "...Which are **a shadow** of things to **come;** but the body is of Christ." (Col. 2:13-14, 17)

AARON'S ROD

Aaron's Rod is a type of **Christ,** being the **High Priest** chosen by **God over all** others. As **Aaron was chosen** over all the company of **Kohath as High Priest in Israel**. (Num. 17)

"And **no man taketh this honor** unto himself, but he that is **called of God**, as *was* Aaron. [5]So also **Christ glorified not himself** to be made a **high priest;** but he that said unto him, **Thou art my Son, today have I begotten thee**. [6]As he saith also Thou art a **priest forever** after the **order of Melchizedec**." (Heb. 5:4-6). **Jesus Christ** of **Nazareth** is **the stone** which was **set at naught** of you builders, which is **become the head** of **the Corner**. (Acts 4:11)

THE MERCY SEAT

(Lev. 25:7-22–KJV)

The **Mercy seat** was the **lid that was place on top of the ark**. This represents **Christ** as being the **mercy of God toward** us, as the **Cherubim looks down** on us **through** Jesus. Jesus **covers the broken law**. He becomes our **Jehovah Tsidkenu**, the Lord **our righteousness** (I Cor. 1:30; Jer. 23:6; Gal. 2:15-21).

Jesus Christ is **the mercy of God extended** to us (I John 2:1-2).

THE CHERUBIM OF GLORY

The Cherubim represents the presence of the shekanah glory of God. Wherever the Cherubim was found, God's **glory** was there, They kept the **way of the tree of life** in Genesis 3:24. **The glory of God** was on **Jesus Christ, His Mercy Seat.**

"And Jesus, **when he was baptized**, went up **straightway out of the water:** and, Lo, **he saw** the **Spirit of God descending like a dove**, and lighting **upon him:** And Lo, **a voice from heaven**, saying, **This is my beloved son**, in whom **I am well pleased.**" (St. Matt. 3:16, 17).

"And he said unto him Verily, Verily, I say unto you, Hereafter ye shall see **heaven open,** and the **angels of God ascending** and **descending upon the Son** of **Man.**" (St. John 1:51).

"That all men should honor the Son, even as they honor the Father. He that honoreth **not the Son** honoreth **not the Father** which hath sent him." (St. John 5:23).

THE SEVEN SON-SHIPS OF CHRIST

Jesus Christ is mentioned **as a Son** in **different perspectives** in the bible. Each position of Son ship typifies **Christ in a certain way**. It is good for us to be able to **see Christ** in **all these positions to understand His manifold work in redeeming man** from **sins**. We have heard of Christ being the **Son of God quite elaborately**. But **in the other** Son ships we have **not heard much**.

We will do our best to give you **a glimpse of these various Son ships**, as follows:

1. Son of God	(Luke 1:35)
2. Son of Man	(Mark 6:3; Luke3:23)
3. Son of Abraham	(Matt. 1:1; Gal. 3:16)
4 Son of David	(Matt. 1:1; Isa.7:14; Luke 1:31-35).
5. Son of God by Resurrection	(Rom. 1:3-4; Acts 13:33).
6. Son of Joseph	(Luke 2:48; 3:23).
7. Son over his own house	(Heb. 3:6; 5:8).

All of these various Son ships are dealing with **His Humanity** and **priestly functions**. Let us examine each one.

SON OF GOD
(St. Luke 1:35--KJV)

"And the **angel** answered and said unto her, The **Holy Ghost** shall come upon thee, and the power of the Highest shall **overshadow thee:** Therefore also that holy thing which shall be born of thee shall be called the SON OF GOD." (St. Luke 1:35).

This area of the Son ship is where many **do not understand**. Many think that Christ has always been the **Son of God from all Eternity**. They **fail to see Christ** as being the **Son of God in flesh,** but **God in Spirit; Christ's flesh** had a **beginning**, but Jesus in **Spirit** is God **the Father who has no beginning** (Micah 5:2).

Christ is not God's **only Son**, but rather, His only **begotten** Son. The bible says, that **Adam was the Son of God** (St. Luke 3:38).

Adam is God's **created** Son. Christ is the **only Son** God has **begotten** or **brought forth** by a woman. "But when the **fullness of time was come**, God sent forth His Son, **made of a woman, made under the law.**" (Gal. 4:4)

The **Son of God is actually God in a body.** "Behold, **a virgin** shall be with child, and shall **bring forth a son**, and they shall call his name **Immanuel**, which being interpreted is, **God with us.**" (St. Matt. 1:23)

"In the beginning was the **Word**, and the **Word was with God**, and the **Word was God.** [14] And the **Word** was **made flesh**, and **dwelt among us**, (and we beheld his glory, **the glory as of the only begotten** of the **Father**) full of **Grace** and truth. [10] He was **in the world**, and the world **was made by him**, and the world **knew him not.**" (St. John 1:1, 14, 10).

At that time, Jesus answered and said, **I thank thee, O Father, Lord of heaven** and earth because thou hast **hid these things from the wise and prudent**, and hast **revealed** them unto babes. [26] Even so, **Father:** for so it seemed good in thy sight. [27] All things are delivered unto me of **my father:** and no man knoweth the Son, but **the Father:** neither knoweth any man **the Father, save the Son,** and he **to whom ever the Son will reveal Him.**" (St. Matt. 11:25-27).

"And **we know** that the **Son of God is come**, and hath **given us** an **understanding,** that we may **know him that is true**, and **we are in him** that is true, *even* in **his Son Jesus Christ. This is the true God**, and eternal life." (I John 5:20; St. John 14:7-11).

So then, Jesus Christ the Son of God, **is God in a body**. This is the meaning of that term (I Tim. 3:16; St. John 10:30-38).

THE SON OF MAN

(Matt. 16:13; Heb. 2:5-9–Kjv)
(Gen. 35:18; 48:13-22; Ps.16:11; 110:1; Matt. 22:42)

The term "**Son of Man**" typifies Christ as being the **representative** of the **human family**. He **became a man** that He might **justifiably take man's place** as a **Sacrifice** for **sins.**

To do this, He had to become **identified with the human** family. [14]"Forasmuch then as the children are **partakers of flesh, and blood**, he also himself **likewise took part of the same;** that through **death He might destroy** him that has the **power of death,** that is, **the Devil;**"(Heb.2:14-18).

"Who, being in the **form of God, thought it not robbery** to be **equal with God:** [7]But **made himself of no reputation,** and took upon him **the form of a servant,** and was **made in the likeness of men:** [8]And being found **in fashion as** a **man,** he **humbled himself,** and became **obedient** unto death, **even the death of the cross."** (Phil. 2:6-8).

When Jesus took upon Himself the form of man, **He inherited all the enemies of man.** He **was made under the law to redeem them from the penalty of the law,** He **became subject to death.** God laid upon Him the **sins of us all.** Whatever He accomplishes, **it was man that accomplished.** When He did that which was righteous, **it was man that did it.** When **He died it was man that died.**

"For the **love of Christ constraineth us;** because we thus judge, that if one **died for all,** then were **all dead:** and *that* **he died for all,** that they which live should not henceforth live unto themselves, but **unto him which died for them** and **rose again."** (2 Cor. 5:14, 15).

Christ **Jesus was born as a man.** (Phil. 2:7, 8), Lived as man (John 19:5), He **died as a man** (I Pet. 3:18), **He rose as a man** (I Cor.15:20, 21). **Ascended** on high and sat down on the right hand of God **as a man.** (Acts 7: 55-60; Eph. 1:20-23; 2:1-6).

"For there is **ONE God,** and **ONE mediator** between **God and men**, the man Christ **Jesus;** [6]Who gave himself **a ransom for all,** to be testified in due time." (I Tim. 2:5).

He is coming back to reign on His Father David's throne, **as a man.**

Jesus saith unto him, "**Thou hast said:** nevertheless I say unto you, **Hereafter** shall you see the **Son of man** sitting on the **right hand of power,** and coming in the **clouds of heaven."** **(St. Matt. 26:64; Luke 1:31-33; I Cor. 15:25-28)**

When Jesus' mission **as a man is completed,** then **man will be placed** in that **position of the son.** And **Jesus the Son of man,** will go **back to the position,** which he was in **before he took on the position of man,** which is the position of **God the Father,** that **God** may **be all in all.**

Where it is said the **Son of Man sitting on the right hand of God,** Jesus is the representation of **man brought back in favor** with God. **Man is** brought from the **left hand** to **the right hand.** He became **God's Benjamin, Son of My Right**

Hand. It is **never said in the bible** that He is **sitting on the right hand** of God, **until after His resurrection** and **ascension**. When Jesus left heaven **man was on the left side**, (dis-favor). When He went **back to heaven, man was brought on God's right side**.

When Jesus left heaven He was **God**, and became **man**. When He went back to heaven he went back as **man**. Though he yet remained God in **Spirit**. (St. John 3:13**)**.

When He comes back, He is coming **as a man**. He will reign **as a man** when He has destroyed the **last enemy**, which is **death.** He is going back to **the position** of **GOD**. And, we would be in the position of the **son of GOD**. Oh! **What favor:** and **Jesus did it all**.

I will quote a few verses from the bible on this particular **point**. If I don't do that, many won't get the point. So, bear with me in my quotations.

"For unto the angels hath he not put in subjection the world to come, whereof we speak. [6]But one in a certain place testified, saying, **What is man**, that thou art mindful of him? Or the Son of man, that **thou visitest him?** [7]Thou madest him a little lower than the **angels;** thou **crownedst him with glory** and **honor**, and didst set him over the **works of thy hands:** [8]Thou hast put all things in subjection under his feet. For in that he put all in subjection under him, he left nothing *that* is not put **under him**. But now we see **not yet all things put under him**.

[9]But **we see Jesus**, who was made a **little lower than the angels for the suffering of death**, crowned with glory and **honor;** that he by the **grace of God** should **taste death for every man**. [14]Forasmuch then as the **children are partakers of flesh and blood**, he **also himself like wise took part of the same;** that through **death he might destroy him that had the power of death, that is, the devil;** [15]And deliver them who through fear of death were all their lifetime subject to bondage.

"For verily he took **not on** *him the nature of* **angels;** but he took on *him* the seed of Abraham...." (Heb. 2: 5-18).

[20]"But now is Christ risen from the dead, and **become the first fruits** of them that **slept**. [21]For since by **man** *came* **death**, by **man** *came* **also the resurrection** of the dead. [22]For as in **Adam all die**, even so in **Christ shall all be made alive**. [23]But every **man in his order:** Christ the **first fruits;** afterward they that are Christ's at his coming.

[24]Then *cometh* **the end**, when he shall have **delivered up the kingdom to God**, even the **Father;** when he shall have **put down all rule** and **all authority** and **power.** For he **must reign, till he hath put all enemies under his feet**. But when he saith all things are put under him, it is manifest that **he is excepted**, which did put all things under him. [28]And when **all things shall be subdued** unto him, then shall the **Son also** himself **be subject unto him** that put all things under him, that **God may be all in all**." (I Cor. 15:20-28)

"And he said unto me, **It is done**. I am **Alpha** and **Omega**, the beginning and the end. I will give unto him that is **athirst of the fountain of the water of life freely**. [7]He that **overcometh shall inherit all things;** and I **will be his God**, and he shall **be my son**." (Rev. 21:6, 7; Ps. 110:1).

SON (SEED) OF ABRAHAM
(Gal. 3:16–KJV)

"Now to Abraham and **his seed were the promises** made. He **saith not,** And to **seeds, as of many;** but as of ONE, **And to thy seed**, which is Christ." **(Gal. 3:16)**

"THE BOOK of the **generation of Jesus Christ**, the son David, the son of Abraham." (Matt. 1:1)

Christ **as the seed of Abraham is man's representative** that **we may receive** the **promise of the inheritance of God** that was made **through Abraham.** If **Christ received the inheritance of Abraham,** then we would have **received it from Christ when He died.** He **is the seed** or Son of Abraham. Therefore, we may receive **salvation by faith** and **not by works** of the law. We **become righteous through faith.** Everything that we **receive must be through faith.**

1. We are **saved by faith.**
2. We are **justified by faith.**
3. We receive **the inheritance by faith.**
4. We are **children of God by faith.**
5. We are **healed by faith.**

"I am **crucified with Christ:** nevertheless **I live; yet not I,** but Christ liveth in **me:** and in the life which I now in the flesh I live by **the faith of the Son of God,** who **loved me,** and gave himself **for me."** (Gal. 2:20; Rom. 8:16, 17)

THE BOOKS of **Romans, Galatians, Hebrew,** and **James are faith books.**

Abraham is the great **figure of faith.** Because he **believed God,** he became **righteous.** His faith was not only from **his heart,** but he **acted out his faith.** Faith without **works is dead.** Our **faith must** not be passive, but **active.**

"I know that ye are **Abraham's seed;** but ye seek to kill me, because **my word hath no place in you...**[39]They answered and said unto him, Abraham is our father. Jesus saith unto them, **if ye were Abraham's children**, ye would do **the works of Abraham."** (St. John 8:37, 39; Rom. 9)

THE SON OF DAVID
(St. Luke 1:32, 33–KJV)

"He shall be great, and shall be called the **Son of the Highest:** and the Lord God shall give unto Him the **throne of his father David:** [33]And He shall **reign over the house of Jacob forever;** And of his **kingdom there shall be no end."** (St. Luke 1:32, 33).

The title, **Son of David,** shows **Christ as the rightful heir to the throne** of David. It was **God's right to rule in the first place.** Israel rejected God from reigning over them in the days of Samuel. **(**I Sam.9:7).

When God **allowed Saul** and **David to take over that throne**, it was His throne. [23]"Then **Solomon sat on the throne** of the LORD **as king instead of David** his father, and **prospered;** and **all Israel obeyed him.**" (I Chron. 29:23). The right to **rule was and is God's.**

God will, through Jesus, **get back the kingdom that man obtained from Him.** Jesus came **through the tribe of Judah,** (David's Tribe), where the **royal line was.** [10]"The **scepter shall not depart from Judah,** nor a **lawgiver from between his feet**, until **Shiloh come;** and unto him shall the gathering of the people be." (Gen. 49:10)

Unto David it is said, "...Also the LORD telleth thee that he will make thee a house. [12]And when thy **days be fulfilled**, and thou shalt sleep with thy fathers, I will set up thy seed after thee, which **shall proceed out of thy bowels**, and I will **establish his kingdom.** [13]He shall build a house for my name, and **I will establish the throne of his kingdom for ever.**" (2 Sam. 7:11, 12, 13).

Jesus Christ was predestinated to come through the **Tribe of Judah to receive the Kingdom back from Israel** and **the world.**

"Thus saith the LORD GOD; **Remove the diadem**, and **take off the crown:** this *shall* **not** *be* **the same:** exalt *him that is* low, and **abase** *him* **that is high**. I will overturn, overturn, **overturn, it:** and **it shall be no** *more*, until he come **whose right it is;** and I will give it *him.*" (Ezek. 21:26, 27).

"And in the **days of these kings** shall the God of heaven set up a kingdom, which **shall never be destroyed:** and the kingdom shall **not be left to other people,** *but* it shall **break in pieces and consume all these kingdoms**, and it shall stand forever." (Dan. 2:44; 7:9-14).

"But thou, **Bethlehem Ephratah,** *though* thou be **little among the thousands** of Judah, *yet* **out of thee shall he come forth** unto me **that is to be ruler in Israel;** whose going forth *have been* from of old, from everlasting." **(Micah 5:2).**

"Rejoice greatly, **O daughter of Zion; shout, O daughter of Jerusalem:** Behold, **thy King cometh unto thee:** he is just, and having **salvation;** lowly, and **riding upon an ass**, and upon **a colt the foal of an ass.**" (Zech. 9:9).

"And the LORD **shall be king over all the earth:** in that day shall there be ONE LORD, and his name ONE." (Zech. 14:9)

"Pilate therefore said unto him, **Art thou a king then?** Jesus answered, Thou sayest that **I am a king.** To **this end was I born**, and **for this cause come I into the world**, that I should bear witness unto the truth. Everyone that is of the truth **heareth my voice.**" (St. John 18:37; 19:19-22).

"Which in his times he shall show, *who* **is the blessed and only Potentate**, the **King of kings**, and the **Lord of lords;**" (I Tim. 6:15).

"And the seventh **angel sounded;** and there were **great voices in heaven**, saying, The **kingdoms of this world** are **become the** *kingdoms* **of our Lord**, and of **his Christ;** and he shall **reign forever and ever.**" (Rev. 11:15).

"And out of his mouth goeth **a sharp sword**, that with it he should **smite the nations:** and he shall **rule them with a rod of iron:** and he treadeth **the winepress of** the fierceness and wrath of Almighty God. ¹⁶And he hath on his **vesture and on his thigh** a name written, KING OF KINGS, AND LORD OF LORDS." (Rev. 19;15, 16). **Amen.**

SON OF GOD BY RESURRECTION
(Rom. 1:3, 4; Acts 13:33–KJV)

"God hath fulfilled the same unto us their children, in that he hath **raised up Jesus again;** as it is also written in the **second psalm,** "Thou art **my Son,** this day **have I begotten thee**." **(**Acts 13:33).

"Concerning his **Son Jesus Christ** our Lord, which was **made of the seed of David according to the flesh;** ⁴And declared to be the **Son of God with power,** according to the spirit of holiness, by the resurrection from the **dead:**" **(**Rom. 1:3, 4).

"Who is the image of **the invisible** God, the **firstborn of every creature:** For by him were all things created, that are in heaven, and that are in earth, **visible** and **invisible,** whether *they* be **thrones,** or **dominion,** or **principalities,** or **powers:** all things were created **by him,** and **for him:** ¹⁷And he is **before all things** and **by him all things consist.** ¹⁸And he is the **head of the body,** the **church:** who is the beginning, the firstborn **from the dead;** that in **all things** he might have the **preeminence."** (Col.1:15-18).

This **Son ship of Christ has to do with his resurrection from the dead.** He is the first **begotten Son** from **the dead.** Which actually means **brought back to life** after being dead. It was the **act of the Father (Spirit),** who **raised his Son to life.** And He **became the Son of God by the resurrection** from the dead. (Acts 3:15; 1 Pet. 3:18)

Paul speaks on this Son ship in **another way by saying:** "But now **is Christ risen from the dead,** *and* **become the first fruits of them that slept.** For since by man *came* death, **by man** *came* **also the resurrection of the dead.** ²²For as in Adam (margin, son of God), all die, even so in Christ (Son of God), shall **all be made alive.** But every man in **his own order:** Christ the **first fruits;** afterward they that are Christ's at his coming." (I Cor. 15: 20-23).

It was **necessary for Christ to become God's resurrection Son;** for it is through the **resurrection that we become the sons of God.** All of us who put our faith in Jesus Christ to our sacrifice for sin **dies with Him on the cross.** In that instance, The **Son of Abraham dies,** The **Son of David dies,** The **Son man dies,** and the **Son of God dies.** All of these Son ships are of **no avail until he becomes the Son of God by resurrection from the dead.** He gives us **new hope** when he **rises** from **the dead.** In Him we become **God's new son** from the dead.

"And if Christ **be not raised,** your **faith is vain;** ye are **yet in your sins.** ¹⁸Then they also which are **fallen asleep in Christ** are perished. ¹⁹If in **this life only** we have **hope in Christ,** we are **of all men most miserable.** ²⁰But now is **Christ risen** from the dead, and become the **first fruits** of them that **slept**." (I Cor. 15:17-20)

"AND You *hath he quickened*, who **were dead in trespasses and sins;** Wherein in time past ye **walked according to the course of this world,** according to the **prince** of the **power of the air,** the spirit that now **worketh in the children** of **disobedience:** [3]Among whom also we **all had our conversation in times past in the lusts of our flesh, fulfilling the desire of the flesh and of the mind;** and were by nature the **children of wrath,** even as others. [4]But God, **who is rich in mercy,** for his **great love where with he loved us,** [5]Even when we **were dead in sins,** hath **quickened us** together **with Christ,** (By grace ye are **saved;)** [6]And hath **raised us up together,** and made *us* sit together **in heavenly** *places* in Jesus Christ." (Eph. 2:1-7)

"IF YE then **be risen with Christ, seek those things which are above,** where Christ sitteth on **the right hand of God.** [2]Set **your affection on things above,** not on things on the earth. [3]For **ye are dead,** and **your life is hid with Christ** in God. [4]When Christ, *who* **is our life, shall appear,** then shall ye also **appear with him in glory."** (Col. 3:1-4; Rom. 6;1-11) AMEN

SON OF JOSEPH
(Luke 2:48)

Jesus as **son of Joseph,** gives him the **position of heir** apparent **for the king line.** For the **king line had come down to Joseph.** Joseph should have been **King Joseph.** Jesus **inherited the right to the throne from Joseph his stepfather.** This **locks in the Kingship in Christ.** And Mary his **Mother was a descendant** from David through **Nathan the Son of David.**

When Joseph was **married to Mary** and **became the Son of Heli,** who was the **Father of Mary.** By Jesus being **born of Mary gives him the right to the king line** through **David through Nathan.** God **made him a promise** to have a **Seed of David to sit on the throne forever** (2 Sam. 7:12; 13). God **swore that He would be the one** who will **sit on that throne.** But he couldn't except he came through **the lineage of David.** "The Lord hath **sworn in truth unto David;** he will **not turn from it;** Of the **fruit of thy body will I set upon thy throne."** (Ps. 132:11)

"For the children of Israel shall **abide many days without a king,** and without **a prince,** and without **a sacrifice,** and without **an image,** and without **an ephod,** and *without* **teraphim:** [5]Afterward shall the children of Israel return, and **seek the Lord** their God, and **David their king;** and shall fear the LORD and **his goodness** in the latter days." Hosea 3:4, 5

"For unto us a **child is born,** unto us **a son is given:** and the **government shall** be upon his **shoulder:** and his **name shall be called Wonderful, Counselor, The Mighty God, The everlasting Father, The Prince of Peace.** [7]Of the increase of *his* government and peace *there shall be* **no end,** upon the throne of David, and upon his kingdom to order it, and to **establish it with judgment** and with justice from **henceforth** even for ever. The **zeal** of the LORD of hosts **will perform this."** (Isa. 9:6, 7).

So it was **necessary for Joseph to marry Mary to tie both lineages together** so that Jesus could **be sealed to be the only king forever.** No one else could ever get that position for **Jesus lives forever.** This is the reason why Jesus **had to become the Son of Joseph.**

SON OVER HIS OWN HOUSE
(Heb. 3:6; 5:8–KJV)

"But **Christ as a Son over his own house**; whose house **are we,** if we **hold fast** the **confidence** and **the rejoicing of the hope firm** unto **the end.**" (Heb. 3:6)

Christ in the position of the Son over His Own House, has to do with his work **as the High Priest.** There was a functioning in the typical **Leviticus priesthood** that required the priest and **his son to minister in the daily ministry. Aaron** was commanded to be brought before the Lord with his sons. "AND THE LORD spake unto Moses, saying, ²Take **Aaron and his sons,** with him, and the **garments,** and the **anointing oil,** and **a bullock** for the sin offering and **two rams,** and a basket of **unleavened bread;...**⁶And Moses brought **Aaron** and his **sons,** and **washed them with water.**" (Lev. 8:1, 2, 6)

Jesus as a Son over His Own House suggests to us that they who **work in the ministry should rule his own house.** His family should be a vital part of the ministry. This will give a good example to the people to follow or **learn a lesson.** There are good lessons to learn and there are **bad lesson to avoid pitfalls,** such as the bad examples left by the **two sons of Aaron;** NADAB and **Abihu,** who brought **strange fire** before the LORD. And therefore the LORD slew them. And Aaron was commanded to hold his peace Leviticus 10.

Another **bad example is shown in Eli** and **his sons,** Who were children of **Belial.** Wherefore **God slew them** (I Sam.. 2, 3, 4).

But the good side is **Aaron's other son Eleazar** was **able to take over** the **priesthood after his father died** (Number 20:25-29).

A priest should be the head of his family. Jesus is the head of his family and we are members of his family **if we hold fast the confidence and the rejoicing of the hope firm unto the end.** We should minister as **under priests** as the function requires. AMEN

TYPOLOGY

EXAMINATION

FIRST WEEK

1. You must be able to define the word "Typology" in a two-page report.
2. You must be able to give five typical Characters.

SECOND WEEK

1. You must study God's Financial plan for construction of the Religious building.
2. You must study God's plan for the support of the poor.

THIRD WEEK

1. You must study God's plan for the support of the Ministry.
2. You must study the purpose of the tithe.

FOURTH WEEK

1. You must bring in a report on the construction of the Tabernacle, and how we are able to determine the length, height, width, and divisions of the Tabernacle into the Holy Place and Holiest of Holies.

FIFTH WEEK

1. You must be able to name the furnishings of the tabernacle in order.

SIXTH WEEK

1. You must be able to name the material of the Tabernacle as they relate to Christ and His Ministry.

SEVENTH WEEK

1. Give a research paper of all the sacrifices that were held in the Tabernacle and what they represent as they relates to Christ.
2. Give the use of each piece of furniture and as each relates to Christ.

EIGHTH WEEK

1. Study the purpose of the Tabernacle as it relates to God's dwelling places: The Wilderness, Solomon's Temple, the Body of Christ, and the Church.

NINTH WEEK

1. You must study a detail lesson on the seven Son ships of Christ.

TENTH WEEK

1. Write 2,000 words Biography of Christ.

EXAMINATION

1. Explain in detail the meaning of the term **Typology**?

   _____

   _____

2. Name the first High Priest.

   _____

Many typical characters of the Old Testament and their possessions were a type of Christ, the Church, the Holy Ghost and the Church Adversary (flesh, Satan, and the world.) Fill in the Chart Below

NAMES	TYPE OF	BACKGROUND SCRIPTURE
3. Abraham		
4. Isaac		
5. Rebekah		
6. Eliezar		
7. Ishmael		
8. Ruth		
9. Boaz		
10. Enoch		
11. Noah Ark		
12. The land of Abraham Kindred		

13. The Jewels that Eliezar gave to Rebekah _____

14. The camel ride to Isaac _____

15. The veil on Rebekah's Head. _____

There was five offering that were offered upon the **Brazen Altar** of the Old

Testament. These offering represented? _____. of the New Testament in a special way, Name them.

16. _____ 17. _____
18. _____ 19. _____
20. _____

There were five articles in the Ark of the Covenant. These articles-furnishing represented the attributes of Christ. Fill in the Chart below.

Material of The Tabernacle

What does the Gold Represent? _____

Silver _____

Brass _____

Wood _____

Shitten Wood _____

Blue _____

Purple _____

Scarlet _____

BadgerSkin _____

Goat'sHair _____

Anointing Oil _____

Inncense _____

Spices _____

ARTICLES   **CHRIST ATTRIBUTES**

21. Pot of manna _____

22. Covenant _____

23. Aaron's Rod _____

24. Mercy Seat _____

25. Two Cherubim _____

Christ has seven Son ships', list them, and give their individual meanings and scripture references.

26. _____

27. _____

28. _____

29. _____

30. _____

31. Name the furnishing of the Tabernacle, and what they are a type of.

_____

32. Give the dimensions of the Tabernacle. _____

33. Name at least ten different materials in the Tabernacle and what they mean in Typology. _____

34. What does the **Brazen Altar** represent?

_____

35. What does the **Brazen Laver** represent?

_____

36. What does the **Golden Lamp stand** represent?

_____

37. What does the **Table of Shewbread** represent?

_____

38. What does the **Altar of Incense** represent?

_____

39. What does the **Holy Place** represent?

_____

40. What does the **Holiest of Holies** Represent?

_____

41. Draw the **Tabernacle,** arranging the furnishings in order, and giving the Correct dimensions of it in the scale of cubits and inches.

VOLUME III

FUNDAMENTAL DOCTRINE
OF SALVATION

CONTENTS

ACKNOWLEDGEMENTS

I thank the Lord for giving me the courage to write this book: "**The Fundamental Doctrine of Salvation**." It is not I, but the Lord.

"I **am crucified** with **Christ:** nevertheless I live; yet not I, but Christ liveth in me: and the life which I now live in the **flesh** I live by the **faith** of the **Son of God**, who **loved** me, and gave Himself for me." (Gal. 2:20)

Special thanks unto Sis. Ann Deourin for typing and proofreading this book in the original.

Special thanks are given to Evangelist Deloris Mimms, for her proof reading and assistance in the editing of the final draft of this book.

This book is dedicated to my wife, **Dr. Zeola Duncan**. I wish to express my sincere thanks for your patience with me during the writing of this book. May the Lord God bless you real good! You have been a loving wife.

To those of you who are reading this book may the LORD cause you to be **blessed**.

The Author

INTRODUCTION

THE FUNDAMENTAL DOCTRINE OF SALVATION

Under this subject, we shall deal with the **Testator**, the **Prophet**, the **Priest,** and the **Sacrifice**. God holds all positions. God is the TESTATOR, and He is **Jesus Christ** who is God **manifest** in the **flesh**.

THE DEATH OF THE TESTATOR

A **Testator** is a person who leaves a **will** in force at his **death**. A **will** *is* a testament. A **testament** is a **written** act by which a person determines the disposition of his property after his death. **Hebrews 9:17**—KJV "For a **testament** is of force **after** men are **dead:** otherwise it is of no **strength** at all while the testator liveth.

THE PROPHET

A **Prophet** is a person who tells of **future** events. He is also **a messenger** of God who tells the people **what** thus saith **the Lord**, and what **God requires** of them. **Moses**, for an outstanding example, was a **Prophet** of God. After **receiving** the **commandments** and promises on **Mount Sinai**, Moses **declared** them unto the **Children of Israel**.

After declaring all the **commandments** and **promises** of God unto the Children of Israel; even the **promises** God **made** unto **Abraham** and his **seed,** Moses gave unto them the commandments concerning the **priesthood** and **sacrifices** wherein the work of the **redemption** of **mankind** was to be made.

Moses and the **Prophets**, and the **commandments** concerning the **law, priesthood, sacrifices,** and nearly all the **positions** and activities that are **recorded** in the **Old Testament** were a **symbol,** or a **type** of Christ and the **church**, which have some comparisons concerning His **redemptive** work for **man** (St. John 5:39).

Galatians 3:19 "The **law** was **added** because of **transgressions**" It was for the purpose of **condemning of sin** that...." **Romans 3:19** "....all the **world** may become **guilty before God."** **Romans 5: 13-14**—KJV (For until the **law sin** was in the world: but **sin is** not **imputed** when there is no **law**. [14]Nevertheless death **reigned** from

157

Adam to **Moses**, even over them that had **not sinned** after the **similitude** of Adam's **transgressio**n, who is the **figure** of him that was to come."

If the **law** had **not** been **given,** there would not have been a way for man to be redeemed **from** the **curse** of **sin.** The evil **deeds** of man were not **condemned** as being sin, without the law. Wherefore Paul said in **Romans 7:7-9,** "What shall we say then? Is the **law sin? God forbid.** Nay, I **had** not **known** sin, but by **the law:** for I had not known **lust,** except the law had said, Thou **shalt** not **covet.** But sin, taking occasion by the commandment, wrought in me all manner of **concupiscence.** For without the law sin *was* **dead.** For I **was alive** without the law once: but when the commandment came, sin revived, and I **died."**

Before the **law** came man was in **bondage** of death when he died, and was **subjected** thereunto while he was alive. Yet, when the **law** came, **man** was **condemned** to die. There was **none** found among **men** who was able to **redeem** man **from** the curse of **the law.** This **redeemer** must be **holy** according to all the **commandments** of the **law. Moses** the prophet, **Aaron** the high priest, and the **sacrifices,** offered under the **law** were not **sufficient** to work and **bring** forth the **redemption** for man.

Moses said in **Deuteronomy 18:15, 18**—Kjv "The Lord thy **God** will raise up unto thee a **Prophet** from the midst of thee, of the brethren, like unto me; unto him ye **shall hearken;"** [18]"I will raise them up a Prophet from among their brethren, like unto thee, and will put my **words** in his **mouth;** and he shall speak unto them all that I **shall command** him."

Hebrews 1:1-2 "**God,** who at **sundry times** and in **divers manners spake in time past** unto the **fathers** by the **prophets,** Hath in these **last** days spoken unto us by *his* **Son..."** Jesus said in **St. John 15:22** "If I had not come and spoken unto them, they **had** not **had sin:** but now they have **no cloak** for their **sin."** In like manner before the law came, **sin** was not **imputed** unto them. But **when** the law **came** they had no **excuse.** Therefore, Moses was a **type of Christ** in his position of a **prophet.** He was not sufficient because of the evil found in him. Jesus said in **St. John 10: 7-8** "Verily, verily, I say unto you, **I am** the door of the **sheep.** All that ever came before me are **thieves** and **robbers:** but the sheep **did** not **hear** them."

Jesus portrayed the part of a **prophet** of God to **tell** the **people** what thus **saith the Lord,** and what **God requires** of them. **Isaiah 59:2** "But your **iniquities have separated** between you and your **God,** and your sins have **hid** *his* face from you, that he will **not hear.** And, because of their **sins,** they were condemned to die, and were in **need** of a **high priest** to go into the presence of the **Almighty** to present their purchased redemption. For he who **enters** into the **presence** of God **must be Ho**

THE PRIEST

PRIEST means a person who serves as a mediator, or an **intercessor** between **God** and man. His principle duties were to **offer gifts** and **sacrifices** unto God for **man,**

which was done in the **tabernacle** of the congregation. He serves as a connector or a **go between** men unto God. Before he can work as a mediator or **intercessor** for man, he **must** be **holy**; otherwise, it is of no connectional **strength** at all.

Exodus 32:1-6—KJV "**Aaron** was not sufficient to be the real **high priest**, because he made an **idol god** for the **children of Israel** to worship; for this and other reasons, he was insufficient to be the real high priest." **Isaiah 59:16** "*There was* no **man** found **qualified** for this office (Jere. 5:1; Ezek. 22:30; Psalm 49:5-9).

Since the **law** had been **given**, and the commandments concerning the sacrifices, and all the **qualifications** of the priesthood had been given, it became **necessary** for a person who would take the office of the **priesthood** to be brought up **under** the **law** to **fulfill** it in every **respect** before he could be an acceptable **high priest**. But, there was **no one found** among **men** who **kept the law** in its **fullness** (Rom. 3:9, 10).

Galatians 4:4-5 the scripture says, "But when the **fullness** of the time **was come, God** sent forth his **son,** made of a woman, made under the law, to **redeem** them that were under the law, that we **might receive** the **adoption of sons**." **Hebrews 10: 1-2** "For the **law** having a shadow of **good things** to **come,** *and* not the very **image** of the things, can never with those **sacrifices**, which they offered **year** by year continually **make** the comers thereunto **perfect**. For then would they not have ceased to be offered? Because that the **worshippers** once **purged** should have **had no** more **conscience** of **sins.**"

Hebrews 10: 3-7 "But in those *sacrifices there is* a **remembrance again** *made* of sins every year. For *it is* not possible that the **blood** of bulls and of goats should take away sins. Wherefore when he cometh into the world, he saith, **Sacrifice** and **offering** thou **wouldest** not, but **a body hast** thou **prepared** me: In **burnt** offerings and *sacrifices* for sin thou **hast had** no **pleasure**. Then said I, Lo, I come (in the volume of the book it is written of me,) to do thy **will**, O God."

Therefore, Jesus said in **St. Matthew 5:17-18** "Think **not** that I am **come** to destroy the **law**, or the **prophets:** I am not come **to destroy,** but **to fulfill**. For **verily** I say unto you, **till** heaven and **earth** pass, one **jot** or one **title** shall in no wise pass **from** the **law, till** all **be fulfilled**."

Hebrews 8:1-3 "Now of the things which we have spoken *this is* the sum**:** We have such an **high priest**, who is set on the **right hand** of the throne of the **Majesty** in the heavens; A **minister** of the **sanctuary,** and of the **true tabernacle**, which the **Lord** pitched, and not **man**. For every **high priest** is **ordained** to offer **gifts** and **sacrifices:** wherefore *it is* of **necessity** that **this man** have somewhat also to offer."

Hebrews 9:14 "**Jesus** is this **faithful** high priest**;** who through the EXTERNAL SPIRIT offered Himself **without spot** to God."

THE SACRIFICE OF TESTATOR

A SACRIFICE is the offering up of something that is **precious,** or **beloved**. A **testator** is a person who leaves a **will** in force **after** his **death**. **A will** is a testament or an act used to determine the disposition of the property of a person after his death. Now, the synonymous expression of the terms *"Sacrifice and Testator"* shall be explained from this manner as follows:

Genesis 12:1-3—KJV "In the first place, God **made** a will unto **Abraham** and his **seed,** saying, "....Get thee out or thy **country,** and from thy **kindred,** and from they father's **house,** unto a land that I **will show** thee: And I **will make** of thee a great **nation,** and I **will bless** thee, and make thy name great; and thou shalt be a **blessing:** And I will bless them that bless thee, and **curse** him that **curseth** thee: and in thee **shall** all **families** of the **earth be blessed**"(Gal. 3:8).

From this we can see that God, (the Testator) **promised** an inheritance to **the entire world** through **Abraham** and his **seed. Galatians 3:-18** "Now to Abraham and his **seed** were the promises **made.** He saith **not,** And to **seeds,** as of many; but as of **one,** And to thy seed, which is **Christ.** [17]And this I say, that the **covenant** that was confirmed before of God in Christ, **the law,** which was **four hundred** and **thirty** years after, cannot **disannul,** that it **should make** the **promise of none effect**. But God gave *it* to Abraham by promise.

Galatians 3:19 "Wherefore then *serveth* the **law**? It was added because of **transgressions,** till the **seed** should come to whom the **promise was made;** *and angels in the hand of a mediator ordained it.* **Galatians 3:20-22** "Now *a mediator is* not *a mediator* of one, but God is one. [21]Is the law then **against** the promises of God? **God forbid:** for if there **had been** a law **given** which could have given life, **verily righteousness** should have been by the law. But the scripture hath concluded all under **sin,** that the promise by **faith of Jesus Christ** might be given to them **that believe**."

Upon the Galatians, (which were Gentiles), Paul said in **Galatians 3:26-28**, "For ye are all the **children** of **God** by faith in Christ Jesus. For as many of you as **have been baptized** into Christ have put on Christ. There is neither **Jew nor Greek,** there is neither **bond** nor **free,** there is neither **male** nor **female**: for ye are all **one** in Christ Jesus..." **Galatians 3:29** "And if ye be Christ's, then are ye Abraham's **seed,** and **heirs** according to the **promise**."

Since we are the **seed** of Abraham (by faith in Jesus Christ), the **Promises** or the **will** was **made to us** also. Therefore, God is our TESTATOR. He made the promises unto us saying that we should be blessed through the seed of Abraham, which is **Christ**.

Remember, we said that a TESTATOR is a person who leaves **a will** in force **after** his death. Since God was the **testator,** it was necessary for **God** to **die** in order for us to **receive** the inheritance. Now we know that God **cannot die** in the **Spirit**. Therefore, He took on Himself a **body** for the **suffering** of death.

Hebrews 2:16-17 "For **verily** he **took** not **on** *him the nature of* angels; but he took *on him* the **seed** of Abraham. [17]Wherefore in all things it **behooved** him to be made like unto *his* **brethren**, that he might be a merciful and **faithful high priest** in things *pertaining* to God, **to make reconciliation for** the **sins** of the **people."** (2 Cor. 5:19)

Through this transition, let me explain the things that took place. God in the beginning was in the position of the **Father** when He made the promises to Abraham and his **seed**. Since He was the Testator in the **position** of the Father, and being a **Spirit**, He could **not die. James 2:26** said, the **body** without the **spirit** is dead, or death occurs when the spirit is separated **from** the body.

Therefore, it was necessary for God to **prepare** him **a body.** Since this body had to serve as a **sacrifice**, it had to be **holy.** Since there were **none** holy **among men**, neither those that were begotten by man; therefore, it was **necessary** for God to beget him a body. This is what took place: "In the **beginning** was the **Word**, and the Word was with **God**, and the Word was God. The same was in the **beginning** with God. **All things were made** by him; and without him **was** not anything **made** that was made" St. John 1:1-3).

St. John 14; St. Matthew 1:23 "And the **Word was made flesh**, and dwelt among us, (and we beheld his **glory**, the glory as of the **only begotten** of the Father,) **full** of **grace** and **truth." Philippians 2:8** "And being found in **fashion** as a man, he **humbled** himself, and became **obedient** unto **death**, even the death of the **cross."**

Through this **process** of the **unification** of **this body** and God **who is a Spirit**, it was called the **Son of God.** Since this was God manifest in **flesh**, everything that God was in the **Father ship** was **transferred** into the **Son ship. St. Luke 10:22** "All things are **delivered** to me of my Father..." "For it pleased *the Father* that in him should all **fullness** dwell." (Col 1:19; 2:9)

So we have the TESTATOR in the Son-ship. For we have shown before that Jesus made the **same promises** that **God** made in the **Old Testament**. Since God **being** in the **Son-ship** and not classified as the **Father**, how could we **receive** the inheritance through Him?

Hebrews 2:17 saith, "Wherefore in all things it behooved him **to be made like unto his brethren**, that he might be a merciful and **faithful high priest** in things pertaining to God, to make reconciliation for the **sins** of the people."

Romans 8:29, "For whom he **did foreknow**, he also **did predestinate** *to be* **conformed** to the **image** of his **Son**, that he might be the **firstborn** among many **brethren**." That is, the church.

Since He was the **firstborn**, it was according to the **law** that the **firstborn** of the flock should be used as **a sacrifice**. Also, the firstborn among **men** was to **receive** the **Father's inheritance**. Since God in the Son-ship was **our brother**, He was in the position to **leave the inheritance** to us, the **church, since He was, the first** in the church.

Numbers 27:8-9 The law concerning the **inheritance** of one who dies says, "And thou shalt speak unto the **children** of Israel, saying, If a **man die**, and have no **son**, then ye shall cause his **inheritance** to pass unto his **daughter**. And if he have **no daughter**, then ye shall give his inheritance to **his brethren**."

Acts 8:33 Jesus did not have any **sons** or **daughters** in the **Son ship**. Therefore, the scripture says, "In his **humiliation** his **judgment** was taken **away:** and who **shall declare** his **generation?** for his **life** is taken from the earth." Since we are His **brethren**, we received the **inheritance** according to the **law** from Jesus our **brother,** or **God** in **flesh** our **brother,** while God was still our **Father** in the **Eternal Spirit**. Oh! How great **a Mystery** this is!

Colossians 1:12 "**Giving thanks** unto the Father, which **hath made** us **meet** to be partakers of the **inheritance** of the saints in **light**. The **Spirit** of God **is** the **earnest** of our **inheritance....**" (Eph. 1:13-14)

Hebrews 9:15 —KJV **"Jesus** is **the mediator** of the **New Testament**. "....by means of **death**, for the **redemption** of the **transgressions** *that were* under the first testament, **they which are called** might receive the **promise** of **eternal inheritance**. [16] "For where a testament is, there must also of necessity **be** the death of the **testator**. For a **testament** is **of force** after men are **dead:** otherwise it is of no <u>strength</u> at all while the testator **liveth**." (Heb. 16-17)

Therefore, since the testator must die; it was necessary for God, the Testator, to be put to death in the flesh, but yet remain **alive** in the **Spirit**. **God is Spirit**, and death occurs when the **spirit** is separated **from** the **flesh** (James 2:26; Acts 20:28; 1 John 3:16).

THE SACRIFICE

A Sacrifice is the offering up of something that is **precious** or **beloved**. The **need** for a sacrifice can **be seen** from this point. That is, when the **law** was given, man was **condemned** to die. Everyone became subjected in bondage to death. (Psa. 49:7, 8) "The **whole world** was in **need** of a **redeemer**, or **a sacrifice** for the **sins** of the world" ".... When God saw that *there was* **no intercessor**, His **own arm** brought salvation unto him: and his **righteousness**, it sustained Him." (Isa 59:16)

In order for His arm to bring salvation, He had to come through the same process as He did as the **Testator**. **Ruth 4:1-8** "Since a redeemer must be the **nearest** of **Kin**," it was necessary for God to **prepare** Himself a **body**.

Hebrews 2:14, 15 "Forasmuch then as the children **are partakers** of **flesh** and **blood**, he also himself likewise took **part of the same**; that through death he might destroy him that had the power of death, that is, the **devil**; And **deliver** them who through **fear** of death were all their **lifetime subject to bondage**."

Hosea 13:14—KJV God said: "I **will ransom** them from the power of the **grave**; I **will redeem** them from death: O death, I will be thy **plagues**; O grave, I will be thy **destruction: repentance** shall be hid from mine eyes."

"Since there was no remission of sin without the shedding of **blood**, and "God is a Spirit, **Luke 24:39 states** "a **Spirit** hath not **flesh**, and **bones** nor blood", it was necessary for God to **prepare** Himself a body."

"The blood of those sacrifices **under the law** was not sufficient to **redeem** man from the **curse** of the law. **Hebrews 9:14** But Jesus, through the **Eternal Spirit**, offered Himself **without spot** to God, purge your **conscience** from **dead works to serve** the **living God**?"

Philippians 2:8 "Jesus, being found in **fashion** as a man, he **humbled** Himself, and became **obedient** unto **death**, even the death of the **cross**." Do I mean God died on the cross? Yes. **I Peter 3:18** "not being put to death in the **Spirit** but in the **flesh**," **James 2:26** ".... as the **body without** the **spirit** is **dead**,

St. John 10:17, 18 "Therefore doth my Father love me, because I **lay down** my **life**, that I might take it again. No man taketh it from me, but I lay it down of myself. I have **power** to lay it down, and I have power to take it again." (Jesus said He had power to lay down His life or His body, and raise it up again. Even when His body would be laying in the grave: Jesus said He would **raise it up**. (But let's see who did raise up His body from the grave.)

Acts 2:24 states, "Whom God **hath raised up**...", Also I **Corinthians 15:15**, saith; "...because we have testified of God that he **raised up** Christ:..." (Read **Acts 3:14, 15; 20:28; I John 3:16; Galatians 2:20; Isaiah 40:11; St. John 10:13-18**). From the aforementioned Scriptures, we can see that it was **God** who **died** and **raised** Himself **from** the **grave**. "For Jesus said, "...**Destroy** this **temple**, and in **three** days **I will raise** it up." (St. John 2:19)

Someone might say: If God **died**, why did **Jesus** say: "My God, my **God** why hast thou **forsaken** me. The sins of the whole **world** were upon the **flesh** of Jesus. This was how Jesus the **Son of God**, or **God** in the **flesh** had to feel in order to pay the penalty for **sin**. "...God was in **Christ**, reconciling the world unto himself..." (2 Cor. 5:19)

Hebrews 9:14 "How much more shall the **blood** of **Christ**, who through the Eternal Spirit offered himself **without spot** to God, **purge** your **conscience** from **dead works to serve** the **living God**?"

St. John 4:24 "God is a **Spirit**:" The **Eternal** Spirit is God Himself. **Ephesians 4:4-5** There is but One Spirit and there is but ONE Lord. **I Corinthians 8:6; 2 Corinthians 3:17; Acts 9:5** "The Lord is that **Spirit**."

Psalm 100:3 "Know ye that the LORD he is God: it is he *that* **hath made** us, and not we ourselves; *we are* his **people**, and the sheep of his pasture."

THE MEDIATOR

To show that **God** is the high priest, or the **mediator** between God and **man**, (that is God being in the flesh, called the son of God), **I Timothy 2:5-6**, "For *there is* ONE **God**, and ONE **mediator** between God and men, the man Christ Jesus; Who gave himself a **ransom** for all, to be **testified** in **due time**." It's important to note that **scripture** hath said there is but ONE intercessor or **mediator** between God and man, who is the man **Christ Jesus**?

Now let us **compare** another scripture with the one we have just used. **Romans 8:9** "But ye are **not** in the flesh, but in the **Spirit**, if so be that the **Spirit** of God **dwell** in you. Now if any man have not the **Spirit of Christ**, he is none of his." More importantly, note the **Spirit** of **God** and Spirit of **Christ** is the **same** Spirit. **Ephesians 4:4** "For there is but ONE **Divine Spirit**. **St. John 4:24** "God is a **Spirit**.

Romans 8:26—KJV "Likewise the **Spirit** also helped our **infirmities**:" (That is **God** which is the Spirit in us), "for we know not what we should pray for as we ought: but the **spirit**," (God), "itself marketh **intercession** for us with groanings which cannot be uttered."

Remember there is but ONE **mediator** between God and man. That is the man **Christ Jesus**. We know that **Romans 8:27** "...the Spirit, which is **God in us**, marketh **intercession** for us according to *the will of GOD*. 1 Corinthians 12:6 "Now a mediator and an intercessor hold the **same** position. Does not this **prove** that God is Jesus the mediator **between** God and man? Yes. **St. John 10:35** "For the **scripture** cannot **be broken**" We must not look on God as being a stationary person. For God **fills** all **space**.

MELCHIZEDEK

There has been somewhat of a great confusion as to who Melchizedek is. **Hebrews 7:3 says,** "Without father, without mother, without descent, having neither beginning of days, nor **end** of **life**; but made like unto the Son of God; **abideth** a priest continually."

It is my conviction that this **Melchizedek**, was a pre-appearance, or pre-manifestation of Jesus Christ who is the only Mediator between God and men, (1 Timothy 2:5-6) The scripture said Melchizedek was made like unto the Son of God. Then if he was made, he was **pre-positioned** in the place where he would afterward appear as the **Son of God**.

It's interesting to note the appearing of **Melchizedek**. **Genesis 14:18-19**—KJV "And **Melchizedek** king of Salem brought forth **bread** and **wine**: and he *was* the **priest** of the **most high God**. And he **blessed** him, and said, **Blessed** *be* Abram of the **most high** God, **possessor** of **heaven** and **earth**:"

Someone might question the **existence** of Jesus back in those days. But we must remember Jesus said in **St. John 8:56-58**, "Your father Abraham **rejoiced** to see my day: and he **saw it**, and was **glad**. Then said the Jews unto him, Thou are **not yet** fifty years old, and hast thou **seen** Abraham? Jesus said unto them, Verily, verily, I say unto you, BEFORE ABRAHAM WAS, I AM." Compare **Hebrews 7:14-17**, with **Genesis 14:18-20**.

THE WAY OF SALVATION

We will now consider the way or **steps** to salvation. There are **six basic** steps to salvation and they are as follows:

1. **Hearing** the Full Gospel.
2. **Believing** the Gospel.
3. **Repentance** From Sins.
4. **Baptism** in the Name of Jesus.
5. **Baptism** of the Holy Ghost.
6. **Maintaining** Good Works.

HEARING THE FULL GOSPEL

Before a person can **be saved**, he **must** hear the Gospel. To hear, brings us in **contact** with God. It puts us in the position **to believe** and know God. If a person does not believe in God, he will not come unto God. **Hebrews 11: 6** "But **without faith** it is impossible to please him: for he that cometh to God **must believe** that he is, and that he is a **rewarder** of them that diligently seek him."

We will consider this point in **Romans 10:12-17** "For there is no difference between the **Jew** and Greek: for the same Lord over all is **rich** unto **all** that **call upon** him. For whosoever shall call upon the name of the Lord shall be saved."

These two verses emphasize the **point** that there is no **respecter of persons** with **God.** Both **Jew** and **Gentile, Black** and **White**, Male and **Female** must be saved the same way. (**Acts 10: 34-35; 11:14-18; 15:7-11**).

Romans 10:14-15 "How then shall they **call on** him in whom they have **not believed**? and how shall they **believe in** him of whom they have **not heard**? and **how shall they hear** without a **preacher?** and how shall they **preach,** except they **be sent**?"

"HOW SHALL THEY HEAR WITHOUT A PREACHER?"

"How shall they hear without a **preacher**?" From this scripture we can see the necessity of having a preacher to tell us the **Word** of God. The reason why many people are in darkness today is because of **not hearing** the preacher. But every **preacher** who claims **to be** a preacher **is not** a preacher.

Jeremiah 23:21 God said, "I have not sent these prophets, yet they ran: I have **not spoken** to them, **yet** they **prophesied**." From this we can see that many preachers who are preaching and God has not sent them. **St. John 3:34**, "The preacher whom God **hath sent** speaketh the **words of God:**"

If God has not sent a preacher, and the preacher goes forth, he will not speak **God's Word,** but his own. **Deuteronomy 18:20-22,** "But the prophet, which shall presume to speak a word in my name, which I have not commanded him to speak, or that shall speak in the name of other **gods**, even that prophet shall die. And if thou say in thine heart, How shall we **know** the word which the LORD hath **not spoken**? When a prophet speaketh in the name of the LORD, if the thing follow not, nor **come to pass,** that **is** the thing which the LORD hath **not** spoken, *but* the prophet hath spoken it **presumptuously:** thou shalt **not be afraid** of him." (Due. 13:1-5)

BEWARE OF FALSE PROPHETS

St. Matthew 7:15-16—Kjv "Beware of **false prophets,** which come to you in sheep's clothing, but inwardly they are ravening wolves. Ye shall know them by their **fruits.** Do men gather grapes of thorns, or figs of thistles?"

The reason why there are so many churches and false religions today is because there are so many **false teachers** and preachers. **St. Matthew 24: 4-5,11, 24 25,** "Jesus said, "**Take heed** that **no man deceive** you. For many shall come in my **name,** saying, I am Christ; and shall **deceive many.** And many false prophets **shall rise,** and shall deceive many. For there **shall arise false Christs,** and false prophets, and shall show great signs and wonders; insomuch that if *it were* possible, they shall deceive the **very elect.** Behold, I have told you before."

We are **not** to **follow** after **signs** and wonders for **false** prophets use **miracles** to **deceive** people. **Matthew 7:22-23** Jesus said, "Many will say to me in that **day,** Lord, Lord, **have** we not **prophesied** in thy **name?** And in thy name have cast out **devils?** And in thy name have done many wonderful **works?** And then **will I profess** unto them, **I never knew** you: depart from me, ye **that work iniquity.**"

2 Corinthians 11:13-15, Paul spoke about false prophets on this wise. "For such *are* **false apostles,** deceitful workers, **transforming themselves** into the apostles of **Christ.** And no marvel; for **Satan** himself is transformed into an **angel of light.** Therefore *it is* no great thing if **his ministers** also be **transformed** as the **ministers** of **righteousness;** whose **end** shall be according to their **works.**"

2 Thessalonians 2:3, 9, 10—Kjv "**Let no man deceive** you by **any means:** for *that day shall not come,* except there **come** a **falling away** first, and that **man** of **sin** be revealed, the son of **perdition;**...*Even him,* whose coming is after the working of **Satan** with all **power** and **signs** and lying **wonders,** and with all deceivableness of unrighteousness in them that perish; because they received not the **love** of the **truth,** that they **might be saved.**"

Romans 16:17-18 "Now I beseech you brethren, **mark them** which cause **divisions** and offenses contrary to the doctrine which ye **have learned;** and avoid them. For they that are such **serve** not our Lord Jesus Christ, but their own belly; and by good words and **fair speeches** deceive the hearts of the **simple.**"

Revelation 13:13-14 John spoke concerning the false prophet working miracles. "And he doeth great wonders, so that he maketh fire come down from heaven on the earth in the sight of men, and deceiveth them that dwell on the earth by *the means of* those miracles which he had power to do in the sight of the beast; saying to them that dwell on **the earth,** that they should make **an image** to the beast, which had the wound by a sword, and **did live.**

From this **we see** that **devils work miracles.** God used signs and wonders in the land of **Egypt** by the hand of **Moses. Devils** did also by the **hands** of the **magicians** of Egypt. Read **Exodus,** Chapter **seven.**

In our day we have the same encounter as Moses' day. 2 Timothy 3:6-8 Paul said, "For of this sort are they which creep into houses, and lead captive **silly women** laden with **sins, led away** with **divers lusts,** ever **learning** and never able to come to the **knowledge of the truth.** Now as **Jannes** and **Jambres** withstood Moses, so do these also resist the truth: men of **corrupt minds, reprobate** concerning the **faith."**

APOSTOLIC WARNINGS

I Timothy 4:1 The Apostles knew that... "some **shall depart** from the **faith,** giving heed to seducing **spirits,** and **doctrines** of devils;" **For that reason, they warned the church of this fact.**

Acts 20:27-30—Kjv Paul said unto the elders of Ephesus, "For I **have** not **shunned to declare** unto you all the **counsel** of God. Take heed therefore unto yourselves, and to all the **flock,** over the which the Holy Ghost **hath made** you **overseers, to feed** the church of God, which he hath purchased with his own **blood.** For I know this, that after my departing shall **grievous** wolves enter in among you, not sparing the **flock.** Also of your own selves shall men arise, speaking **perverse** things, to draw away disciples after them."

2 Peter 2:1-2 Peter said, "But there were false prophets also among the **people,** even as there shall be **false teachers** among you, who **privily shall bring in damnable heresies,** even **denying** the **Lord that bought** them, and bring upon themselves swift **destruction.** And many shall follow their **pernicious ways;** by reason of whom the **way of truth shall be even spoken of."**

I John 4:1 John said, "Beloved, **believe** not every **spirit,** but try the spirits whether they are of God: because many false prophets are gone out into the **world." I John 2:19** "They went out from us, but they were not of us; for if they had been of us, they would *no doubt* have continued with us: but they *went out,* that they **might be made manifest** that they were not all of us."

Jude 4 said, "For there are certain men **crept in unawares,** who were before of old ordained to this **condemnation, ungodly men,** turning the **grace** of our God into **lasciviousness,** and **denying** the only **Lord** God, Jesus Christ."

From the **Apostolic Warning,** we see that many false **preachers** and churches shall **arise.** I must say they have come forth and have **deceived** many. But we that have the **truth** must stand **firmly** on the **Word** of God and refute every false church and **doctrine.** The best way to do this is from the **written Word** of God. For the **Isaiah**

8:20 said, "To the **law** and to the **testimony**: if they **speak not** according to this **Word, it is** because **there is not light** in them."

To refuse every **false doctrine,** we must do it under the light of the **Word** of God. **I Timothy 6:3, 5d** Paul said to Pastor Timothy, "If any man **teach otherwise,** and **consent** not to wholesome words, *even* the words of our Lord Jesus Christ, and to the **doctrine** which is **according to godliness;**...from such **withdraw thyself.**"

Hebrews 2:1-3 "THEREFORE WE ought to give the more earnest heed to the things which we have heard, least at any time we should **let** *them* **slip.** For if the **Word** spoken by **angels** was **steadfast,** and every **transgression** and **disobedience** received a **just recompense of reward;** How shall we escape, if we neglect so great **salvation;** which at the first began to be spoken by the Lord, and **was confirmed** unto us by them that heard *him;*

Galaians 1:6-8 Paul said to the Galatians, "I marvel that ye are so soon removed from him that called you into the **grace** of Christ unto **another gospel:** Which is not another; but there be some that **trouble** you, and would **pervert** the **gospel** of Christ. But though we, or an **angel** from **heaven, preach** any other **gospel** unto you than that which we **have preached** unto you, let him be **accursed.**"

2 Thessalonians 3:6, "Now we command you, **brethren,** in the **name** of our Lord Jesus Christ, that ye **withdraw yourselves** from every brother that walketh **disorderly,** and not after the **tradition** which he received of us."

Titus 3:10, 11 "A man that is a **heretic** after the first and second **admonition reject;** Knowing that he that is such is subverted, and **sinneth,** being **condemned of himself.**"

2 Peter 3:1-2 Apostle Peter said, "This second **epistle,** beloved, I now **write** unto you; in both which I stir up your **pure minds** by way of **remembrance:** That ye may be mindful of the **words** which were spoken before by the holy **prophets,** and of the commandment of us **the apostles** of the **Lord** and **Saviour:**"

2 John 7-11 Apostle John said, "For many deceivers are entered into the world who **confess** not that Jesus **Christ** is come in the **flesh.** This is a deceiver and an **anti-Christ.** [8]Look to yourselves, that we lose not those things which we **have wrought,** but that we **receive** a **full reward.** [9]Whosoever **transgresseth,** and abideth not in the **doctrine** of Christ, hath **not** God. He **that abideth** in the doctrine of Christ, he hath both the Father and the Son.

If there come any unto you, and bring not this doctrine, receive him not into *your* house, neither bid him **Godspeed:** [11]For he **that biddeth** him Godspeed **is partaker** of his **evil deeds.**"

We therefore see from these scriptures that the apostles knew that they had received the **full truth** of God's **plan of salvation,** and the church that was established in their day was the church that would **remain** until the **rapture.**

Romans 10:14b, "...How shall they **hear** without a preacher?" We can see the need of having a preacher to speak unto us the words of the Lord. God has put this gospel into the hand of the preacher. God will not use an angel to preach.

Acts 10:5, 6, 25, 26 "For the angel that appeared unto **Cornelius** to **tell him** to "…
Send **men to Joppa**, and call for *one* Simon, whose surname is **Peter:** He lodgeth with
one Simon a tanner, whose house is by the seaside: He Shall Tell Thee Wʜᴀᴛ Tʜᴏᴜ
Oᴜɢʜᴛᴇꜱ Tᴏ Dᴏ." When **Jesus** appeared unto **Saul** He did **not tell** him how to be
saved, but He said; "…**Arise**, and go into the city, and it shall be told thee what thou
must do." (Acts 9:6)

Acts 18:24-26 **No preacher can take you any farther than he has gone himself.**
"And a certain Jew named **Apollos**, born at Alexandria, an **eloquent** man, *and* mighty
in the **Scriptures**, came to **Ephesus**. This man was instructed in the **way** of the
Lord; and being fervent in **the spirit**, he spake and **taught** diligently the things of
the Lord, **knowing** only the **baptism** of John. And he began to speak boldly in the
synagogue: whom when **Aquila** and **Priscilla** had heard, they **took** him unto *them*,
and **expounded** unto him the **way of God** more perfectly."

From this we see how some **preachers** can be very sincere, but still **not have** the
fullness of the truth. The people to whom these preachers **preach** to will believe only
as much as **that preacher** believes.

There was **a group** of **people** in **Acts 19:1-6,** who only had heard about the
baptism of John. They had not heard of the **baptism** in the **Name** of **Jesus Christ**
and being **filled** with the **Holy Ghost** speaking in other tongues as the **Spirit** of God
gives **utterance. Paul** said unto them, "…Have ye received the **Holy Ghost** since ye
believed?" And they said unto him, We have not so much as heard whether there
be any Holy Ghost. And he said unto them, Unto **what then were ye baptized**? And
they said, Unto John's baptism.

Acts 19:1-6 Then said Paul, John **verily** baptized with the baptism of **repentance**
saying unto people, that they should believe on him which should come after him,
that is, Christ Jesus. When they **heard** *this*, they were baptized in the **name** of the
Lord Jesus. And when Paul had laid *his* hands upon them, the Holy Ghost **came** on
them; and they spake with **tongues**, and **prophesied**." How can they **hear without
a preacher.**

Bᴇʟɪᴇᴠɪɴɢ Tʜᴇ Gᴏꜱᴘᴇʟ

Aꜰᴛᴇʀ Hᴇᴀʀɪɴɢ Tʜᴇ Gᴏꜱᴘᴇʟ, **The Next Step To Salvation ɪꜱ Tᴏ Bᴇʟɪᴇᴠᴇ Tʜᴇ Gᴏꜱᴘᴇʟ.**
Ephesians 1:13, "In whom ye also *trusted*, after that ye heard the **Word** of **truth**, the
gospel of your **salvation** in whom also **after** that ye **believed**, ye **were sealed** with
the **Holy Spirit** of **promise." Acts 8:12,** "But when they **believed** Philip **preaching**
the things concerning the **kingdom** of God, and the name of Jesus Christ, they were
baptized, both men and women."

Acts 8:36-37, "And as they went on *their* way, they came unto a certain water: and
the eunuch said, See, *here is* water; what doth hinder me **to be baptized**? And Philip

said, if thou **believest** with all thine heart, thou mayest. And he answered and said, I **believe** that Jesus **Christ is the Son** of God."

Mark 16:15-16, "And he said unto them, Go ye into all the **world,** and **preach** the **gospel** to every **creature.** He **that believeth** and **is baptized shall be saved**; but he that **believeth not shall be damned**." (Acts 16:31)

The above-mentioned **scriptures** should **suffice** in showing the **necessity** of **believing** the gospel. We must define **what is** believing, and **how much salvation** has a person **received** at the point of **believing?**

To **Believe** one must accept the gospel as the **truth,** and be **convinced** without prior **personal** knowledge. Since this is the case where a person does **not have** a personal **knowledge**; then, he should believe the **report** or the **evidence** given of someone who has had a personal **experience** of that which is being declared.

Hebrews 11:6, "He **that cometh** to God must **believe** that **He is,** and *that* he is a **rewarder** of them that diligently **seek** him."

Before a person can **believe** in God, he must first **hear** the gospel. There must be a spirit-filled **preacher** or a spirit-filled person who **declares** the gospel. **Romans 10:14-15,** "How then shall they **call** on him in whom they **have** not **believed?** and how shall they **believe** in **him** whom they have not **heard?"** **St. John 3:34,** "For he whom God **hath sent** speaketh the **words** of God:" This person who is sent by **God** must have **knowledge** or a firm **conviction** of the gospel.

For a striking example, Acts 17:22-24, "when **Paul** came to **Athens,** and beheld their **devotions,** he found an altar with this inscription, "To the UNKNOWN GOD." He said unto them, "...Him **declare** I unto you. God that made the **world** and all things therein, seeing that he is LORD of **heaven** and **earth,** dwelleth not in **temples** made with hands;"

It's **Interesting to note Paul's declaration** as he introduced unto them the **God** that they had **never heard** of. He gave unto them the **proof** of God's **existence** by **declaring** unto them the **things God** hath **done.** He gave unto them the **evidence** of God.

Romans 1:19-20 "Because **that which may be known** of God is **manifest** in them; for God **hath showed** it unto them. For the invisible things of him from the **creation** of the **world** are clearly seen, **being understood** by the things that are made, *even* his **eternal** power and **Godhead**; so that they are without excuse:"

This **must** be the **process** of all **those** that **declare** the **gospel of God,** so they that **hear** it **will have no excuse** not to **believe it.** St. John 3:33-34, "He that hath received his **testimony** hath set to his **seal** that **God is true.** For he whom God hath sent **speaketh** the **words** of God: for God giveth not the **Spirit** by measure unto him."

When a person **receives** this (that is that **God** is **true) he will accept** whatever **God says,** as being **truth.** Any promise that God makes unto him, would **impute** a certain spirit of **expectation** for such thing that is **promised** to come to pass. He **will have faith** toward **God.**

To believe does not mean that a person is saved at that point. Many people misunderstand that **particular** point. The amount of **salvation** that a person **receives**

at that **point** is that he has **only** turned to the **source** of his salvation. He can now look to **Jesus** for his salvation. He is the **author** and finisher of our **faith** (Heb 12:2).

To believe on the Lord Jesus means to accept Christ as your only hope of salvation. He alone can save us. Our **works** cannot save us. The **law** cannot save us. The Levitical **priesthood** could not save us. What can wash away my sins? Nothing but the **blood** of Jesus. What can make me whole again? Nothing but **the blood** of **Jesus.**

Romans 10:4 We no longer look to the law for our righteousness. "For **Christ** is the end of the law for righteousness to every one that believeth."

Romans 8:3-4 "For what the law could not do, in that is **was weak** through the **flesh**, God sending his own **Son** in the **likeness** of **sinful** flesh, and for sin, **condemned** sin in the flesh: That the **righteousness** of the law might be fulfilled in us, who walk not after the flesh, but after **the Spirit**."

Believing simply means we don't **work** for our salvation. **God gives it to us by His grace** through **our faith in Him.** "For by grace are ye saved through faith; and that not of yourselves: it is the gift of God: Not of works, lest any man should boast (Eph. 2:8-9).

"For what saith the **Scripture?** Abraham **believed** God, and it was counted unto him for **righteousness.** Now to him that worketh **is the reward** not **reckoned** of **grace,** but of **debt.** But to him that worketh not, but **believeth** on him **that justifieth** the **ungodly,** his **faith is counted** for righteousness." (Rom. 4:3-5)

THE WORK OF FAITH

There is a **process** by which we are to obtain this **salvation**, not by the **work** of the **law,** but by the **obedience** of **faith.**

"What *doth it* profit, my brethren, though a man say he hath **faith,** and have not works? Can faith **save** him?...Thou **believest** that there is one **God;** thou doest well: the **devils** also believe, and tremble. But wilt thou know, O **vain** man, that faith without works is dead? **Was** not Abraham our father **justified** by works, when he had offered Isaac his son upon the altar? Seest thou how faith wrought with his works, and by works **was** faith **made perfect?** And the Scripture was fulfilled which saith, Abraham **believed** God, and it **was imputed** unto him for **righteousness**..." James 2:14, 19-23.

Here **James** is **speaking** about the **works** of **faith.** Let's **understand.** If Abraham **believed** God, then he would be **obedient** to what God would **tell** him. He would **act** according to his **faith.**

When God tells us to **Believe, Repent,** be **Baptized** and be **filled** with the **Holy Ghost** in order to have **salvation applied** unto **our souls,** that will **we do** if we **believe** in **Him.** This work would not be the work of the **law,** but rather the **obedient** or work of **faith.**

When the Israelites heard Peter saying they had crucified the Lord of glory, because they had **confidence** in **God,** they were **pricked** in their hearts, and said unto Peter and to the rest of the apostles, "Men and **brethren,** what shall we DO?" Peter gave them the work of **process** to go back to **obtain** salvation.

"Then Peter said unto them, **Repent,** and **be baptized** every one of you in the **name** of Jesus Christ for the **remission** of **sins,** and ye shall receive the **gift** of the **Holy Ghost.**" (Acts 2:38)

"In the last day, that great *day* of the feast, Jesus stood and cried, saying If any man thirst, **let** him **come** unto me, and drink. He **that believeth** o me, as the **Scripture** hath said, out of his belly shall flow rivers of **living** water. (But this spake he of the Spirit, which they that believe on him should receive: for the **Holy Ghost** was not yet *given*; because that Jesus **was** not yet **glorified.**" (St. John 7:37-39)

This is not the **works** of the **Law,** but rather the **obedience** of **faith. Acts 6:7,** "And the Word of God **increased:** and the number of the disciples multiplied in Jerusalem greatly; and a great company of the priests **were obedient** to the **faith.**" **Acts 5:32** said: "And we are His **witnesses** of these **things;** and *so* is also the **Holy Ghost,** whom God hath given to them that obey Him."

REPENTANCE

Repentance means to become godly sorrowful for the things you have done against God, which is accompanied with the complete **surrendering**, or giving up of **sins.** Before a person can give up his sins he must **become sorrowful** and **ashamed** of the **things** he has **done.** With this **conviction**, he gives up his sins: but before a person can **repent**, he must **be willing** to give up his **sins.**

Repentance is a very **necessary step** in **salvation.** Matthew 1: 21, JESUS came to **save** his **people** from their **sins.** Jesus said, "The **time is fulfilled,** and the **kingdom** of God **is at hand**: **repent** ye, and **believe** the gospel." (Mark 1:15)

St. Luke 13:2, 3, "And Jesus answering said unto them, Suppose ye that these Galileans were **sinners** above all the Galileans, because they suffered **such things**? I tell you, Nay: but, except ye **repent,** ye shall **all** likewise **perish.**"

"And the **times** of this **ignorance** God **winked at**; but now **commandeth** all **men** every where **to** REPENT." (Acts 17:30)

"**Repent** ye therefore, and **be converted,** that your **sins may be blotted out**, when the **times** of **refreshing** shall come from the **presence** of the **Lord.**" (Acts 3:19)

Let us consider this: A person who gives up **his sins** must have **power** to **replace** what he has **given up.** Otherwise, the **things** that he **gave up** will become **a part** of him **again** (St. Luke 11:24-26).

Just to believe and **repent is not enough.** A person must **be baptized** as **Peter** says, "**Repent,** and **be baptized** every one of you in the **name** of Jesus Christ for the **remission** of **sins,** and ye shall receive the **gift** of the Holy Ghost." (Acts 2: 38)

BAPTISM

Baptism is the **immersion** in **water,** or the plunging **beneath** and **out of water,** (like the **burial** and **resurrection** of a person**),** of a **believer** who has confessed **faith** in the **death, burial** and **resurrection** of the **Lord** Jesus Christ. This person, when repented of all his sins, hopes to receive **eternal** salvation through the God given **plan.**

The **true baptism** is not administered by pouring, or sprinkling. **Romans 6:4-5,** "For he that is **baptized** is **buried** with **Christ,** and is brought up in the likeness of his **resurrection** to walk in the **newness** of life. A person who is baptized, is a person who has been **completely covered** by **water,** in the **name** of the Lord Jesus Christ. The same manner as **St. Matthew 3:16,** when **Jesus was baptized**, He came **up out of the water.**

When **Philip** preached unto the **Ethiopian eunuch, he believed** and said; "...See, here **is water**; what doth hinder me to be **baptized**? And he commanded the chariot **to stand still**: and they went **down both into the water,** both **Philip** and the **eunuch**; and he **baptized** him." (Acts 8:36, 38)

No one is qualified to **be baptized,** but he **who has repented** of **his sins,** and **believed** the **gospel.** As **Philip** said unto the Eunuch: "If thou **believest** with **all** thine **heart,** thou mayest. And he answered and said: **I believe that Jesus Christ is** the **Son of God.**" (Acts 8:37) Therefore, no one should **be baptized** unless he **believes** personally. **Infants** should **not be baptized**; because they have not the ability to **hear** the **gospel** and **believe it.** Neither should it be done by **proxy,** for there must be a **personal** belief. (Mark 16:16)

THE FORMULA OF BAPTISM

St. Matthew 28:19-20, Baptism must be done in the **name of the Father,** and **of the Son,** and **of the Holy Ghost.**

If we **carefully note** there has not been a **NAME** called in these **phrases;** name of the Father, and of the Son, and of the Holy Ghost. Also, we must note, in particular, the word **name** is **singular.** But, there are **three** titles or **positions** mentioned – Father, Son, and Holy Ghost. Then we must consider that the **name** of the person in these **three** positions, **is** ONE. If we know not **what** the **name** is, we **must look for the name** of the Father, Son, and Holy Ghost.

Now the **terms Father, Son, and Holy Ghost are not names,** but **titles** of **positions.** For **the word** _name_ is not plural. They are titles of positional relationships. The Son is **related to** the Father, because He brought the Son, (that is the flesh) into **existence.** The Holy Ghost is the **Spirit** of the **Father** and the **Son** (Rom. 8:9; Acts 5:3, 4; Eph. 4:4, 5; 2 Cor. 3:17.

The person who **fills** these **positions, Father, Son,** and **Holy Ghost** bore the name of **JESUS.** If I say the Father's name is Jesus, what do I say about the Scriptures which say the Father's name is Jehovah?

In the **Old Testament, Genesis 1:1,** God was called by many different names such as **Elohim,** which is the Hebrew name which means God the **Creator. Elyon,** which means the **Most High God** (Psalm 7:17). **Shaddai,** which means **Almighty. Exodus 6:2, 3,** "And **God spake** unto Moses, and said unto him, I *am* the **LORD:**" (or Jehovah). "And **I appeared** unto Abraham, unto Isaac, and unto Jacob, by *the name of* **God Almighty,**" (or Elshaddai) "but by my name JEHOVAH was I not known to them."

From this we can see that God used **many** different **names,** but in these **last days;** He has used the name of **Jesus** (Hebrews 1:1-4; Zech. 14:9).

The name of Jesus was a secret name of God before the revelation of it. It was God's **saving name** for us today. **Jacob** wanted to know what that **name** was when he **wrestled** with the **angel of the Lord,** saying; "...**Tell** *me,* I pray thee, thy name. And he said, Wherefore is it *that* thou dost ask after **my name?** And he blessed him there. And Jacob called the name of the place **Peniel:** for I have seen **God** face to face, and my **life is preserved.**" (Gen. 32: 29, 30)

Manonah wanted to know what that name was, but the angel said unto him: "**Why** asketh thou thus after my name, seeing it is **secret?**" (Judges 13:18)

That name was to be revealed in its proper time. In Psalm 22:22, the Scripture spake concerning Christ saying: "I will declare thy **name** unto my **brethren:...**" **Isaiah 7:14,** it is said: "Therefore the Lord himself shall give you **a sign;** Behold, a **virgin** shall **conceive,** and **bear a son,** and shall call his name Immanuel." (St. Matt. 1: 23)

Isaiah 9:6, "For unto us **a child** is born, unto us **a son** is **given:** and the **government** shall be upon his **shoulder:** and his **name** shall be called **Wonderful, Counselor, The Mighty God, The Everlasting Father, The Prince of Peace.**"

Zechariah 14:9, lets us know by prophecy there would be only **one name.** He said: "and the LORD shall be king over all the earth: in that day shall there be ONE LORD, and his name ONE.

The angel of the Lord brought that long **awaited revelation** by saying unto **Joseph:** "And she shall bring forth **a son,** and thou shalt call his **name JESUS:** for he shall **save his people** from **their sins.**" (Matt. 1:21, 23)

Truly Jesus said in **St. John 5:43** "I am come in my **Father's name...**" And again in **St. John 17:26,** "And I have declared unto them thy **name,** and will declare it..." Fulfilling the Scriptures in Psalm 22:22.

Acts 4: 10-12, There is no other name under heaven whereby we must be saved but **the name** Jesus. "Of whom the whole family in heaven and earth is named." (Eph. 3:15) "And whatsoever ye do in word or deed, do all in the **name** of the Lord Jesus, giving thanks to God and the Father by Him." (Col. 3:17)

All of God's **names** are included in this ONE name **JESUS.** For Psalm 138:2 says: "... thou has magnified thy **word** above all thy **name.**" **Yes, Jesus is the word of God.** "... All things were made by him; and without him was not anything made that was made.

"…And the **Word** was made **flesh**, and dwelt among us, (and we beheld **his glory**, the glory as of the **only begotten of the Father**,) full of grace and truth. (St. John 1:1, 3, 14)

All other manifestations that God used in **times past have ceased** since Jesus came. **Hebrews 1:1, Jesus** is the name **God is using today.** "But as many as received him, to them gave he **power to become the sons** of God, even to them that **believed** in the **name** of the only **begotten Son** of God." (St. John 1:12)

Philippians 2: 9-11, "Wherefore God also hath highly exalted him, and **given** him **a name** which is above every **name:** That at the **name of JESUS** every knee should bow, of *things* **in heaven**, and *things* **in earth**, and *things* under the earth; And *that* every tongue **should confess** that Jesus Christ is LORD, to the **glory** of God the **Father**."

WHICH IS THE CORRECT BAPTISMAL FORMULA?

IN THE NAME OF THE FATHER, SON AND HOLY GHOST
OR
THE LORD JESUS CHRIST?
(Matthew 28: 19, 20 – Acts 2: 38, 39 ---KJV)

There have been **questions** asked as to when the **baptism** in the **name of Jesus** started. Or, when did the baptism using the term; *"In the name of the Father, and of the Son, and of the Holy Ghost,"* begin?

In answering these questions, we must go to the **Bible** and **Church History.**

The first **Historical account** that anyone should note is **the Bible.** It is the only **authoritative** account that should be **believed.** All others should be believed as they correspond with the Bible.

Now concerning the subjects under discussion: There is no place in the Bible where the Apostles **baptized** using the term: *"In the name of the Father, and of the Son, and of the Holy Ghost.* "The **book of Acts is** the **Historical book** of the **New** Testament. It shows us **how** the Apostles carried out the **commandment** of Jesus. The statement in **St. Matthew 28:19, 20** is a command **given** by Jesus to his disciples **to baptize.** They carried out that **command** in the book of Acts.

The first baptism that was administered after Jesus gave His command was, in the **name** of Jesus, **for** the **remission** of **sins** (Acts 2:38; 8:12-17; 10:48, 36; 19:1-6).

If Peter and the rest of the disciples understood Jesus to speak of **three distinct** NAMES, would he not have included them in these **statements**? But he knew what Jesus meant. That is, that **baptism** was **to be** done in **Jesus' name**, and not in **three distinct names.** St. Luke 24:45-48, Jesus **opened** up the **understanding** of the disciples that they might understand **the Scriptures.** Not only that, Jesus said that the **Holy Ghost** would bring back to their **remembrance** whatsoever He had **commanded** them (St. John 14:26; Acts 1: 2).

Inasmuch as the Apostles were the ones to whom Jesus taught directly, Jesus said we should believe on Him through the **apostles words** (St. John 17:20).

The **book of Acts is the Biblical History of what went on in the early days of the Church.** It covers a history of about **thirty years** of Church history. **Acts 19:1-6,** Paul **baptized** the disciples at Ephesus in the **name** of the Lord Jesus Christ, about twenty years **after** the **day of Pentecost.** This should be enough **evidence** to let us know that **baptism** was done **only** in the **name of Jesus Christ,** in the **early days** of the church.

The Book Of Acts is a **record** of how the Apostles fully **implemented** the **commands** of Jesus. If you want to know what Jesus Taught his disciples, go to the four gospels. If you want to know **how** the Apostles carried out His **commands,** go to The Book Of Acts and the epistles to the Church.

When Jesus said, "...**Baptizing** them in the **name** of the Father, and of the Son, and of the Holy Ghost," His disciples **obeyed** it by **baptizing everyone** in the **name** of Jesus. If we don't **believe** the Apostles, we don't **believe** Jesus (St. Jhn. 17:20; Mt. 10:40,41).

Therefore, **baptism** was done in the **name of Jesus** from the **day of Pentecost** on and especially to the **third Century A. D.** when the mode and **Formula** were changed to the so-called Trinitarian Formula.

The **Encyclopedia Britannica,** the eleventh edition vol. 3, page 365, section 5, on the **Baptism Formula** it is said: "The **Trinitarian** Formula and **Triune** Immersion were not **uniformly used** from the **beginning,** nor did they always go together. The **teaching** of the **Apostles** indeed, prescribes **baptism** in the **Name** of Father, Son and Holy Ghost, but on the next page **speaks** of those who have been **baptized into the name** of the Lord, * which is the normal **formula** of the **New Testament.**

In the **Third Century baptism** in the **name** of Christ was still so widespread that **Pope Stephen,** in opposition to Cyprian of Carthage, **declared** it to be **valid.** From **Pope Zachariah** we learn the Celtic Missionaries in **baptizing** omitted one or more persons of the **Trinity,** and this was one of the **reasons why** the church of **Rome** Anathematized them."

Pope Stephen was **Bishop** over the **Roman Catholic Church** from 253-257 A. D. **Baptism in Jesus' name** was still being practiced. But **Pope Zachariah 741-752,** who was also a Bishop of the **Church of Rome, rejected** those who **baptized** in **Jesus' name.** We see between 253 A. D. there has been a **drastic** change from the **formula** of baptism in the **name** of **Jesus** Christ to the formula in the **name** of the terms **Father, Son** and **Holy Ghost.** This influence came chiefly **from** the **Nicene Council,** when they instituted the **Creed of the Trinitarian** doctrine **325 A. D.**

They that question the baptism in Jesus' name should check throughout church **history,** and **above all,** the **Bible.** And, they will **find** that **baptism in Jesus' name** didn't **start** just a few **years** ago but **on the Day of Pentecost.**

Four Parts To The Great Commission

Whenever we think about the **Great Commission** when Jesus sent His disciples to **evangelize** the world, we often go to the **28th** chapter of **St. Matthew.** But after **examining** the commission a little **closer,** I find that the commission **was** given unto us in FOUR **parts** as follows:

(1) Teach & Baptize in the Name_____   **St. Matthew 28:19**
(2) Preach, Believeth & **is** Baptized———   **St. Mark 16:15-17**
(3) Repentance & remission of Sins———   **St. Luke 24:45-49**
(4) Holy Ghost Power & Witnesses———   **Book of Acts 1:8**

We cannot obtain a **good** understanding of the **Great Commission,** unless we examine **all** the **Scriptures** that **contain** it.

Let's turn to the FIRST **scripture on this subject. St. Matthew 28:19, 20,** "Go ye therefore, and **teach** all nations, baptizing them in the **name** of the **Father,** and of the Son, and of the **Holy Ghost: Teaching** them to observe all things whatsoever I have commanded you: and, lo, I am with you always, *even* unto the **end** of the world. **Amen."**

*The teaching of the Apostles is **a spurious** book circulated claiming to be written by the apostles. **Historians** know this to be a **forged** document.*

The SECOND **scripture-reference is St. Mark 16:15-17. "And** he said unto them, GO ye into all the **world,** and **preach** the **gospel** to every creature. **He that believeth** and **is baptized shall be saved;** but **he that believeth not shall be dam**ned. And these **signs** shall follow them **that believe;** IN my **name** shall they cast out **devils;** they **shall speak** with **new tongues;** They shall take up **serpents;** and if they drink any **deadly** thing, it shall not hurt them; they shall lay hands on the **sick,** and they shall recover."

The THIRD **scripture-reference is St. Luke 24:45-49.** "Then opened he their **understanding,** that they **might understand** the **Scriptures,** And said unto them, Thus **it is written,** and thus it **behooved Christ to suffer,** and **to rise** from the **dead** the third day: And that **repentance** and **remission** of sins **should be preached** in his name among all nations, beginning at Jerusalem. And ye are witnesses of these things. And, behold, I send the **promise** of my Father upon you: But tarry ye in the city of Jerusalem, until ye be endued with power from on high."

The FOURTH **scripture-reference is Acts 1:8.** "But ye shall receive **power,** after that the Holy Ghost is come upon you: and ye shall be **witnesses** unto me both in Jerusalem, and in all Judea, and in Samaria, and unto the **uttermost part** of the earth."

These are **the Scriptures** that deal with the **GREAT COMMISSION.** We shall **examine** each part **to** determine what **benefit** it gives unto us.

MATTHEW 28: 19-20 - - KJV

The first thing that is mentioned in the commission is to go into all the world. The word "**Go**" signifies unto us that the gospel was to be carried unto the **people**, not the people brought unto the gospel. There must be a **missionary** or **evangelistic endeavor initiated** by the **church** for the **lost.** If not, **many** souls will go into **eternity** and possibly be lost because of the laxity on the part of the church. Therefore, we see in each scripture on this subject of the great Commission, that **emphasis** is placed on **evangelizing** the world.

The next point is to **teach** all nations. This term "**Teach'** merely means to **make disciples** of all men. Cause all **to understand** the way of salvation. Whether they be **Jew** or **Gentile**, Black, Yellow, Red, or White, Rich or Poor, Learned or Unlearned, we must cause them to **understand** the **gospel**.

The next point was to **baptize** them in the **Name** of the **Father**, and of the Son, and of the **Holy Ghost**. **All believers** are to **be baptized**. Anything that Jesus commands us to do, it must be done if it be for no other reason than the mere fact that Jesus said it. But there are other **reasons** for **baptizing** all **believers** which we shall examine in the **other** Scriptures on the Great Commission.

The next point about **baptism** in this scripture is that it must be done in the **name** of the **Father**, Son, and **Holy Ghost**.

The terms, in the **Name** of the Father and of the Son, and of the Holy Ghost have been a subject of great debate. Some have used this **scripture** to establish a doctrine of Triune Immersion. That is, to **baptize** a candidate once in the name of the Father, once in the name of the Son, and once in the name of the Holy Ghost. For they thought this meant to **baptize in three different Names**. But if we consider the Scriptures **carefully**, we should see that the term *name* is **singular,** signifying that there is only ONE NAME under consideration.

There is a **threefold** relationship to this ONE NAME, the Father, Son, and Holy Ghost. For we know that the **Son's name** is not Son, but **His name** is **Jesus**.

St. Matthew 1:21, "And she shall bring forth a **son,** and thou shall call his **name** JESUS: for he **shall save** his **people** from their **sins.**" Jesus said, he came in **His Father's** name. **St. John 5:43.** He said that the **Holy Ghost** would be **sent in His name.** **St. John 14: 26** From this it can be seen that Jesus has reference unto **only** ONE **name.**

The **next point** in this scripture is that Jesus told his disciples to **teach** all nations whatsoever He had **commanded** them. This is to say, whatever Jesus **taught** His disciples to **preach, teach**, and the way to **baptize,** and we must **do the same**.

The Great Commission in **St. Matthew** only told the disciples to go, **teach**, and **baptize.** It didn't mention **faith, repentance,** and **receiving the Holy Ghost.** Therefore, from this Scripture in St. Matthew, we don't receive the **complete understanding** on the way of **salvation.**

St. Mark 16: 15-18--KJV

The SECOND **scripture** which is in **St. Mark 16:15-18,** He said **Go** into all the **world** and **preach** the **gospel** to every **creature**. This also supports **evangelism**. The next part said, "He **that believeth** and **is baptized shall be saved**."

The SECOND **portion of the Great Commission** let's us to know the **necessity** of **believing** and being **baptized** in order to be **saved**. The person **to be baptized** must **confess faith** in **Jesus Christ**. He must **believe before** he **is baptized (Acts 8:12-37)**. The next portions of this scripture are the **signs** following:

1. Casting **out devils** in **the name** of Jesus.
2. Speaking in **new tongues**.
3. **Protection** from **snakes,** and **poison**.
4. Laying **hands** on **the sick** for their **healing**.

Everywhere the gospel was to be preached, **these signs** follow them that **believe**. The casting out of devils, speaking in new tongues etc. was to continue throughout the time of the preaching of the gospel.

From the Scriptures in **St. Matthew** and **St. Mark**, we have included in the Great Commission **Evangelism, Teaching, Preaching, Baptism, Believing,** and **Signs** Following.

St. Luke 24:45-49--KJV

The **Third scripture** in **St. Luke 24:45-49,** tell us "That **repentance** and remission of **sins** should be **preached** in his **name** among **all nations,** beginning at Jerusalem." This scripture add REPENTANCE to the list in the Great Commission. It also clarifies **what name** to **use** in the **Baptismal formula.** Jesus said, "That **repentance** and **remission of sin** should be preached, in **his Name**." This let's us know that **Jesus** didn't have reference to **three names** in the baptismal **formula**.

St. Luke 24:46 said, that this **gospel** must be **preached** beginning at **Jerusalem.** Jesus said, if any man (disciples) thirst, let him come unto me and drink, not only disciples must **be filled** with the Holy Ghost, but **all believers**. St. John 7:37, 38. However, these **signs** of **speaking** with **new tongues** shall **follow** them that **believe,** which is associated with the receiving of the **Spirit** of God **(St. Mark 16:17)**.

Now we have in the Great Commission, **Evangelism,** through the process of **preaching** in the name of Jesus for the **remission** of **sins**; being filled with the Holy Ghost, with **signs** following.

BOOK OF ACTS 1: 8--KJV

The FOURTH **scripture** is **Acts 1-8, reaffirms** the other **scriptures, saying:** "But ye shall receive **power**, after that the Holy Ghost is come upon you: and ye shall be **witnesses** unto me both in Jerusalem, and in all Judea, and in Samaria, and unto the **uttermost part** of the earth."

To get a good **understanding** of the Great Commission, we must examine how the Apostles implemented the commands in accordance with the wisdom and knowledge God gave them. Jesus said in **St. John 17:20** that we should **believe** on him through the **Apostles' words**.

There are about **three places** we must look to see whether the Apostles carried out the Great Commission as Jesus has said:

A. Jerusalem and all Judea.
B. Samaria.
C. The uttermost part of the earth. (Gentiles)

FULFILLMENT

Fulfillment of **Number** ONE – **Acts 2:1-4.** The disciples were all filled with the Holy **Ghost** and begin **to speak** with **other tongues** in the upper room **at Jerusalem.** This was **fulfilled** in the following Scriptures: St. Luke 24: 49, and Acts 1: 8.

Fulfillment of **Number** TWO – **Acts 2:14.** The gospel began to be **preached** at **Jerusalem.** "But Peter, standing up with the eleven, lifted up his **voice**, and said unto them, Ye men of **Judea,** and all ye that dwell at **Jerusalem,** be this **known** unto you, and hearken to my **words**..."

Fulfillment of **Number** THREE – **Acts 2:37,** The people must **believe, repent, be baptized** in Jesus' **name**, for remission of **sins**, and receive the Holy **Ghost,**

Acts 2:37-38 "Now when they heard *this*, they were pricked in their heart," signifies faith. "Then Peter said unto them, **Repent,** (Acts 2; 38) and **be baptized** every one of you (Mark 16:16) in the **name** of Jesus Christ (Matt. 28:19) for the **remission** of **sins,** (Luke 24:47) "and ye shall receive the **gift** of the Holy Ghost." (St. Luke 24: 49; Acts 1:8; St. John 3: 5; 7: 37-39)

Fulfillment of **number** FOUR – **Acts 8:4-7.** "Therefore they that were scattered abroad went every where **preaching** the **Word**. Then Philip went down to **Samaria,** (Acts 1:8) and preached **Christ** unto them. ⁶And the people with ONE ACCORD gave heed unto those things which Philip spake, hearing and seeing the **miracles** which he did. For **unclean spirits**, crying with loud voice, came out of many that were possessed *with them*: and many **taken with palsies**, and that were lame, were **healed**." Mark 16: 17, 18

Acts 8:12, "But when they **believed** Philip **preaching** the things concerning the **kingdom** of God, and the name of Jesus Christ, they **were baptized,** both men and **women**." Verse 17, "Then laid they *their* hands on them, and they **received** the Holy Ghost." (Luke 24: 45, 47; Acts 1:8; 2: 39; Mark 16:15, 16; Matt. 28: 19)

Fulfillment of **Number** FIVE – **Acts 10:34-37, 42** To the Gentiles, going into all the world. **Peter** went to **Caesarea,** to **Cornelius** the **Gentile,** to carry the Word. "Then Peter opened *his* mouth, and said, Of a truth **I perceive** that **God** is no **respecter** of **persons:"** [35]"But in every nation he **that fearth** him, and **worketh righteousness,** is **accepted** with him. [36]The Word which *God* sent unto the **Children** of Israel, **preaching peace** by Jesus Christ: (he is Lord of all:) "That **Word,** I *say,* ye know, which was published throughout all **Judea,** and began from **Galilee,** after the **baptism** which John **preached;** "…And he commanded us **to preach** unto the people, and to **testify** that it is he **which was ordained** of God *to be* the **Judge** of **quick** and dead." (**Acts** 10: 34-39, 42; Romans 10:12; 1:14-16)

Acts 10: 44-48; the **Gentiles** believed and were **filled** with the **Holy Ghost** (Acts 2:4; 1:8; 11:15; St. John 7:37, 38). They too were **baptized** in **Jesus' name** (Acts 2:38; Mark 16:16).

All these **Biblical** historical accounts show us that the disciples **implemented** the **Great Commission** just as Jesus **commanded** them to do.

Acts 4: 17-20, "But that is spread no further among the people; let us **straitly** threaten them, that they **speak** henceforth to no man in this **name.** And they called them, and **commanded** them not **to speak** at all nor **teach** in the **name** of Jesus. But Peter and John answered and said unto them, Whether it be **right** in the sight of **God to hearken** unto you more than unto God, **judge ye.** For we cannot but **speak** the things which we **have seen** and **heard**."

We conclude therefore in saying that in order to grasp a complete understanding of the **Great Commission,** we must consider **all** of the **scriptures** relating to the subject.

Remember, that which is contained in the **Great Commission** is as follows:

1. **Preaching** and **teaching** the gospel to **every creature**.
2. **Faith** and **belief** in the gospel.
3. **Repentance** from **sins.**
4. **Baptism** in the **name** of Jesus Christ.
5. **Baptism** of the Holy Ghost speaking in **other tongues**.
6. **Signs** and miracles following the **believers. Amen.**

THERE IS ONE BAPTISM

Ephesians 4:4 Paul states, *There* is ONE **body,** ONE **Spirit,** "...ONE LORD, ONE FAITH, ONE **Baptism.** Since there is only ONE baptism, why did John the Baptist say in Matthew 3:11 "I indeed **baptize** you with water unto **repentance:** But he that cometh after me is mightier than I, whose **shoes** I **am** not **worthy** to bear: he shall baptize you with the **Holy Ghost,** and *with* fire:" The baptism in the **name of Jesus** took the **place** of the baptism administered by **John the Baptist (Acts 19:1-6).**

Considering what John the Baptist said concerning the Baptism, there seems to be **three** baptisms: with **water,** with the **Holy Ghost** and with **fire.** But the scripture said there is but ONE **baptism.** Then what does this mean, i.e. what John said concerning the baptism? I shall explain. There is but ONE **baptism,** but there are **three parts** to this ONE baptism. There is but ONE BAPTISM with **water,** with **Holy Ghost,** and **with fire.** . Now, let us take this **concept** to another level.

The **purpose** of baptism is to **purify** or **cleanse,** as we shall discuss later. May we consider, and know this, that ONE **part** of Baptism is just as **important** as the **other** Two.

Each part must be **connected** with the other in order for a person to whom it is **applied** to be saved. For this reason, baptism is **essential** to salvation.

Jesus said unto **Nicodemus:** "...Verily, verily, I say unto thee, Except a man **be born** of the water, "(that is baptism)," and *of t*he **Spirit,**" (baptism of the Holy Ghost), "he cannot enter into the kingdom of God." (St. John 3: 5)

Paul said in **Galatians 3:27,** "For as many of you as **have been baptized** into Christ have **put on** Christ." Also I Corinthians 12:13 "For by ONE **Spirit** are we all **baptized** into ONE body, whether we be Jews or Gentiles, whether *we be* **bond** or **free:** and **have been** all **made to drink** into **one Spirit.**"

Peter said in **Acts 10:47, 48,** "Can any man forbid water, that these **should** not be **baptized,** which have received the Holy Ghost as well at we? And he **commanded** them to be baptized in the **name** of the Lord..."

"The **like figure** whereunto *even* **baptism doth** also now **save** us (not the putting away of the filth of the flesh, but the answer of a good conscience toward God,) by the **resurrection** of Jesus Christ." (I Pet. 3:21)

Ananias said to **Paul,** "And now why tarriest thou? Arise, and be baptized, and wash away thy sins, calling on the name of the Lord." (Acts 22:16)

St. Mark 16:16, If we are not **baptize** in **water,** in the **name of Jesus,** for the **remission** of **sins,** we cannot be saved. If we don't have the baptism of the Spirit: We must get it to be **saved** (Rom. 3:9; I Cor. 12:13; Gal. 3:27).

Acts 19:1-6 When we receive **the Spirit of God,** we are baptized with the **baptism** of the **Holy Ghost** (Eph. 1:13).

The baptism of fire, occurs when we **experience** our **trials** and **tribulations.** Peter said in **I Peter 4:12,** "Beloved, think it not strange concerning the **fiery trial** which is to **try** you, as though some strange thing happened unto you:"

I Peter 4:1, "Forasmuch then as Christ hath suffered for us in the **flesh**, arm yourselves likewise with the same **mind:** for he that hath suffered in the flesh hath ceased from sin;" (Mark 10:38, 39)

James 1:12 said, "Blessed is the man that **endureth temptation**: for when he is **tried,** he shall receive the crown of **life**, which the Lord **hath promised** to them **that love** him."

It does not matter if a person has received the **baptism** of the **Holy Ghost** if he has not been **baptized** in **water** in the **name of Jesus**. But, he **must be** Baptized, in order for his salvation to be **complete.**

For an interesting example, **Cornelius,** and they that were with him, **received** the **baptism** of the **Holy Ghost** before they were **baptized** in **water in Jesus' Name.** But **Peter** immediately said; "Can any man **forbid water**, that these **should** not be baptized, which have **received** the Holy Ghost as well as we? And he commanded them to be baptized in the **name** of the Lord..." (Acts 10:47, 48)

MODE OF BAPTISM

There is but **one-way** to be **baptized;** that is by **immersion** in the **name** of **Jesus Christ.** There is nowhere in the **Bible** where the **Apostles baptized** in **any other mode.**

Please find below notes from various Church **Leaders** and Church **History** as follows:

BRITANNICA ENCYCLOPEDIA
Vol. 1, Pg. 82

Everywhere in the oldest sources it states that **baptism** took place _ In the **name** of Jesus Christ.

CANNEY ENCYCLOPEDIA OF RELIGIONS
Pg. 53

The **early church** always **baptized** in the **name** of the **Lord Jesus** until development of **Trinity doctrine** in the **2nd Century.**

CATHOLIC ENCYCLOPEDIA
Vol. 2, Pg. 263

Here the **Catholics** acknowledge that **baptism** was changed by the **Catholic Church.**

HASTINGS ENCYCLOPEDIA OF RELIGIONS

Vol. 2, Pg. 377, 378, 379.

   Christian **baptism** was **administered** using the **words, "In the name of Jesus"** The use of a Trinitarian formula of any sort was not suggested in **early** church **history.** Baptism was always in the **name** of The Lord Jesus until the time of Justin Martyr when the triune formula was used.

HASTINGS ENCYCLOPEDIA OF RELIGIONS
Vol. 2, Pg. 377 on Acts 2:38
   NAME was an ancient synonym for "Person". Payment was always made in name of some person referring to ownership. Therefore, one being baptized in Jesus' Name became his Personal property.

IMMERSION

JOHN CALVIN
Presbyterian
"The word Baptize signifies to **immerse.** It is certain that immersion was the practice of primitive church."

MARTIN LUTHER
Lutheran
Baptism is a Greek word, and may be translated "**Immerse**." "I would have all who are to be baptized to be altogether dipped."

JOHN WESLEY
Methodist
"The Bible term, **buried** with Him by baptism alludes to the ancient manner of **baptizing** by **immersion."**

WALL
Episcopal
"**Immersion** was in all probability the way in which our blessed **Savior**, and for certain the way in which all **early Christians** were baptized."

BRENNER
Catholic
"For the first thirteen hundred years, baptism was an **immersion** of the person **under water."**
STOUDZA
A native Greek

"The verb 'Baptize' has only one meaning. It signifies to **plunge** beneath. Baptism and **immersion** are identical. To say baptism by sprinkling would be to say immersion by sprinkling."

JERIMIAH
A Greek Patriot
"The **ancient** did not sprinkle the candidate, but **immersed** him."

WHITFIELD
Methodist
It is certain that the word **buried** in the text, **Romans 6:4** alludes to the matter of Baptizing by **Immersion**.

BAPTISM FOR THE REMISSION OF SINS

Let us go to **Acts 2:38**, where **Peter** said: "**Repent**, and **be baptized** every one of you in the **name** of Jesus Christ for the **remission** of **sins**, and ye shall **receive** the **gift** of the Holy **Ghost**."

Act 22:16, "And now why tarriest thou? Arise, and **be baptized**, and **wash away** thy **sins**, calling on the name of the Lord."

I Corinthians 6:11, "And such was some of you: but ye **are washed**, but ye **are sanctified**, but ye **are justified** in the **name** of the Lord Jesus, and by the **Spirit** of our God."

Ephesians 5:26 "That He **might sanctify** and **cleanse** it with the **washing** of **water** by the **Word**,"

Before God could have a **holy people**, He had to **clean up** those that **surrendered** themselves unto **Him**. For man was a **sinner** from his birth. The only way for him to be **cleansed** from this **sins**, was by the **blood of Jesus** that was shed on **Calvary**. The way **God** has **chosen** to get this blood **applied to our hearts** is through **believing, repenting,** and **baptism**. As it is said in **Revelation 1:5**;" ...Unto him that **loved** us, and **washed us** from sins in **his own blood**."

If the **Apostle Paul** had received remission of sins When he became **a believer,** on the road to **Damascus, why** was he told to "...Arise, and **be baptized**, and **wash away** thy **sins**, calling on the **name** of the Lord." (Acts 22:16)

We see the remission of sins associated with water baptism. Someone might say, "How can we be washed in the **blood** of the **Lamb**?" This is how; by **faith** in the name of Jesus, the **blood applied** unto our **hearts** when we are **baptized** in the **name** of Jesus. For the blood is brought in by **faith** in **the name** of Jesus **when** it (the name) is **called** over the **candidate**. The **blood** is **associated** with the **name** (Acts 5:28, 22:16).

For an interesting example, my name is **Duncan**. I am not a Duncan because of my **parents** named me Duncan, but I am a Duncan because I **inherited the Duncan**

blood at the time of **conception**. That was my name before I was born. If I would have my name changed, biologically, I would still be a Duncan. Despite the passing of generations, I have **inherited** the Duncan **Blood** and I am passing it on to my **off springs** and they will pass it on to their **generation**.

From this we can see that the **name** and the **blood** are **associated** together. It is a necessary thing to use the **name** of Jesus to **bring** in the **blood** when a **candidate is baptized.** It is more than that, it's **a command.** "...and without **shedding of blood** is no remission." (Heb. 9:22)

Baptism is for the **remission** or forgiving of **sins.** His blood in water cleanses us by the **baptism** in the **name** of Jesus.

When Moses **administered** in the **sanctuary,** he took **blood** and **water,** and used it in his ministry of **sanctifying** the **people** and vessels under the law. Not water alone but also with **blood.** The law purges almost all things with **blood**, and with out the **shedding of blood**, there is **no remission** (Heb. 10:18-23; 9:22). **Baptism** is for **remission** of sins, or the **removing** of **sins** (Acts 22:16).

Under the **law,** the **blood** of those **sacrifices** that were used are the **atonement** for **man, purified** the **flesh** but not the **conscience** (Heb. 9:13) **Since** those sacrifices **purified** the **flesh:** How much more shall the **blood** of **Christ**, who through the eternal **Spirit** offered himself **without spot** to God, PURGE YOUR CONSCIENCE, from **dead works to serve** the LIVING GOD." (Heb. 9:14)

We conclude by saying that **baptism** is for the **remission** of **sins.** If you have not been baptized in the **name** of Jesus Christ, you have not been **cleansed** from your **sins** (Acts 4:10-12).

YE SHALL RECEIVE THE HOLY GHOST

The **Holy Ghost** is **God** in us, or the way **God applies salvation** to the **heart** of the **believer** (Rom. 8: 9-11; Eph. 1:13; Gal.4:4-6).

The Holy Ghost is for everyone. Because God said He will **pour** out the **gift** of His **Spirit** upon all flesh (Joel 2:28). Peter said, "For the **promise** is unto you, and to your children, and to all that are afar off, *even* as many as the Lord our God **shall call.**" (Acts 2:39; 10:44-48) The Holy Ghost is for **Jews** and **Gentiles** alike. For **Cornelius,** being a **Gentile, received** the **Holy Ghost** (Acts 10:45-48; 11:15; 15:6-12).

Some people say the **moment** a person **believes he has** the **gift** of the Holy Ghost, or **Spirit** of God. But this is **not so.** Yes, a person must believe in order to get the Holy Ghost; but because he believes **that is not a sign** the Holy Ghost **has come in.** To prove this, let us read in the **book of Acts** where **Philip** preached the gospel unto the **Samaritans.**

"But when they **believed** Philip **preaching** the things concerning the **kingdom** of God, and the **name** of Jesus Christ, they **were baptized**, both men and women. [14]Now when the **apostles** which were at Jerusalem heard that **Samaria** had received the **Word** of God, they sent unto them **Peter** and **John**: [15]Who, when they were come down, **prayed** for them, that they might receive the **Holy Ghost:** (For **as yet** he was **fallen** upon **none** of them: only they were **baptized** in the **name** of the Lord Jesus." (Acts 8:12-16; 19:1-6)

Some people **think** the Holy **Ghost** and the Holy **Spirit** are two **different Spirits.** But that is not so. For in **St. Matt. 3:16,** the Scripture said that **he saw** the Holy **Spirit** descending like a **dove,** and **lighting** upon **him.** While in **St. Luke** doing the same **incident** the Scripture said, the Holy **Ghost** descended in a **bodily shape** like a **dove** upon him **(St. Luke 3:22).**

Hence, the **Holy Spirit** and the **Holy Ghost are the same Spirit.** You cannot have the Holy **Spirit** without having the Holy **Ghost.** If you don't have the Holy Ghost, you don't have the Holy **Spirit.**

It is **very necessary** to **have** the **Holy Ghost** to **go** to **heaven. Romans 8:9,** "But ye are not in the flesh, but in the Spirit, if so be that the **Spirit** of God **dwell** in you. Now if any **man** have **not** the **Spirit** of **Christ,** he is **none of his."**

Romans 14:17, "For the kingdom of God *is* not meat and drink; but **righteousness,** and **peace,** and ʝoʏ in the Holy **Ghost."** 2 Corinthians 13:5 "**Examine** yourselves, whether ye be in the **faith; prove** your own selves. Know ye not your own selves, how that Jesus **Christ** is in you, except ye be **reprobate?"**

BAPTISM OF THE HOLY GHOST

There is a **misconception** going about **today** as to whether it is **necessary** to have the **baptism** of the Holy Ghost **to be saved.** Some think it is possible to receive the Holy Ghost and baptism of the Holy Ghost with different experiences. They think it is possible to **receive** the Holy **Spirit** without being **baptized** with the **Holy Ghost.** The **receiving** of the Spirit of God is the **same** as being **filled** with the Holy Ghost. Being filled with the **Holy Ghost** is the **same** as being **baptized** with the **Holy Ghost.**

Joel 2:28, 29 prophesied, "And it shall come to pass afterward, *that* I **will pour out** my **spirit** upon all **flesh;** and your **sons** and your daughters **shall prophesy,** your **old men** shall dream dreams, your young men **shall see visions**: and also upon the **servants** and upon the handmaidens in those days will I pour out my **Spirit."**

This **promise** was **fulfilled** in **Acts 2:14-15,** when the disciples were **filled** with the **Holy Ghost,** and began **to speak** with **other tongues** as the **Spirit gave** them **utterance.** "But Peter, standing up with the eleven, lifted up his voice, and said unto them, Ye men of **Judea,** and all *ye* that dwell at Jerusalem, be this **known** unto you, and hearken to my **words**: for these **are** not **drunken** as ye **suppose,** seeing it is *but* the third hour of the Day.

Acts 2-16-17, "But this is that which **was spoken** by the prophet **Joel;** And it shall come to pass in the **last** days, saith God, I will pour out my **Spirit** upon all **flesh**: and your **sons** and your daughters **shall prophesy."** **Acts 2:39** "…For the **promise** is unto you, and to your children, and to all that are afar off, *even* as many as the LORD our God **shall call."**

This **promise** is for the **Jews, Samaritans, and Gentiles** and to **everyone.** This **same Holy Ghost,** was given to the **Samaritans.** The same act of giving the Holy Ghost was to the Jews, Samaritans, **and Gentiles** alike. On the day of **Pentecost,** it is said they were **filled** with the **Holy Ghost**. It is said that they **received** the Holy Ghost. (**Acts 2:4; 8:17**). With the **Gentiles** it is said the Holy Ghost **fell on them,** that is on the Gentiles, as on us at the **beginning**. [17]"Forasmuch then as God gave them the like **gift** as *he did* unto us, **who believed** on the Lord Jesus Christ; what was I, that I could withstand God? (**Acts 11:15, 17**) "…And God, **which knoweth the hearts,** bare them **witness,** giving them the Holy Ghost, even as *he did* unto us; And **put** no **difference** between us and them, **purifying** their **hearts** by **faith."** (Acts **15:8, 9**)

Acts 19:6 With the **Ephesians** saints, it said; it **came upon** them. Now all these statements: they were **filled** with the Holy Ghost, they **received** the Holy Ghost, the Holy Ghost **fell on them**, and the Holy Ghost **came upon them**, mean the **same thing**. They all **spake with other tongues**.

I Corinthians 12:13, "For by one Spirit **are** we all **baptized** into **one** body, whether *we be* Jews or Gentiles, whether *we be* **bond** or **free**; and **have been** all **made to drink** into one Spirit." **All of these** terminologies are the **same** as the **term, baptism** of the **Holy Ghost.**

Ephesians 4:4, 5 *"There* is one **body,** and **one Spirit,** even as ye are called in one **hope** of your **calling;** One **Lord,** one **faith** one **baptism." Galatians 3:27, 28** "For as many of you as **have been baptized** into Christ have put on Christ. There is neither Jew nor Greek, there is neither **bond** nor **free**, there is neither **male** nor **female:** for ye are all one in Christ Jesus."

Galatians 4:6 "And because yea are sons, God hath sent **forth** the **Spirit** of his Son into your **hearts,** crying **Abba, Father."** In order to be sons of God, we must be **filled** with the **Spirit** of God." Everyone must receive the **baptism** of the Holy **Ghost.**

Romans 8:14-15 "For as many **are lead** by the Spirit of God, **they are** the **sons** of **God.** For ye **have** not **received** the **spirit** of **bondage** again to **fear**; but ye have received the Spirit of **adoption,** whereby we cry, **Abba, Father."** THIS CONSTITUTES THE BAPTISM OF THE HOLY GHOST THAT EVERYONE MUST RECEIVE.

SPEAKING IN OTHER TONGUES

God has **given** us **a sign,** that we may **know** when the **Holy Ghost** comes into **our hearts.** Some think when a person has great joy, he has received the Holy Ghost. But this is **not so**. For in **Acts 8:8**, the Samaritans had **great joy**, but they did not received the Holy Ghost until **Acts 8:17.** "The Apostles returned to **Jerusalem** with **great joy**."

(St. **Luke 24:52**) In **Acts 13:52**; "And the disciples were **filled** with **joy,** and with the **Holy Ghost."**

At the time a person receives **the gift** of the **Holy Ghost,** he will **speak in other tongues** as the **Spirit gives** utterance. St. Mark 16:17, 18 Jesus said: "And these **signs** shall **follow** them that **believe;** In my name shall they **cast out devils**; they shall speak with **new tongues;..."**

Now **some** will **say** today that **all do not speak with tongues** when they get the **Holy Ghost.** Using the scripture in **I Corinthians 12:30,** where Paul said: "Do all speak with tongues?" But I say, not in contradiction to this scripture, but apart from it: That everyone who receives the Holy Ghost speaks at that time with **other tongues** or languages **as the Spirit** of God **gives** utterance. Though he may not ever speak again; he **will speak when he receives the Holy Ghost**; for the scripture said, they **all** spake with **other tongues (Acts 2:4; 10:46; 19:6).**

This subject has been a **subject of debate** for quite some **time** in our **past Apostolic Church History.** Many have **questioned** the doctrinal fact of speaking in **other tongues.** Many **believed** that the speaking in **other tongues** have ceased since the days of the Apostolic Church.

In **Apostolic times,** whenever an individual **received** the **gift** of the **Holy Ghost,** the **initial sign** that **followed** was the **speaking** in **other tongues** as the **Spirit** of gave them utterance. The fact that we want to take under consideration is, "Will believers speak in **other tongues** as the **Spirit** of God gives utterance, when they receive the baptism of the Holy Ghost?"

The only **way** we may find out this **fact** is to **study** what the **Bible** says about this subject. Just because an individual has not **spoken** in **other tongues** is no **proof** that **tongues** have ceased.

OLD TESTAMENT PROPHESYING AS SIGN OF THE PRESENCE OF THE SPIRIT

Let us examine the **Scriptures** of the **Old Testament. The prophets, Kings and** the **seventy elders** are listed as **receiving** the Holy **Spirit.** (In other words, the Holy Spirit was given to a select few). Whenever they received the Holy Spirit there was a **verbal sign** following them to show that they had been **filled** with the **Spirit** of God. This sign was PROPHESYING.

Our first scripture we would **consider** is **Numbers 11:16, 17,** which reads as thus: "And the LORD said unto Moses, **Gather** unto me seventy **men** of the **elders** of Israel, whom thou **knowest** to be elders of the people, and officers over them; and bring them unto the **tabernacle** of the **congregation,** that they may stand there with thee. And I will come down and **talk** with thee there: and I will take of the **spirit** which *is* upon thee, and will put *it* upon them; and the shall bear the burden of the people with thee, that thou bear *it* not thyself alone."

²⁴"And Moses went out, and told the people the **words** of the Lord, and gathered the seventy men of the elders of the people, and set them round about the **tabernacle.** ²⁵And the Lord came down in **a cloud,** and **spake** unto him, and took of the spirit that *was* upon him, and gave *it* unto the seventy elders: and it came to pass, *that,* when the Spirit rested upon them, they **prophesied,** and **did not** cease.

²⁶But there remained two *of the* men in the camp, the name of the one *was* **Eldad,** and the name of the other **Medad:** and the spirit rested upon them; and they *were* of them that were written, but went not out unto the tabernacle: and they prophesied in the camp. And there ran a young man, and **told** Moses, and said, Eldad and Medad **do prophesy** in the camp.

²⁸And Joshua the **son** of Nun, the **servant** of Moses, *one* of his young men, answered and said, my **lord** Moses, forbid them. And Moses said unto him, **Enviest** thou for my sake? Would God that all the Lord's people were **prophets,** *and* that the LORD would put his spirit upon them!" (Numbers 11:24-29)

Samuel said that the **sign of Prophesying** would **follow Saul** when he **received** the **Spirit of God.** Let us read **I Sam. 10:6-10:** "And the **Spirit** of the Lord will come upon thee, and thou shalt prophesy with them, and **shalt be turned** into another man. ⁷And let it be, when these **signs** are come unto thee, *that* thou do as occasion **serve** thee; for God is with thee. "... And it was so, that when he had turned his back to go from Samuel, God gave him another heart: and all those Signs came to pass that day. ¹⁰And when they came thither to the hill, behold, a company of prophets met him; and the Spirit of God came upon him, and he **prophesied** among them."

I Sam. 19:20, 21-24 said: "And Saul sent messengers to take David: and when the **saw** the company of the **prophets** prophesying; and Samuel standing *as* **appointed** over them, the Spirit of **God** was upon the **messengers** of Saul, and they also **prophesied."**

Thus **we see** that whenever the **Holy Spirit** was **given** in the **Old Testament, A verbal sign** *was* accompanied in **prophesying.**

Elizabeth, the mother of **John the Baptist,** "...was filled with the Holy Ghost: and she spake out with a loud voice, and said, Blessed art thou among women, and blessed is the fruit of thy womb." "And his Father Zechariah was **filled** with the Holy Ghost, and Prophesied..." (Luke 1:41-42, 67).

These people **prophesied** in their **native** or **Hebraic tongue.** But God **Said,** in the **time to come,** He would **speak** unto **them** in **another tongue.** In other words, they would not prophesy in their **native** tongue. He said in **Isaiah 28:11, 12;** "For with **stammering lips** and another tongue will he **speak** to this people. To whom he **said,** this is the rest *wherewith* ye may cause the weary to rest; and this is the refreshing: yet they **would** not **hear."**

This speaking in other tongues is **connected** with the prophesy of **Joel 2:28, 29,** when he said: "And it shall come to pass afterward, *that* I **will pour out** my **spirit** upon all **flesh;** and your **sons** and your **daughters shall prophesy,** your **old men** shall dream dreams, your young men **shall see visions:** And also upon the **servants** and upon the handmaids in those days will I pour out my spirit."

Remember the **desire** of **Moses who wished,** "...that **all** the LORD's people were **prophets,** *and* that the LORD would put his spirit upon them!" (Num. 11:24-29)

This wish came true in the prophesy of **Joel 2:28. Ezekiel speaks** about it on this wise: "And I will give them ONE **heart,** and I will put a new spirit **within** you; and I will take the stony heart out off their flesh, and will give them a heart of flesh: That they may walk in my **statues,** and **keep** mine **ordinances,** and **do** them: and they shall be my people, and I will be their **God.**" (Ezekiel 11:19, 20; 36:25, 26)

NEW TESTAMENT TONGUES AS INITIAL SIGN OF RECEIVING THE HOLY GHOST

In the **New Testament,** Jesus began teaching the **new birth** or the **necessity** of **receiving** the **Holy Ghost** by saying; "Ye must be born again." A Pharisee by the name of Nicodemus heard this teaching of Jesus.

St. John 3:2-5, 8, "The same came to Jesus by Night, and said unto him, Rabbi, we know that thou art a teacher come from **God:** for no man can do these **miracles** that thou doest, except God be with him. ³Jesus answered and said unto him, **Verily,** verily, I say unto thee, Except a man **be born again**, he cannot **see** the **kingdom** of God. ⁴Nicodemus saith unto him, How can a man be born when he is old? Can he enter the second time into his mother's womb, and be born?

⁵Jesus answered, Verily, verily, I say unto thee, Except a man **be born** of water and *of* the **Spirit**, he cannot enter into the kingdom of God."

⁸"The **wind bloweth** where it **listeth,** and thou hearest the **sound** thereof, but canst not tell whence it cometh, and whither it goeth; so is every one that is born of the **Spirit.**" Nichodemus wanted to know how this could be.

Jesus said in so many words, it is like the **wind**. You **can't see it**, but you hear the **sound** thereof, for the Holy Ghost **will speak** through you in **another** tongue. Tongues is a **sound** from **within,** by the **Spirit** of God.

We studied in the Old Testament that whenever the Holy Spirit was **given,** they spake a verbal **sound,** (*Prophesying*). This was the **initial** sign that they had received the Holy **Spirit.**

Jesus said in **St. Mark 16:15-17,** "...**Go** ye into all the **world,** and **preach** the **gospel** to every **creature.** He **that believeth** and **is baptized shall be saved; but** he that **believeth not shall be damned.** And these **signs** shall follow them **that believe;** In my **name** shall they cast out **devils;** they **shall speak** with **new tongues;"**

I Corinthians14:21, 22, Paul spoke in reference to **tongues** being **a sign** on this wise: "In the **law** it is written, With *men of* **other tongues** and other lips **will I speak** unto this **people** and yet for all that **will** they not **hear** me, saith the Lord. ²²Wherefore **tongues** are for a **sign,** not to them **that believe,** but to them that

believe not: but **prophesying** *serveth* not for them that believe not, but for them which believe."

So **we see** from these **scriptures,** that **tongues** are **a sign.** And this **sign is associated** with the **receiving** of the **Holy Ghost.**

The place where Paul said, it is not for those, which believe, but for **those** that **believe not.** The reference is to the **Nation** of **Israel.** That is that God did a **miraculous** thing by causing his **believers** to **speak** in those various **tongues** on the day of **Pentecost.** But **yet** the **nation of Israel** would **not believe.**

Tongues are **continuously associated** with the **reception** of the **Holy Ghost.**

Let's consider the first **incident** of speaking in other **tongues** as recorded in **Acts 2:1-4.** "And when the day of **Pentecost was fully come** they were all with one accord in one place. ²And suddenly there came a "S O U N D" from **heaven** as of a **rushing** might "W I N D" and it filled all the house where they were sitting. ³And there appeared unto them cloven **tongues,** like as of fire, and it sat upon each of them. ⁴And they were all filled with the Holy **Ghost,** and began **to speak** with **other tongues,** as the **Spirit** gave the utterance."

This was the beginning of the **New Testament** account of the outpouring of the **Holy Ghost.** All of them that were in the **upper room** were filled with the Holy Ghost with the **sign** of speaking in **other tongues.** They all spoke in different **languages.** These are other **tongues** of **Isaiah 28:11.**

Acts 2:16 Peter also said, "But this is that **which was spoken** by the prophet Joel; ¹⁷"And it shall come to pass in **last** days, saith God, I will pour out of my **Spirit** upon all **flesh**; and your sons and daughters **shall prophesy,** and your young men shall see **visions** and your **old men** shall dream dreams: ¹⁸And on my **servants** and on my **handmaidens** I will pour out in those days of my Spirit: and they SHALL PROPHESY." (Joel 2:28; Acts 2:4, 14-18).

These **One Hundred** and **Twenty believers** were prophesying in other **tongues.** This is the **fulfillment** of the **Old Testament** Scriptures. Also where **Jesus said,** "And these **signs** shall follow them **that believe;** In my **name** shall they cast out **devils;** they **shall speak** with **new tongues.**" (St. Mark 16:17)

Some say that the speaking in **tongues** were **only** as a sign for the nation of **Israel.** But we know for a fact that the **Gentiles** also **received** the **baptism** of the Holy Ghost and spoke in **other tongues** as the Spirit gave them utterance (**Acts 10: 44-48; 11:15, 16, 17, 15:8, 9).**

Some think the **moment** a person **believes** he has the Holy Ghost. But this is not so when we **search** the Apostolic **record.** For an **outstanding example: Acts 8:12,** the people **believed** Philip **preaching** and **were baptized** but they **did not** receive the **Holy Ghost** at the **same time (v. 16).** "(For as **yet** he was fallen upon **none** of them: only they were baptized in the **name** of the Lord Jesus.)"

It is quite **evident** that they had not spoken in other **tongues.** Therefore when the Apostles Peter and John came down they **laid** their **hands upon them** and they were **filled** with the **Holy Ghost.** Some say, in this particular **incident,** it is not recorded in the Scripture that they spoke in other **tongues**. I say, "Neither is it **recorded** that they **did not speak** in other **tongues**."

It is quite **obvious** that they did **speak** in **tongues** for they went through **all** the other **requirements**. Act 8:12 They **Believed**. Acts 8:12, 14 They were **baptized. They** had **joy** (Act 8:8). There was **some** sort of public **sign** or awareness for **Simon** the **sorcerer** saw the **reception** of the **Holy Ghost** (Acts 8:17, 18).

Another event is **recorded** where the **Gentiles** were **filled** with the **Holy Ghost. Acts 10:44-48** "While Peter yet spake these words, the Holy Ghost fell on all of them which heard the **word**. And they of the **circumcision which believed** were astonished, as many as came with Peter, because that on the Gentiles also was poured out the **gift** of the Holy Ghost. ⁴⁶For they heard them **speak** with **tongues**, and magnify God. Then answered Peter, ⁴⁷Can any man forbid water, that these **should** not **be baptized**, which have received the Holy Ghost as well as we?"

This is a factual **Biblical** historical account that the speaking in **other tongues** was continued after the day of **Pentecost** to the non-Jews. Peter, speaking in relation to this incident when he returned to **Jerusalem**, said: "And as I began **to speak**, the Holy **Ghost** fell on them, as on us at the beginning." (Acts 11:15)

About 22 years **after** the day of **Pentecost**, in **Acts 19:2, Paul** asked those **disciples** of Ephesus, "…Have ye received the **Holy Ghost** since you **believed**? And they said unto him, We have not so much as heard whether there be any Holy Ghost." After this question and answer, **Paul preached** unto them the **baptism** in the **name** of Jesus and the **necessity** of receiving the **Holy Ghost.**

Acts 19:5 says, "When they heard *this,* they were baptized in the name of the Lord Jesus. And when Paul had laid *his* hand upon them, the Holy Ghost **came** on them; and they spake with **tongues, and prophesied**." Do All Believers Speak With Tongues?

Now for the question, "Is speaking in **tongues** for us today? And, do all believers who receive the Spirit, speak in **other tongues** as they did on the day of Pentecost?"

St. Mark 16:15-17 Jesus said unto his disciples, "**Go** ye into all the **world,** and **preach** the **gospel** to every **creature**. He **that believeth** and **is baptized shall be saved;** but he **that believeth not shall be damned**. And these signs shall follow them that believe; In my name shall they cast out **devils**; they shall speak with **new tongues;**"

From these **scriptures, we see** that Jesus said the sign of speaking in **new tongues** will **follow** all that **believe** wherever the gospel is to be preached.

Joel 2:28 said, everyone would **prophesy**. Peter said their speaking in other tongues was the **fulfillment** of Joel's prophecy. ³⁹"And that promise God made to Joel, was for the **Jews** and **their Children**, and to all that are far off (The Gentiles), *even* as many as the Lord our God **shall call**." (*i.e. anybody/everyone*) (Acts 2:14-39; 10:44-48; 11:15; 15:8, 9)

There is no **Biblical** record to **prove** that the speaking in other **tongues** have **ceased**. The Scripture that is so often used by those that believe that speaking in tongues has ceased is found in **I Corinthians 13:8**, which says: "**Charity** never **faileth:**

but whether *there be* **prophecies**, they **shall fail**; whether *there be* **tongues**, they shall cease; whether *there be* **knowledge**, it shall vanish away."

This scripture is interpreted by some to mean, "That the Bible was not complete in those days. For this, they say is the reason God gave us various gifts in the Church. But since the **Bible** is completed, there is no need for **tongues** and other **gifts** to be used in church."

This scripture **does not** mean when the **New Testament** Bible is completed the church will stop speaking in **tongues**. For not only **tongues** are included in this scripture, **prophecy** is included as well. Prophecy is one of the **gifts** for the **edifying** of the **body** of Christ.

Paul in this **chapter** and **verse** is only showing the church the **greatness of Love**. Therefore this scripture is not to be used to say that **tongues** have ceased.

We conclude that the **sign** of speaking in other **tongues** shall **follow** them that **believe.**

THE DIFFERENCE IN OTHER TONGUES AND GIFTS OF TONGUES

For quite sometime, **many** have been **confused** over this **question.** We shall give unto you the Biblical **difference**. For there is **evidence** that there is a **difference.**

We will quote the first scripture from **Acts 2:4**, "And they were all filled with the Holy Ghost, and began to speak with **other tongues**, as the Spirit gave utterance. And there were dwelling at Jerusalem Jews, **devout** men, out of **every nation** under heaven. Now when this **was noised** abroad, the multitude came together, and were confounded, because that every man heard them: (The Apostles) "speak in his" (Jews, devout men, out of every nation under heaven) "**own language**." (Acts 2:4-6).

There is **one** significant **point** that I want you to note, **in particular,** from this **scripture** and **event.** On the day of **Pentecost, One hundred** and **twenty** people were **filled** with the **Holy Ghost** and spoke in **a language** that they did not **know** themselves. But they spoke the **languages** of about **sixteen** different **nations** that **were present** at Jerusalem. These nations understood what these **Galileans** were saying. But they **that were speaking** didn't know what they were saying, for they were speaking in **another tongue** that they had not **learned.**

This kind of **tongue** is **called** the "Sign" tongues speaking as the **Spirit gives utterance.** The **difference** in this kind of **tongue** is that the tongues that they spoke in, was a **known language**. That is, the people that were born in that language **understood** what was **said.** While on the other hand, the **Gift** of **tongues** in **I Corinthians 14:1, 2,** "Follow after **charity**, and desire **spiritual** gifts, but rather that ye may prophesy. For he that speaketh in a unknown tongue **speaketh not** unto men, but unto God: for **no man** understandeth him; howbeit in the spirit he speaketh **mysteries**."

This kind of **tongues** speaking can plainly **be seen** to be **different** tongues than the **other tongues** of **Act 2:4.** For this tongue here **is** an **unknown** tongue and the other a **known** tongue.

Everyone does not receive the **Gifts** of Tongues as recorded in **I Corinthians 12:10, 28, 29,** but do speak in the **"Sign"** tongues of **Act 2:4.** But more importantly, it is striking to note these six verses as follows:

1. **"I will pour out** my **Spirit** upon all **flesh;** and your **sons** and your daughters **shall prophesy..."** (Joel 2:28).
2. "For with **stammering lips** and another tongue **will** he **speak** to this people." (Isa. 28:11)
3. "And these **signs** shall follow them **that believe;** In my **name** shall they cast out **devils;** they shall **speak** with **new tongues."** (Mark 16:17)
4. "And they were all filled with the Holy **Ghost,** and began **to speak** with **other tongues,** as the Spirit gave them utterance." (Acts 2:4)
5. "For they heard them **speak** with **tongues,** and magnify God**."** (Acts 10:46)
6. "And when Paul had laid his hands upon them, the Holy Ghost **came** on them; and they spake with **tongues,** and **prophesied."** (Acts 19:6)

Gifts In The Church

With all these Scriptures saying that all spake in tongues, why did Paul ask the question; **"do all speak** with tongues?" I shall express my version of explanation.

When Paul was speaking these words, he was speaking unto the **Corinthian church** who had been **baptized** and **filled** with the Holy Ghost. Paul was talking about the **diversities** of gifts in the church **after** a person has been **saved.** All are saved the same way. But after they are **saved, all** don't receive the **same gifts.**

I Corinthians 12:13, "For by One Spirit **are** we all **baptized** into One body, whether *we be* Jews or Gentiles, whether *we be* bound or free; and **have been** all **made to drink** into One Spirit."

I Corinthians 12:7-11, "But the **manifestation** of the Spirit is given to **every man** to **profit** withal. [8]For to one is given by the Spirit the **word** of **wisdom;** to **another** the word of **knowledge** by the same Spirit; To **another faith** by the same Spirit; to **another** the **gifts** of **healing** by the same Spirit; [10]To **another** the working of **miracles;** to another **prophecy;** to another **discerning** of spirits; to **another** *divers* kinds of **tongues;** to **another** the **interpretation** of tongues; [11]But all these worketh that One and the selfsame Spirit, **dividing** to every man severally as he will."

The Difference Between The Holy Ghost Tongues
And
The Gifts Tongues

There is **a Major difference** between the **tongues** in **Acts 2:4,** and **I Corinthians 14:2.**

The **tongues** in Acts 2:4 are the **sign** to show that the **believer** has **received** the **Holy Ghost.** All **believers** speak in the **sign** tongue when they receive the **Holy Ghost.** Note this in particular: "And they were all filled with the Holy **Ghost,** and began **to speak** with **other tongues,** as the Spirit gave them utterance." (Acts 2:4)

The Scripture said emphatically that they **all** spoke in **other tongues.** Not some of them but **all of them.**

The **tongues** in **I Corinthians says:** "To another the **working of miracles**; to **another** prophecy; to **another** discerning of spirits; to **another** divers kinds of tongues; to **another** the interpretation of tongues." (1 Cor. 12:10) In these **gifts** all don't speak in **tongues.**

These tongues have a **Noted** difference; these tongues are classified as an *unknown* **tongue** (I Cor. 14:2). No man **understandeth** these languages except a **gift** of **interpretation** is given to *him.* On the other hand, in **Acts 2:4** they speak in the **tongues** of **other nations** (Acts 2:8). These **tongues** follow everyone that receive the Holy Ghost. **The scripture said:** "For with **stammering** lips and **another tongue** will He speak to this **people.**" (Isa. 28:11; Joel 2:28; Mark 16:17; Acts 2:4, 8, 14)

These are **sign** tongues, and is **activated** when the **gift** of Holy Ghost comes in. It's interestingly enough that we should note the following: "While Peter yet spake these words, the Holy Ghost fell on **all them** which heard the **Word.** And they of the **circumcision which believed** were astonished, as many as came with Peter, because that on the Gentiles also was poured out the **gift** of the Holy Ghost. For they **heard** them **speak** with **tongues,** and magnify God. Then answered Peter, can any man forbid **water,** that these should not **be baptized,** which have received the Holy Ghost as well as we? (Acts 10:44-47; 11:15)

All spoke in tongues in this incident and in every **incident** when they **received** the Holy Ghost. In approximately twenty-three years **after** the day of **Pentecost,** the Ephesians **believers** all spoke in tongues **when they received** the Holy Ghost (Acts 19:1-6).

When a person **receives** the Holy Ghost **God speaks through him** as a sign that this person has received the Holy Ghost. However, when a person speaks in an unknown tongue **this is not God speaking through him,** but rather, it is **the gift** of **tongues** that the **Spirit gave** him to use as **he will.** This gift must be used in order and not out of order as the Corinthian were doing. Paul said: "For if I **pray** in an *unknown* **tongue, my spirit prayeth,** but my **understanding is unfruitful.** What is it then? I will pray **with** spirit, and I will pray **with** the understanding also: I will sing **with the spirit**, ant I will sing **with the understanding** also." (1 Cor. 14:14-15)

The Corinthians were using this **gift** of tongues **out of order.** Certainly they were not speaking as the **Spirit** of God gives utterance. For God is not *the author* of **confusion,** but of **peace** (1Cor. 14:33, 40)

THE GIFTS IN THE CHURCH

FOUR MINISTERIAL GIFTS
(The gifts that deals with the Word)
Ephesians 4:11

APOSTLES
PROPHETS
EVANGELISTS
PASTORS
TEACHERS

NINE SPIRITUAL GIFTS IN CORINTHIANS

Three **revelation** gifts: (Those that **reveals** something)	The word of **Wisdom** The word of **Knowledge** The **discerning** of spirits
The Three **power** gifts: (Those that **Do** something)	The gift of **faith** The gift of **Healings** Those working of **miracles**
Three **utterance**, or Inspirational gifts **Those that say some thing**	**Divers** kinds of **tongues** **Interpretation** of tongues

GIFTS FOUND IN ROMANS
Romans 12:6-8–KJV

Prophesy	According to the **proportion** of faith;
Ministry	*Wait on our* ministering;
Teaching	Wait on our teaching;

Extort	Wait on Exhortation
Giving	*Do it* with simplicity;
Ruleth	With diligence;
Mercy	With cheerfulness.

THE CHRISTIAN WALK - - HOLINESS

I Peter 2:1-3says, "Wherefore laying aside all **malice**, and all **guile**, and hypocrisies and envies, and all evil speakings, As **newborn babes,** desire the **sincere milk** of the **Word**, that ye may grow thereby: If so be ye **have tasted** that the Lord is gracious."

The church of God is Holy. Ephesians 1:4 states, "According as he hath chosen us in him before the foundation of the **world**, that we should be **holy** and **without blame** before him in love:" (I Pet. 1:14-16)

To be holy means *to be* **sinless: without spot, blemish, or any such thing.** The Scripture said, "...Christ also loved the church, and gave himself for it; That he **might sanctify** and **cleanse** it with the **washing** of water by the **Word**, That he might present it to himself a **glorious church,** not having **spot**, or wrinkle, or any such thing; but that it should be **holy** and **without blemish.**" (Eph. 5:25-27)

From these scriptures we can see that the church is holy**; i.e.** without **sin.** Paul said in **Ephesians 5:3, 4:** "But **fornication,** and all **uncleanness**, or **covetousness**, let it not **be** once **named** among you, as becometh **saints;** Neither filthiness, nor **foolish talking,** nor **jesting,** which **are** not **convenient:** but rather giving of thanks."

There are some people saying that no one can live on this earth without sinning. **Titus 2:11, 12,** "For the **grace** of God that **bringeth salvation hath appeared** unto all **men, Teaching** us that, **denying ungodliness** and **worldly lusts,** we should live **soberly, righteously**, and **godly,** in this present **world;**"

1 John 3:9 saith; "Whosoever **is born** of God doth not commit sin; for his **seed** remaineth in him: and he cannot sin, because he is born of God**."** (v. 8) **"**He that commietteth sin is of the devil; for the **devil** sinneth from the beginning.

There has been a scripture used in **contradiction** to **I John 3:9,** by some who **oppose** the **fact** that a person can live free from sins **Rom. 6:22.** The Scripture that they used is **I John 1:8.** "If we say that we have **no sin,** we **deceive** ourselves, and the **truth** is not in us.

Let us remember that the **same writer** who wrote **I John 3:8, 9,** also wrote **I John 1:8.** There is no **contradiction** between these two scriptures. We should find out what is the **meaning** of these two scriptures. Since we have considered **I John 3:8, 9,** let us consider **I John 1:8.**

My explanation concerning this scripture is as follows: If a person has committed a sin, he cannot say that he has not done so. Or else, he will be **a liar.** If he **acknowledges** or **confesses** his sin, God will **forgive** him:

In **I John 3:8, 10,** where it is said, "Whosoever **is born** of God doth not commit sin; for his **seed** remaineth in him: and he cannot sin, because he is born of God," the not committing sin is based upon the **point** of the **seed remaining** in him. I consider **the seed** *to be* the **Word of God.** As long as we **keep the Word of God** in our **hearts** we will not **sin against** Him. Psa. 119:11 says, "Thy **Word** have I hid in mine **heart,** that I **might** not **sin** against thee."

I John 2:4 said, "He that saith, I know him, and keepeth not his **commandments,** is a **liar,** and the truth is not in him."

The **foregoing study** has been "**How to become saved,**" or what **constitutes salvation.** The **various steps of salvation** were **demonstrated** throughout the study. We have learned that to become saved one must do the following:

1. Hear the Full Gospel.
2. Believe the Gospel.
3. Repent of one's sins.
4. Be baptized in Jesus' Name.
5. Be filled with the Holy Ghost by speaking in tongues.
6. The Christian Walk, Holiness.

We are now **studying** the **last step** of **salvation.** "**The Christian Walk, Holiness.**" This step shows that when a person is saved, he must be careful to **maintain good works. Titus 3:8** says, "*This is* a **faithful saying,** and these things I will that thou **affirm constantly,** that they **which have believed** in God might be careful to maintain good works. These things are good and profitable unto men."

Romans 6:1, God never intended for His **Church** *to be* **save** and **continue** in their **sins.** He does not **save** a person **in** his **sins,** but **from** his **sins** (St Matt. 1:21).

Inasmuch as we have all sinned who were born of **Adam**; likewise, every one that doeth **righteousness is born** of God (I John 2:29)"

SAVED BY GRACE

Ephesians 2:8-10 tells us: "For by **grace** are ye **saved** through **faith;** and that not of yourselves: it is the **gift** of God: Not of **works,** lest any man should boast. For we are his workmanship, **created** in Christ Jesus unto **good** works, which God hath before ordained that we should walk in them."

Being saved by grace does not give us the license to **continue** in **our sins,** Rom.6:1 says, But rather, we that are saved by grace ought to be holy. [11]"For the **grace** of God that **bringeth salvation hath appeared** to all **men. Teaching** us that, **denying**

ungodliness and **worldly lusts**, we should live **soberly, righteously,** and **godly,** in this present **world:**" (Titus 2:11, 12)

To be saved by grace means that there was **no righteousness** on our **part** to **become** saved. We did **not do** good works to become saved. We are **saved** to do good works.

OLD MAN ADAM

Colossians 3;5-10 says, "Mortify therefore your members which are upon the earth; **fornication, uncleanness, inordinate affection,** evil **concupiscence,** and **covetousness,** which is **idolatry:** For which things' sake the **wrath** of God cometh on the children of **disobedience:** In the which ye also walked some time, when ye **lived** in them.

But now ye also put off all these; **anger, wrath, malice blasphemy,** filthy communication out of your mouth. **Lie not one to another,** seeing that ye have put off the OLD MAN with **his deeds**; And have put on the NEW MAN, which is renewed in **knowledge** after the **image** of him that created him:"

The Old Man was crucified with Christ. Romans 6:6, "Knowing this, that **our** OLD MAN **is crucified** with *him,* that the **body of sin** might be destroyed, that HENCEFORTH we **should** NOT SERVE SIN."

Romans 6:22, "But now being made FREE FROM SIN, and become servants to God, ye have your fruit of holiness, and the end **everlasting life.**" We are **not to live** any **longer** in **sin.**

Some **people say** that to **sin after** you are **saved** only **breaks** your **fellowship** with **God,** but does not cause you to **lose y**our salvation. But **I Corinthians** 6:9-11 said: "Know ye not that the **unrighteous** shall not **inherit** the **kingdom** of God? Be not deceived: neither **fornicators,** nor **idolaters,** nor **adulterers,** nor **effeminate,** nor **abusers of themselves with mankind,** Nor **thieves,** nor covetous, nor drunkards, nor revilers, nor **extortioners, shall inherit** the kingdom of God. And such WERE some of you: but ye **are** WASHED, but ye **are** SANCTIFIED, but ye **are** JUSTIFIED in the **name** of the LORD JESUS, and by the **Spirit** of our God." (5:19-21)

SINOLOGY
(The study of Sins)
SAVED BY GRACE

INTRODUCTION

There is a **necessity** to study the subject that is called **Sinology**. This simply means the **study of** sins. There are so many terms and usages in the **Bible** that need to be defined for the average reader. For an **interesting example**, what is **inordinate affections?** What is **superfluity** of naughtiness? What is the **meaning** of the term **lasciviousness**? What is the term **evil surmising?**

If these things are evil, and they are, we must by all means **determine** the definite and intended **meaning** of these and **other** words.

Sinology is the study of **immorality**. This must be explained **to the new convert**. These sins are taught to **warn** the detriment of **returning** to the **old life style**.

Could it be thought that a **saved** person can be in danger of **sinning** again? Why is this possible? Yes, it is **true** that a saved person *can be* in **danger** of sinning again. The reason is because God did not mean to save us that would be **incapable** of sinning; But rather that we would **not be willing to sin**. So that we will **sincerely serve** Him on our **own free will**. This takes us back to the way God made man in the beginning.

Genesis 2:16-17 God said: "And the Lord God **commanded** the man, saying, Of every tree of the garden thou mayest freely eat: But of the tree of the knowledge of good and evil, thou shalt not eat of it: for in the **day** that thou eatest thereof thou shalt surely **die**." "This is the object **teaching** on **free** will. He may freely eat of **every tree** of the **garden** excepting the tree of **good** and **evil**. The commandment of warning him **not** to eat of the **knowledge** implies **freedom** of **will**.

God does not **force** anyone to be **saved**. **He** does **gives us power** to keep us **from** sinning if we **want** *to be* **kept**. Therefore He **saves** us and **gives** us our **free will** to **continue** in Him. **Philippians 2:13** states, "For it is God which worketh in you both **to will** and **to do** of *his* good pleasure." **God saves** us and keeps us **from sins**. He does **not take** away our **free will**.

Revelation 22:17, "And the **Spirit** and the bride say, **Come**. And let him that heareth say, come. And let him that is athirst come. And **whosoever will**, **let** him **take** the water of life freely. **Titus 3:8,** *"This* is a **faithful saying**, and these things I will that thou **affirm constantly**, that they **which have believed** in God might be careful to maintain good works. These things are good and profitable unto men."

We must study the things that are **determent** to our **salvation** and **avoid them**.

THE SINS OF THE FLESH

GALATIANS 5:19-21

I. SINS OF UNCHASITY

- Now the **works** of the flesh are **manifest,** which are *these*:
- **Adultery**
- **Fornication**
- **Uncleanness**
- **Lasciviousness**.

These sins are called the **unchasity**. They have to do with **sexual impurity,** Sins which are against the body (I Cor. 6:16-18). These sins are at the top of the list. We will define the **meaning** of each Sin:

A. ADULTERY

- This word taken form the Greek word *MOICHOS*. Denotes one who has **unlawful** intercourse with the spouse of another. (Luke 18:11; I Cor. 6:9; Heb. 13:4 (Vine)

- After **two** persons have become **married** there must not be a **third party** who comes in and **separate** the married couple with **any** sexual act. **Who** ever does this act commits Adultery, and the marriage bond and *vow* is **broken**. The marriage becomes *adulterated,* or a mixture of a **strange flesh** has come into the marriage and therefore pollutes it.

- The strange flesh is always that **person** who comes **into** the marriage, being **foreign** or unrelated sexually to neither married **partner**. (Prov. 7:5-27.) This is the meaning of the term Adultery.

B. FORNICATION

1. Taken from the Greek word *PORNEIA*, meaning **illicit sexual** intercourse. **Pre-marital** relationships or to commit **whoredom** and whore mongering. There must **not** be any **pre-marital** relationship. Although this term has to do in this context with premarital relationships; it's a term also used in the Greek for **all sexual sins**.

C. UNCLEANNESS

1. Taken from the Greek word, *AKATHARSIA*. This is still dealing with sexual **impurity**, but on a wider range. This takes in the sins of **Homosexuality**, sodomy lesbianism, **masturbation**, in-ordinate affections, **oral** sexuality and such like. (Rom. 1: 24-27; I Cor. 6:9)

2. The term **Uncleanness** has to do with the unclean approach to **sexuality**. That is placing the sexual **organs** in places where it **ought not to be**. The **sexual** organ is not to be **placed in** or on **the mouth**. Neither is it to be placed **within** the **anus** or **rectum**. This is **unnatural** and **sinful**.

3. When Paul wrote to the Romans concerning the **misuse of the body** by men and women, he uses the **sexual** term for **woman**, by saying in the Greek *THELEIAI*, which means **female** and not just the term woman. For this is **to show** that the **context** means **sexual organ**. The woman change the **natural** use of the body to that which was **unnatural** and began to have **sex** with the same female **gender** and **abused** the purpose of the female **body.** "Wherefore God also gave them up to **uncleanness** through the lusts of their own **hearts,** to dishonour their own bodies between themselves:

4. Who **changed** the **truth** of **God** into a lie, and **worshipped** and **served** the **creature** more than the **Creator,** Who is **blessed** for ever. **Amen.** For this cause God gave them up unto **vile affections**; for even their **women** (*females*) **did change** the natural **use** into that which is against nature: (Rom. 1: 24-26)

5. This **context** deals with **females** ignoring the productive purpose of their **gender** and **became lesbians** instead of having **a male sexual partner.** This sexual sin is classified as uncleanness and unnatural. In fact it is perverted. **Paul** continue on and deals with the **males** by saying: "And likewise also the men, (*Greek, 'Arsen'*) leaving the **natural use** of the **woman** (*Greek, 'Theleiai,' females*), **burned** in their lust one toward **another**; men with **men** working that which is **unseemly,** and receiving in themselves that recompense of their error which was meet." (Rom. 1:27)

This is to be *understood* that **men began** to **practice** *homosexuality*, and became **interested** in sexual **satisfaction** with the **same gender. This** has to do **with a mental** condition and **not a physical** change. This is called **affections.**

We must **conclude** that **uncleanness** has to do with **perverted sexuality contrary** to **nature. Leviticus** 18:22 **says:** "Thou **shalt** not **lie** with mankind, as with womankind: it is **abomination**" "If a man also lie with **mankind,** as he lieth with a **woman,** both of them have committed an **abomination**: they shall surely be put to death; their blood *shall be* upon them." (Lev. 20:13)

D. Lasciviousness

1. Taken from the Greek word *Aselogeia*, denotes excess. **Lasciviousness,** absence of restraint, **indulgency** wantonness. In this case, it means **uncontrolled** lustful passion. Burning lust, incontinent. **A sexual maniac.** From this **kind** of sexual **lust** derives, **incest, pornography** material, **child molestations,** and auto **sexuality.**

2. These are the **sins of Unchasity,** which are the **signs** of **sexual impurity.** These are the **traits** of any **kingdom** or **nation** that is about to be **destroyed.**

II. Sins Of Irreligiousness (Galatians 5: 20)

A. Idolatry

1. Taken from the **Greek word,** *Eidolatria,* **meaning** service or **slave** to **religious practices** of **demons.** Heathen sacrifices were sacrificed to demons (I Cor. 10:19). In Romans 1: 22-25, **idolatry is** the **sin** of the **mind** against **God.**

2. **No man** can **serve two masters:** for either he will **hate** the **one,** and **love** the **other;** or else he will hold to the one, and **despise** the other. Ye cannot serve God and mammon." **(Matt. 6:24.)**

B. Witchcraft

1. **Sorcery**

   a. Taken from the **Greek** word *Pharmakia.* Primarily signified the use of **medicine; drugs, spells;** then **poisoning;** then **Sorcery.**
   b. In sorcery, the **use** of **drugs** was **generally** accompanied by **incantations** and appeals to occult **powers. (W. E. Vine)**
   c. We must stay out from around **spiritualism** and **occultism** (Isa. 8:18, 20).

III. SINS OF MALIGNITY (Galatians 5:20, 21)

A. HATRED

Taken from the **Greek word** MESEO. To hate, is used especially of **malicious** and **unjustifiable** feeling towards **others**, whether toward the innocent or by mutual **animosity. (Vine)**

B. VARIANCE

Taken from the **Greek word** DICHAZO, to cut **apart**, divided in **two. (Vine)** This has to do with **forming groups** out of **groups.** Drawing **away disciples after** oneself **Acts 20:28-30).**

C. EMULATIONS (JEALOUSY)

Taken from the **Greek word** ZELOS. "Zeal" **(in favorable sense, and or;** in an **unfavorable** one, **Jealousy,** as of a **husband** or an **enemy, malice).** Emulation, envy, **fervent mind, indignation, Jealousy, Zeal (Strong).** In other words, to go **against** one because of **Jealousy.**

D. WRATH

Taken from the **Greek word** THUMOO. **To put in passion, i.e. enrage: -** be wroth. **(Strong).** Lasting **anger** against **another.**

E. STRIFE

Taken from the **Greek word** ERIS. **A quarrel, i.e.** wrangling, **contentions, debate, strife, variance. (Strong).** In this case it means quarrel.

F. SEDITIONS

Taken from the **Greek word** DICHOSTASIA. Disunion, **i.e. dissension; -** division, **sedition. (*Strong).*** In other words, to go **against that which is** organized **authority.**

G. HERESIES

Taken from the **Greek word** *HAIREOMAI.* **Denotes a choosing, a choice; then, that which is chosen and hence,** an opinion, especially a self-willed opinion, which is substituted for submission to power of truth, and leads to division and formation of sects. (Vine). That is to originate some doctrine contrary to the truth **(Titus 3:10).**

H. ENVYING

Taken from the **Greek word** *PHTHONOS.* **Envy** is the **feeling of displeasure** produced by witnessing or hearing of the advantage of prosperity of others. (Vine). Or in other words, wishing what someone else has, was yours.

I. MURDERS
Taken form the **Greek** word **PHONOS,** to kill.

IV. THE SINS OF EXCESSIVENESS (GALATIANS 5:21)

A. DRUNKENNESS

Taken from the **Greek word** *METHUO.* **Signifies** to be **drink with wine. (Vine).**

B. REVELLINGS

Taken from the **Greek word** *TRUPHE.* **Luxuriousness, daintiness. Parties, bars... (Vine)**
All of these **sins** are **sins** of the **FLESH.** Being Christians, we are not to be **partakers** of them: **Paul** said, "…that they which do such thing **shall not inherit** the **kingdom** of God." (Gal 5:21)

THE SANCTIFIED CHURCH
LOVOLOGY
(INTRODUCTION)

This subject has to do with the **Christian walk** which deals with the **positive** side of Holiness. It is the result of the infilling of the **Holy Ghost**. This then is the uttermost **purpose** of the **plan of salvation**. That is to cause all to love **one another**. This is the **practical side** of salvation. Not a religious myth but a **sincere demonstration** of **kindness** to **one another**. This is not demonstrated in **rituals, pilgrimage**s, or some **acetic** life-style. On the other hand, this is where we **treat one another** as should be treated, or **do unto others** as we would have them **to do unto us**.

The TOTAL **message** of **Jesus** was to TEACH us how to **love one another**. St. John **13:34-35 Jesus** said: "A **new** commandment I give unto you, That ye **love** one **another**; as I have loved **you,** that ye also **love** one **to** another. By this shall all *men* **know** that ye are My **disciples,** if ye have **love one to another**."

The **walk** of the **Christian** would be in the **fruit** of the **Spirit**. Galatians 5:22-**25** says: "But the fruit of the Spirit is **love joy, peace,** long-suffering, **gentleness, goodness,** faith, meekness, temperance: against such there is no law. And they that are **Christ's have crucified** the **flesh** with the **affections** and lusts. If we **live in the** Spirit let us also **walk** in the Spirit."

The **Spirit** brings into our lives **nine** great **principles**:

1. LOVE, taken from the **Greek, (Agape/Agapao) The love** that **loves all,** the **universal** care for **all.** As God so love the world that He gave His only begotten son that whoever **believes** in Him should not perish. This is an **unselfish love, the divine Love of God.**

2. PHILEOI **(Greek)** is to be **distinguished** from **agapao** in this, that **phileo** more nearly represents **tender affection, Friendship love, Such** as loving an object. Not **so** much as an act of service but rather an **expression** of fondness of **another.** Hence, the questions that Jesus asks Peter were: **Peter, lovest** thou **me more** than **these? Jesus uses Agape,** Peter answers back and said, **I Phileo you.** Agape **gives** and **serves** while **Phileo** holds one in **admirations, Joy__**Taken from the **Greek:** CHARA, joy, **delight,** to rejoice.

3. PEACE _ **SHALOM, (Heb.),** Eirene, **(Grk.)** This definition can be **understood** in **two dimensions:**

   (1) **Peace** *with* God, and the **peace** *of* **God**
   (2) **The peace** *with* **God** has to do with *the penalty* **of sins paid for.**
   (3) Hence, the **hostilities** between God and man cease. Therefore, we have the **peace** *of God,* which gives great **comfort** and **confidence (**Rom. 5:1; 2; Thess. 3:16**).**

- Long Suffering __Makro-Thumia (Grk) Meaning Long (Makro) Thurmia (Temper) In other words, **patience, forbearance,** *not* **short temper.**

- Endurance -To **wait patiently** without **murmuring** and **complaining.**

- Gentleness __Epieikeia—Epi__unto this has to do with **how we treat one another** in **kindness, fairness,** and **humanely.** Not holding to the **letter** of **the law, but** how one may **reconcile, forbear,** and **forgive another.**

- Goodness __Chrestotes (Greek) this denotes **kindness** *of* **heart in acts** of **good deeds.**

- Meekness __Prautes __**Feeling little as** relates to **others.** Not **self assuming.** Has to do with **a yielding** as it is to the **will of God** without **resisting.**

- Temperance _ _Enkrateia __(Greek) **Kratos, -Strength, Self Control,** not unbalanced, and Not pull by **outside influences.**

These are the **virtues** that *come with* the **Holy Spirit.** These are the **opposite** of the **deeds** and **works** of the **flesh.** When these **beatitudes** are **exemplified** by the **church** under **grace** there is no need for the **law.** For **Love** works no ill to its **neighbor.**

A Sanctified Church

Ephesians 5:26--Kjv

Ephesians 5:26-27 says: "That he **might sanctify** and **cleanse** it with the washing of water by the **Word,** That he might present it to himself a **glorious church,** not having **spot,** or wrinkle, or any such thing; but that it should be **holy** and **without blemish.**"

Sanctification

Taken from the **Greek word** *Hagiasmos.* **Sanctification** is used of **separation** to **God** (I Cor. 1:30; II Thess. 2:13; I Pet. 1:2). Sanctification is also used in **N.T.** of the separation of the **believer** from evil things and ways **(Vine).**

God wants **His** church to be a **separated** body from the **world,** and from **false religious systems.** No one has the right to be **fellowshipped** into the **body** but those that **have been** taught the **fundamental doctrines** of **salvation.**

2 Corinthians 6:14-18 God said to His Church, "Be ye not **unequally yoked together** with unbelievers: for what **fellowship** hath **righteousness** with **unrighteousness**? And what **communion** hath **light** with **darkness**? And what concord hath Christ with Belial? Or what part hath **he that believeth with** an **infidel**? And what agreement hath the **temple** of God **with idols**? For ye are the temple of the **living** God; as God hath said, I will dwell in them, and walk in *them;* and I will be their God, and they shall be my **people.** Wherefore come out from **among** them, and **be** ye Separate, saith the Lord, and touch not **the unclean** *thing;* and I **will receive you**, and will be a **Father** unto you, and **ye** shall be my **sons** and daughters, saith the Lord **Almighty."**

Anyone that does not **teach** the **true doctrine of God** is not to be **fellowshipped** by the **Church.**

2 John 9-11, "Whosoever **transgresseth**, and abideth not in the **doctrine** of Christ, hath not God, He that **abideth** in the **doctrine** of Christ, he hath both the Father and Son. [10]If there come any unto you, and bring not **this doctrine**, receive him not into *your* house, neither bid him **God's speed**: For he **that biddeth** him God's speed *is* **partaker** of his **evil deeds**."

We know that there has **been a falling away** from **the faith,** as our beloved **Paul said would happen.** I Timothy 4:1, "Now the **Spirit** speaketh expressly, that in the latter **times** some **shall depart** from the **faith,** giving heed to seducing **spirits,** and **doctrines** of **devils;**" God is **against** His church **accepting** anyone into its **fellowship** who does **not practice** or **teach** the **true doctrine.**

Galatians 1:8 Paul said, "But though we, or an **angel** from **heaven, preach** any **other gospel** unto you than that which we **have preached unto you,** let him be **accursed."**

I Timothy 6:3, 5 says: "If any man **teach otherwise,** and **consent** not to wholesome words, *even* the words of our Lord Jesus Christ, and to the **doctrine** which is **according to godliness;** "... from such withdraw thyself."

2 Thessalonians 3:6 states, "Now we command you, **brethren,** in the **name** of our Lord Jesus Christ, that ye **withdraw yourselves** from every brother that walketh **disorderly,** and not after the **tradition** which he received of us."

Romans 16:17 says: "Now I beseech you, brethren, **mark** them which cause **division** and offense Contrary to the doctrine which ye **have learned;** and avoid them:"

I Corinthians 5:11 Paul writes, "But now I have written unto you not to keep company, if any man that is called a **brother** be a **fornicator**, or covetous, or an idolater, or a **railer,** or a drunkard, or an extortioner; with such a one, no, not to eat."

Titus 3:10, 11 states," A man that is **a heretick** after the first and second **admonition reject;** Knowing that he that is such is subverted, and **sinneth**, being **condemned of himself**."

2 Peter 2:1 Peter said, "But there were false prophets also among the **people,** even as there shall be **false teachers** among you, who **privily shall bring in damnable**

heresies, even **denying the LORD that bought** them, and bring upon themselves swift **destruction."**

ETERNAL SECURITY?

Much argument has been presented on the subject of **Eternal Security.** This argument has been advanced from the dawn of the **reformation** period when **Martin Luther** presented his **ninety-five thesis** against the fallacies found in the **Catholic** dogma and the practice of the sale of indulgencies for the remission of sin after ones conversion. Many others Join him such as, **John Calvin, John Knox, and Zwingwi,** to protest the erroneous doctrine of doing penance of the absolution of temporal sins. They taught the **justification by faith without works.**

However by saying this, they opened a school of thought as whether works ever will be necessary to be maintained in a Christian life so that he may retain his eternal life.

Is it true that a person is **Eternally Secured,** once he has been saved; whether he lives a consistent holy life or not? This question has baffled many for so long a time. The thought that a person is eternally secured comes to us from so many who take some **passages** in the Scripture that they say suggests that once a person becomes save he is then placed into the hands of God where no man or power can pluck him out. (St. John 10:29). The famous quotation that said: "Verily, verily, I say unto you, he that **believeth** on me hath everlasting life." (St. John 6:47)

Do these statements declare unto us that a person is saved regardless to what he does? We will **examine these questions** in our presentation.

There are other scriptures, on the other hand, that **challenge** the **understanding** that some get from the **Eternal Security** scriptures such as: **2 Peter 2:20-22,** "For if after they have escaped the **pollutions** of the **world** through the **knowledge** of the **Lord** and **Saviour** Jesus **Christ,** they are again entangled therein, and overcome, **the later end** is worse with them than the beginning. [21]For it had been **better** for them not to have known the **way** of **righteousness,** than, after they have known *it,* to turn from the **holy commandment** delivered unto them, [22]But it is happened unto them according to the true proverb, The **dog** *is* **turned** to his own **vomit** again: and the **sow** that **was** washed to her wallowing in the **mire."**

Another scripture which warns us of the possibility of falling or failing. Hebrews 12:15-17, "**Looking diligently** lest any man **fail** of the **grace** of God: lest any root of bitterness **springing up** trouble *you,* and thereby many be defiled; Lest there *be* any **fornicator,** or **profane person,** as Esau, who for one morsel of meat sold his birthright. For ye know how that afterward, when he would have **inherited** the **blessing,** he **was rejected**: for he found no place of **repentance,** though he sought it carefully with tears."

This then gives us **two plausible accounts** as we **consider** the truth of **pros** and **cons** about the subject of **Eternal Security. There** is a place we can get in **God where** we will **never fall. Peter** tells us to **add** to our **faith.**

2 Peter 1:5-8, 10, "And beside this, giving all diligence, add to your **faith** virtue; and to **virtue knowledge**; and to knowledge **temperance**; and to temperance **patience**; and to patience **godliness**; and to godliness **brotherly kindness**; and to brotherly kindness **charity.**

[8]For if these things **be** in you, and abound, they **make** *you that ye shall* **neither** *be* **barren** nor unfruitful in the **knowledge** of our Lord Jesus Christ. "…Wherefore the rather, brethren, give diligence to make your **calling** and **election sure**: for if ye do these things, **ye shall** never **fall:**"

There is a **place** we can get **in God** where we will **never fall.** The idea that we can sin continuously and still **be saved eternally**, is foreign to the **Word** of God. It also **limits** the **power** of **God** to keep us from **falling.** It's striking to note **Jude 21, 24**: "**Keep** yourselves in the **love** of God, looking for the **mercy** of our Lord Jesus Christ unto **eternal life.** "…Now unto him that is able **to keep** you from falling, and to present *you* **faultless** before the presence of his **glory** with **exceeding joy.**"

We who are save by **grace** are **kept by grace. Titus 2:11-12, 14 says,** "For the **grace** of God that **bringeth salvation hath appeared** to all **men, Teaching** us that, **denying ungodliness** and **worldly lusts**, we should live **soberly, righteously,** and **godly**, in this present **world;** "…Who gave himself for us, that he **might redeem** us from **all iniquity,** and **purify** unto himself a **peculiar** people, zealous of **good works.**"

Another place in this book__Titus 3:7-8 it is said: "That **being justified** by his **grace,** we should be made **heirs** according to the **hope** of **eternal life.** *This* is a **faithful saying**, and these things I will that thou **affirm constantly**, that they **which have believed** in God might be careful to **maintain** good works. These things are good and profitable unto men."

It appears, from these **scriptures,** that G ʀ ᴀ ᴄ ᴇ **saved us from** our pass **sins, so** that we might **walk** in the **newness** of life **(Eph. 2:8, 9).**

These scriptures should be affirmed **hermeneutically,** this **is to say:** "How does **good works** play-out in our **salvation process?**

We must **understand** that no one **was able** to do good works to **merit** salvation. The Scripture said: "There is none that understandeth, there is none that seeketh after God. "…Therefore by the deeds of the law there **shall** no flesh **be justified** in His sight; for by the law is the knowledge of sin." (Rom. 3:11, 20)

In order for God to save us, He concluded all to be classified as unholy and **not worthy of salvation. God us** did not save by mere **Grace** alone. Though **grace** is used as a means of **Justification** according to **Romans 3:24,** and **Ephesians 2:8,** it was not done by grace only. Justification is also meted out to us through or by **faith. (Rom. 4:1).** This means that we must put our trust in the O ɴ ᴇ Jesus Christ, who is accredited as **keeping** the Law, and was **declared by God** to be **righteous.** And therefore the **propitiation** and the **gift** of His righteousness for our sins were to be given to everyone who **believes** in **Jesus Christ**.

Yet another means of **Justification** must be underlined, that is, the **Justification** by **Blood**. As the Scripture said: "Much more then, **being** now **justified** by His **blood, we shall be saved** from **wrath** through Him." (Rom. 5:9)

This is to be understood that the **shedding of blood** has to be **realized** for the **removing** of the **penalty** of **sins**. God did not just save us **without** someone **paying** for the **penalty** of **sin, which is death.** So then, these **three** means of **justifications, by** GRACE**, by** FAITH**,** and **by** BLOOD has to be **exercised** to **obtain** the **forgiveness** of **sins** so that **God** may **save** all from **sins.**

Since we could not live right to be **saved, and could** not be **excused** from the **death penalty**, so **Christ** came and did all of this for us **without** any works on our part. This is the whole point that must be understood; that is, there were **no works** performed **by us** by which we were **saved**. This is before our salvation, and it does not license us to sins after our salvation and still claim **Eternal** Salvation practicing sin.

This is the reason Paul said in Romans 6:1, 2, 15 "What shall we say then? Shall we **continue** in **sin,** that **grace** may abound? **God forbid.** How shall we, that **are dead** to sin, **live** any longer therein?…What then? **Shall** we sin, because we are not under the law, but under grace? God forbid." Romans 6:21-23, "What fruit had ye then in those things whereof ye are now ashamed? for the **end** of those things *is* **death**. But now being made free from sin, and become servants to God, ye have your **fruit** unto holiness, and the end **everlasting life**. For the **wages** of **sin** is **death**; but the **gift** of God is **eternal life** through Jesus Christ our Lord."

SONS OF GOD

The idea and the Scriptures that say we are **sons of God** should not blind our eyes concerning this **truth**. That is, our **life** style must be **holy** without blame before him in love.

A lesson of son-ships can be understood from the Allegory of **Ishmael** and **Isaac.** Ishmael was a son of Abraham by the bondwoman Hagar. **Isaac** was a son of Abraham by the **freewoman** Sarah (Genesis 16:17). This is a **lesson on eternal inheritance,** and the **rights of a son** versus the **rights of a servant**. The Scripture tells us that the son of the bondwoman was **cast out** (Gen. 21:6-12; Gal. 4:21-31). This shows us that because a person is called **a son,** it does not necessarily mean that he is entitled to **eternal life**. It is dependent on the **action** of that **son,** as to whether he will be **classified** as the **son** of the freewoman or of the bondwoman. **Our lifestyle will determine** this.

Jesus made mention of this in St. John 8:31-36 by saying: "Then said Jesus to those Jews which believed on him, if ye continue in my **Word,** *then* are ye my **disciples** indeed; and ye shall know the **truth,** and the truth shall **make** you **free.** They answered him, we be Abraham's **seed,** and **were** never **in bondage** to any man:

how sayest thou, ye shall be made **free?** Jesus answered them, **Verily,** verily I say unto you, whosoever **committeth sin** is the **servant** of sin. [35]And the **servant abideth** not in the house **for ever;** *but* the **Son** abideth ever. [36]If the Son therefore shall make you free, ye shall be free indeed.

From this passage, **we see that a person** that **committeth sin is classified as Ishmael (***Servant***),** who did not receive the **inheritance** of his father. Those that do the **will of God,** after their **salvation,** are **classified** as Isaac **(***Son***) who received** the **inheritance of the father.**

"Now we, brethren, as Isaac was, are the **children** of **promise**. [29] But as then he that was born after the flesh persecuted him *that was born* after the Spirit, even so it is now. [30]Nevertheless, what saith the **Scripture?** Cast out the bondwoman and her son: for the son of the bondwoman **shall** not **be heir** with the son of the freewoman. So then, brethren, we are not **children** of the bondwoman, but of the free." (Gal. 4:28-31)

Paul further mention concerning fleshly sins: "*This* I say then, Walk in the **Spirit,** and ye **shall** not **fulfill** the **lust** of the **flesh.** [17]For the flesh **lusteth** against the Spirit, and the Spirit against the flesh: and these are contrary the one to the other: so that ye cannot do the things that ye would. But if ye **be led** of the Spirit, ye are not under the law.

Now the **works** of the flesh are **manifest,** which are *these;* Adultery, **fornication, uncleanness, lasciviousness, Idolatry,** witchcraft, hathred, **variance, emulations, wrath,** strife **seditions, heresies,** envyings, **murders, drunkenness, revelings,** and such **like:** the which I **tell** you **before, as I have** also told *you* in **time past,** that they **which do** such things **shall** not **inherit** the **kingdom** of God." (Gal. 5:16-21)

Those that are **practicing sin** though they were **once saved** are not **classified** as the **sons of God.** For the **Scripture said in Romans 6:6, 7:** "Knowing this, that our **old man is crucified** with *him,* that the **body** of **sin** might be destroyed, that henceforth we **should** not **serve** sin. [7]For he **that is dead is freed** from sin." [5]"For **they** that are after the flesh **do mind** the things of the **flesh;** but they that are after the **Spirit** the things of the Spirit. For to be **carnally** minded *is* **death;** but to be spiritually minded *is* **life** and **peace.**" (Rom. 8:5-6)

You are not a **son of God** if you are **not led** by the **Spirit of God.** [14]"For as many as **are led** by the Spirit of God, they are the **sons** of God. [15]For ye **have** not **received** the spirit of **bondage** again to **fear;** but ye have received the Spirit of **adoption,** whereby we cry, **Abba, Father.** [16]The Spirit itself beareth witness with our **spirit,** that we are the **children** of God: And if children, **then heirs;** heirs of God, and **joint heirs** with Christ; if so be that we **suffer with** *him,* that we **may be** also **glorified together.**" (Rom. 8:14-17)

In another place the Scripture said: "Know ye not that the **unrighteous shall** not **inherit** the **kingdom** of God? Be not deceived: neither **fornicators,** nor **idolaters,** nor adulterers, nor **effeminate,** nor **abusers of themselves with mankind,** [10]Nor thieves, nor covetous, nor drunkards, nor revilers, nor **extortioners, shall inherit** the kingdom of God. [11]And such were some of you: but ye **are washed,** but ye **are sanctified,** but ye **are justified** in the **name** of the Lord Jesus, and by the **Spirit** of our God." (I Cor. 6:9-11)

"But **fornication**, and all **uncleanness,** or **covetousness, let** it not **be** once **named** among you, as becometh **saints;** Neither filthiness, nor **foolish talking,** nor **jesting,** which **are** not **convenient**: but rather giving of thanks." (Eph.5:3,4)

[5]For this ye know, that no **whoremonger, nor unclean person,** nor covetous man, who is an **idolater,** hath any **inheritance** in the **kingdom** of Christ and of God. **Let** no man **deceive** you with **vain words**: for because of these things cometh the **wrath** of God upon the children of **disobedience.** [7]Be not ye therefore **partakers** with them. For ye were sometimes **darkness,** but now *are ye* **ligh**t in the Lord: walk as children of light. (For the fruit of the **Spirit** is in all **goodness** and **righteousness** and **truth;).** (Eph. 5:5-9)

Galatians 5:21 it is said, "Envyings, murders, **drunkenness, revellings,** and such like: of the which I **tell** you **before,** as I **have** also **told** *you* **in time past,** that they **which do** such things **shall** not **inherit** the **kingdom** of God.

"Whosoever hateth his brother is a murderer: and ye know that no murderer hath eternal life abiding in him." (1 John 3:15)

My concluding point is this, if we want **our salvation** to be **secured** we must do the following:

2 Peter 1:5-11 tells us: "And beside this, giving all diligence, add to your **faith** virtue; and to **virtue knowledge;** [6]And to knowledge **temperance;** and to temperance **patience;** and to patience godliness; [7]And to **godliness** brotherly kindness and to **brotherly kindness charity.** [8]For if these things **be** in you and abound, they **make** *you that ye shall* neither **be barren** nor unfruitful in the **knowledge** of our **Lord Jesus Christ.**

[9]But he that lacketh these things is blind, and cannot see afar off, and hath forgotten that he was purged from his **old sins.** [10]Wherefore the rather, bretheren, give diligence to make your **calling** and **election sure:** for if ye do these things, ye **shall** never **fall:** [11]For so an entrance shall be ministered unto you abundantly into the **everlasting kingdom** of our Lord and Saviour Jesus Christ".

2 Peter 2:20-21, "For if after they have escaped the **pollutions** of the **world** through the **knowledge** of the **Lord** and **Savior** Jesus **Christ,** they are again entangled therein and overcome, the **latter end** is worse with them than the beginning. [21]For it had been better for them not to have **known** the way of **righteousness,** than after they have known *it,* to turn from the **holy commandment** delivered unto them. [22]But it is happened unto them according to the true proverb, the dog *is* turned to his own vomit again; and the sow that was washed to her wallowing in the **mire.**"

"We therefore, beloved, seeing ye **know** *these things* before, **beware** lest ye also, being led away with the **error** of the **wicked,** fall from your own steadfastness. [18]But grow in **grace,** and *in* **the knowledge** of our Lord and Savior Jesus **Christ.** To Him *be* glory both now and **forever. Amen.**" (2 Pet. 3:17-18)

CURRICULUM STUDY GUIDE

The Redemption Process

First Week

1. For this week you must learn the four necessities that are required to purchase salvation for mankind (The Prophet, Priest, Sacrifice, and Testator).

Second Week

1. Write a report on the Death of the Testator.
2. You must study the role of the Mediator.
3. Who was Melchisedek?

Third Week

1. Learn the ways or Steps of Salvation with the appropriate scriptures.
2. You must study the Hearing of the Gospel.
3. Under this subject you must study: a) The role of the Preacher or the Evangelist is to motivate the people to action through transmitting the Word of God to them.

Fourth Week

1. Study the subject: "Beware of False Prophets."
2. Write a scriptural report: "How to determine a False Prophet."

Fifth Week

1. Study the booklet: "Questions and Answers concerning "The Way of Salvation, until you are able to explain the way of salvation in your own words with scripture references.
2. Write the Steps of Salvation in a three-page report.

Sixth Week

1. You must study the subject: "Which is the correct Baptismal Formula in the name of the Father, the Son and the Holy Ghost, or in the name of the Lord Jesus Christ?" Matt. 28:19, 20 and Acts 2:38.

Bishop Willie J. Duncan Ph.D.

2. Write a report__The four parts to the Great Commission (Matthew, Mark, Luke, and Acts).

SEVENTH WEEK

COMPARATIVE RELIGIONS

1. Do a research paper on three different religious bodies such as: Catholics, Baptist, and Jehovah Witnesses. You must refute or support your findings on their doctrines.

EIGHTH WEEK

2. You must study whether it is necessary to possess the Baptism of the Holy Ghost in order to be saved. b) Is this baptism a second work of Grace?

3. You must study whether there is a difference in the Baptism of the Holy Ghost, and being born again.

NINTH WEEK

4. You must study the role of the **"Sign Tongue"** and its function that has to do with the way of salvation.

TENTH WEEK

5. You must study the functioning of the **"Nine Spiritual Gifts"** in the Church.
   a. You must learn the –**Classifications**– of the Gifts.
   b. You must learn the –**Purpose**– of the Gifts.

6. You must learn the **"Five Ministerial"** Gifts.

SINOLOGY
Galatians 5:19-21–KJV

FIRST WEEK

1. You must study:
   a) The **meaning** of the term Sinology.
   b) The **Classifications** of different kinds of Sins.

216

SECOND WEEK

2. **THE SINS OF UNCHASTITY**
A. Adultery
B. Fornication
C. Uncleanness
D. Lasciviousness

THIRD WEEK

1. **SINS OF IRRELIGIOUSNESS**
A. Idolatry
B. Witchcraft (Sorcery)

FOURTH WEEK

2. **SINS OF MALIGNITY**

a) Hatred,	b) Variance	c) Emulations (Jealousy)
d) Wrath,	e) Strife,	f) Seditions, g) Heresies
h) Envying,	i) Murder.	

FIFTH WEEK

2. **SINS OF EXCESSIVENESS**
A. Drunkenness
B. Reveling

SIXTH WEEK

ETERNAL SECURITY

1. To study whether a "**Believer**" is eternally saved, if he continues in Sins.
2. Restoration and Counseling.

LOVOLOGY

SEVENTH WEEK

1. The Christian Walk.
2. The Fruit of the Spirit.

EIGHTH WEEK

1. The Positive Side of Holiness
2. The Christian Duty (Religion).

NINTH WEEK

1. The Christian's Perfected Growth (II Peter Chapter 1; Ephesians Chapter 4).

TENTH WEEK

1. Personal Evangelism
2. Review.

FUNDAMENTAL DOCTRINE OF SALVATION

1. What is the purpose of Salvation? _____
   _____

2. How is salvation accomplished? _____
   _____

3. What role does the position of the prophet play? _____
   _____

4. What role does the Priest play? _____
   _____

5. For what purpose or reason there is a need for the sacrifice? _____
   _____

6. What particular function does the Testator has? Explain. _____
   _____

7. Explain the position of the Mediator. _____
   _____

8. Who is Melchisedec? _____

9. Name the steps to salvation with scripture references. _____

   _____
   _____
   _____
   _____
   _____
   _____

10. What does the Apostolic Warning consist of? _____
   _____
   _____

11. Explain the approach on the subject of the work of faith. _____
   _____
   _____

12. Baptism was done by what particular mode? _____

13. Compare Matthew 28:19,20, with Acts 2:38. What should be the conclusion there from?

_____

_____

_____

14. Name the four parts to the Great commission, with scripture reference.

_____

_____

_____

15. What is speaking in other tongues?

_____

16. Give four scriptures on tongue speaking.

_____

_____

17. What was prophesying a sign of in the Old Testament? _____

_____

18. What were tongues a sign of in the New Testament?

_____

19. Do all speak in tongues? _____Explain. _____

_____

_____

20. 20. Explain the difference in the gifts of tongues and the other tongues.

_____

_____

_____

21. What is the Christian Walk? _____

22. What does Grace do for us? _____

23. What happened to the Old Man? _____

SINOLOGY

24. What is meant by the term "Negative side of Holiness?" _____

25. Name the Classification of the Sins of the Flesh. _____

26. What are the Sins of each Classifications? _____

27. What is the meaning of the term "A Sanctified Church?" _____

28. Name the fruit of the Spirit. _____

29. Is a Christian eternally saved if they continue in sin? Explain. _____

30. What is meant by the term LOVOLOGY? _____

31. What is the main expression of a saved life? _____

32. What is eternal Security? Could it be obtained?"

Explain _____

Could you ever lose your Salvation? _____

_____

VOLUME IV

NAMOLOGY

CONTENTS

PREFACE

The intent of this book is to provide biblical knowledge and offer remarkable depictions that illustrate certain of **God's characteristics** that one may study "HE WHO IS" through the **divine Revelation** of His **names**. This is to show that **the names** of God are not to be understood by sounds only, but more so as to the **meanings**. Many people have made God **an object of** worship more than **to worship** a **living Person**. The **great majority** of people have restricted God to **a place** of worship, rather than **a Person** to worship in **Spirit** and in **truth**. Our God, the Great Yah, Elohim, Yehovah is **a living** Spiritual **Being**. He must **not be** considered an object to be adored, nor as a **pendulant** to be worn or hung on a wall. Neither is He to be set-aside for a day or time to be worshiped. **He is alive**, for **in him** we **live, move**, and have **our being**.

The Revelation of His name is **progressive**. The study is **enlightening**. This study will bring us to **a personal relationship** with the Great God Our Savior **Jesus Christ**. To know that the **Person** we call **Jesus** is none other than **Jehovah** our **Savior,** Shalom! Eth Shalom!

My first regard is given to the **Lord Jesus Christ the Savior** of the world. I appreciate my wife **Zeola Duncan** for being my constant companion while writing this book.

Special thanks, is given to **Deacon Marvin Bacon**, and his son **Korey Bacon** for lending their time and talents in proofreading this book.

Special thank are given to Evangelist Deloris Mimms for the final draft.

This is the **first** edition; any flaws will be corrected in the **second edition**.

The Author

THE REVELATION OF GOD THROUGH HIS NAMES

EXODUS 6:4 (KING JAMES VERSION)

YAH	HE WHO IS	PS 68:4
ELOHIM	GOD THE CREATOR	GEN. 1:1
JEHOVAH JI-REH	GOD WILL PROVIDE	GEN 22:14
ELSHADDAI	GOD ALMIGHTY	GEN. 17:1
EH-YEH-ASHER-EH-YEH	I WILL BE THAT I WILL BE WHILE I AM	EX. 3:13
YAHVEH	GOD OF THE COVENANT	EX. 6:3
JEHOVAH ROPHEAKA	GOD THAT HEALS	EX. 15; 26
JEHOVAH NISSI	GOD MY BANNER	EX.17:15
JEHOVAH MEDKADISKIM	GOD WHO SANCTIFIES	EX. 31:13
JEHOVAH SHALOM	**GOD OF PEACE**	JUDG. 6:24
JEHOVAH TSIDKENU	GOD OUR RIGHTEOUSNESS	JER. 23:6
JEHOVAH SHAMMAH	THE LORD IS THERE	EZEK. 48:35
JEHOVAH TSAIOT	THE LORD OF HOSTS	IS. 1:3
JEHOVAH ROI	THE LORD MY SHEPHERD	PS. 23:1
JEHOVAH ELYON	GOD MOST HIGH	PS. 17:9
JEHOVAH GMOLAH	GOD OF RECOMPENSE	JER. 51:56
JEHOVAH MAKKEH	GOD THAT SMITETH	EZEK. 7:9
JEHOSHUA	JEHOVAH SAVES	IS. 43:11
ADONAI	GOD WHO RULES HIS OWN	PS. 110.7
EL-OLAM	THE EVERLASTING GOD	PS. 90:2
EL-GIBOR	THE MIGHTY GOD	IS. 9:6
EL-OHEENU	THE LORD OUR GOD	DEUT. 6:4
EL-OHEEKA	THE LORD THY GOD	EX. 20:1
EL-OHAY	**THE LORD MY GOD**	PS. 63:1
EL-IJAH	**MY GOD IS JEHOVAH**	2 KI. 18:39
EL-ISHA	**MY GOD IS SAVIOUR**	2 KI. 6:17
Y'SHUA	YAHVEH IS SAVIOUR	LUKE 2:11
JESUS	**JEHOVAH**	ST. MATT. 1:21

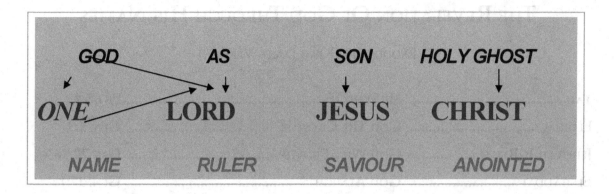

NAMOLOGY

THE REVELATION OF GOD
Through His Names

WHAT IS A NAME?

A name is an appellative by which a person is known. Hence, the term known is taken from the Greek word *O-known-ma*, and the Latin *O-know-en.* This is where we get the word **O-'Known'-ma.** It is a designation by which a person is known. Although, a name in biblical treatise, goes beyond the title, and lays heavier on the **characteristic of a person,** place or thing **named** or famed.

For **an outstanding example**, when **Jacob** was fleeing from his brother **Esau,** he lit upon a place previously named *Luz.* He had a vision of God and he changed the **name** of that place to **Beth-El.** Bethel means the house of God. He found that God was in that place **(Gen. 28–KJV).**

The place where **Uzza** reached forth his hand to **stabilize the Ark** of the Lord unwittingly when the **oxen stumbled,** the Lord smote him that **he died.** That place was **named** *Perez or (Pharez)-Uzzah:* Which means **breaking** or **breaching forth:** Signifying, the **coming forth** of the **hand of the Lord** because of **Uzza's mistake** (2 Sam. 6:8–KJV). When **Tamar** gave birth to the sons of **Judah,** the first who was being born, **put forth his hand,** and they tied **a ribbon around it** to **mark the firstborn:** but before he came out **his brother broke out ahead** of him, and became the firstborn. His name was called **Pharez,** which means **breaking forth.** His brother was named **Zarah,** which means offspring or **dawning light** (Gen. 38:29-30–KJV).

When Naomi was returning home from her sojourning in the land of **Moab,** her acquaintances said, *"Here comes Naomi." Naomi replied and said: "Don't call me Naomi, but call me Mara, for the Lord had done very bitter toward me."*(Ruth 1:20) Hence, the name **Naomi means pleasant,** while the name **Mara means bitter.** In reference to her bitter experiences she had by **losing** her **family** in **Moab,** she called herself **Mara.** The fulfillment of her name did follow with **Ruth** marrying **Boaz.** From **Boaz** comes **Obed,** from Obed comes **Jesse,** from Jesse comes **David,** and **David** is in the **lineage of Christ.** When **Boaz** begot **Obed,** the child is attributed as being the **Child of Naomi.** "And the women her neighbours gave it a name, saying, "There is a son

born to Naomi; and they called his name **Obed:** he is the father of **Jesse,** the father of **David."** (Ruth 4:17–Kjv)

This **lineage** gives the list of the **Names** in the **Generation of Christ** from **Judah** to **David**. It is **interesting to note** the **meaning** of names such as:

1. **(Judah:** *Praise*)
2 **Pharez:** *Breach*
3. **Hezron:** *Enclosed Wall*
4. **Aram:** *Height*
5. **Amminadab:** *People of the Prince*
6. **Naahshon:** *Enchanter*
7. **Salmon:** *Shady*
8. **Boaz:** *Fleetness*
9. **Obed:** *Worshiping (God)*
10. **Jesse:** *Gift*
11. **David:** *Beloved*

The generation, from other persons, that was **named** in the biblical record is **Abram**, which simply means **father**. Moreover, later his name was changed to **Abraham**, which means a **father** of a **multitude**. Sarai was changed to **Sarah**, which means a **mother** of **nations** (Gen. 17:15–Kjv**).**

When **Isaac** was **born**, he was named **Isaac**, simply because his **name** means **laughing**. For when God told **Abraham** that he was blessing him with a child through **Sarah**, he **fell on his face** and **laughed** (Gen. 17:17–Kjv). According to Genesis 18:12; 21:6), **Sarah** also laughed. Therefore, this son's name is called **Isaac**, which means laughing.

When **Jacob** and **Esau** were born, their names became characteristically as it relates to their **actions**. **Jacob** means **sub-planter**, while **Esau** means **hairy,** for he was hairy all over (This was indicative of his **wilderness** involvement in hunting). Eventually, **both** of their **names** were **changed** to suggest other characteristics. **Esau's** name was **changed** to Edom, meaning redness concerning the **red bean lentil** he ate when selling his birthright. **Jacob's** name was **changed** to Israel, meaning **prince of God**, after he **prevailed** in a wrestle with an **Angel**. He later called the place **Peniel,** which means **face of God**.

The name Isaiah means the **salvation of Jehovah**. **Daniel** means **God** is **Judge**. **El I Jah** means my **God** am **Jehovah**. The name of **El-I-Sha** means **My God is Savior**.

The names of the **Hebrew** boys are significant in their meanings. **Hananiah** means **My God Is Gracious**. **Mishael** means there is **none** like **God**. **Azariah** means **God is my-helper**.

Unfortunately, time will not permit to labor any further in presenting any other names other than our **particular study**. This should suffice to show how that **names were significant** concerning a **person, place** or **thing** in the biblical times. But **more**

importantly, I will now present **the meaning** of God's **names** as recorded in the following biblical account:

THE MEANING OF GOD'S NAMES CHARACTERISTICALLY

God does his **mighty works** according to the **meaning** of his **names**. To be more emphatic, his works **declare** his names. There are **names** that deal with **God's past, present,** and **future** works. His names are **not** to be **understood** as human **names;** this is to say, not just **a title:** but a **functioning.**

The names of God in **Scripture** were **not** primarily a **word** given by a specific sound, without a **meaning:** But more so in reference to his **characteristics** in various functions. His names, *Jehovah, El, Eloah, Elohim, Adonai, Adon, Yah, Nissi, and Gmolah* are not sounding words, but rather **various functions** and **relationships.**

No one **will gather** the main or whole **intent** of the names, unless he/she **studies** them from this approach. God is **progressive** in his **actions** and **revelations.** Just to get a **verbal** sound of the names of God is **not** the **intent** of this book, but to **observe** God in his **various functions** unto our day.

God can be one thing to one *person and something else to another.* In **other words,** *He is Ado*n to others that are **not his;** while He is *Adonai* to his **own.** He is *Elshaddai* unto **Abraham, Isaac,** and **Jacob;** however, He is *Jehovah* unto **Israel.** Hence, he said, "I appeared unto **Abraham,** unto **Isaac,** and unto **Jacob,** by the *name* of **God Almighty,** but by my name JEHOVAH was I **not** known unto them." (Exd. 6:3)

Some say that God's **name** should be called *Jehovah* instead of the term LORD, as is primarily used in the **King James** Translation. The Old **Hebrew** used only consonants and no vowels. Hence, if you used the consonants in the name *Jehovah,* they would be "*YHVH*". If you used the consonants in the name Yahweh, would be *YHWH*. In **ancient Hebrew,** there was no "*J*" in the *name* Jehovah, but there was a "*Y*" in *Yehovah.* On the other hand, there was no "*W*" in the name *Yahweh,* but a "*V*" was used instead. Thus, the letters would be "*YHVH*" instead of "*YHWH*". There were **no vowels** between the letters of **either** name. In the **Hebrew,** the Ancient writing would be "*YHVH*".

THE REVELATION OF GOD THROUGH HIS NAMES

We will now follow the **revelation of the names of God** as they are **unfolded** or as they are revealed in the **Holy Scriptures.**

ELOHEEN (ELOHIM)

This name is an extension of the name *"El"*. *"El"* means the **Omnipotent** or the **Almighty-One**. It is found at **the end** of many **proper names** such as *Dan-El*, which means **God is Judge**. The name *Beth-El*, means the **house of God**. *Emanu-El, which means* **God, is with us** (St. Matt. 1:23; Isa 7:14–Kjv). It may also begin with a name such as *El-i-Jah* (Elijah), which **means:** *"My God is Jehovah"*. It may be seen in the name of *El-i-Sha* (Elisha), which **means:** *"my God is Savior"*.

Elohim means **God the Creator**. It suggests plurality simply because **all** of God's **characteristics** are present in the creative acts. It has no suggestion of a pluralistic personality. Though the phrase *"Let Us"* is used in Genesis 1:26–Kjv); it does not translate into the sense of **personality**. For the plural pronoun *Us* corresponds with the **singular** pronoun *His*. For the **Scriptures** said, "Let Us make man in *"Our"* image, after *"Our"* likeness: So God created man in *His* own *image*, in the image of God created *He* him; **male** and **female** created *He* them." (Gen. 1:26-27)

Since the plurals *"Us"* and *"Our"* and the **singular** *"His"* and *"He"* are used interchangeably, a distinction should be made or **observed**. Are the plurals in reference to **personality** or **attributes**? I think it has to do with characteristics rather than with personality. **Note this statement carefully:** "And the LORD God said, Behold, the man is become as **One** of *Us*, to know good and evil:" (Gen. 3:22) What is that **One** of *Us* mentioned in **reference** to here? Why not say that man has become as **All of us?** This statement is what **Satan said to Eve**, so that she would become **AS God** (Elohim). "For God doth know that in the day ye eat thereof, then your eyes shall be opened, and ye shall be as **gods**." (Gen. 3:5–Kjv) The small **"gods"** is **not** found in **the Hebrew**. The small gods is a translation **blunder** that is not rendered in the Hebrew but rather the term **God or Elohim**. God **acknowledged** that **man** has become **as One of us**.

How do we determine the phrase *"One of Us"*? This entire phrase suggests its meaning, **"to know good** and **evil."** The knowledge of **good** and **evil** is an **attribute**, and **not** a **personality**. This is to say, that man has increased in **intelligence** rather than **acquiring** another **personality**. This is in the area of **character** or that his **behavior** is characteristically **different** than before. Hence, the counterpart Scripture found in Colossians 3:9, 10 states: **"Lie not one to another**, seeing that ye have **put off** the **old man** with **his deeds;** [10]And have put on the **new man**, which is **renewed** in **knowledge** after the **image** of him that **created him:"** In this **renewal**, it has to do with **deeds** and **knowledge**. **Notice** the **Scriptures** did **not** say in the **image** of *them*, but in the **image** of *Him*. The language is **never they** who **created** man, but *HE* Who created **male** and **female. Note this interesting point:** *"...He* who made them at the **beginning** made them **male** and **female."** (Matt. 19:4; Gen. 1:27, 28__Kjv)

Let's look at the **illustrated point** of the **name** *Elohim* found in Exodus, chapter 32, and verse 4, "And he received *them* at their hand, and fashioned it with a **graving tool**, after he had made *it* a **molten 'calf:'** and they said, "These *be* thy gods, O Israel, which brought thee up out of the land of Egypt. [5]And when **Aaron saw *it*,** he **built** an altar before **it;** and **Aaron** made **proclamation,** and said, tomorrow is a feast to the LORD." (v. 5)

THE NOUNS AND PRONOUNS EXAMINED
THEM
IT
CALF
THESE
GODS
LORD

Noun: This grammatical term comes from **Anglo-Norman French,** from **Latin** *nomen* **'name'.** It is a **common name** of a person, place or thing. **A** pronoun **is a** word **used instead of a noun** in reference to the same person, place or thing. **This is** from pro **'on behalf of'** and noun, **suggested by:** French *pronoun,* Latin *pronomen* **(from pro 'for in place of'** and *nomen* **'name'.** A Pronoun **stands in the stead** of a **noun** to designate objects **without naming them,** when the reference is clear from the **context** or situation.

Now, we have before us **six titles** or **names** to examine. Our efforts shall be to **examine** a correspondence between **singular** and **plural** to seek whether each corroborates with one another in a **transitive sense.**

Them: What are those **parts that** suggests the **'them'?** It is evidence that they are the **jewels** that the people **broke off** or **took out** of their **ears** and gave them to **Aaron** for the **fashioning** of the **molten calf.** From a variety of sources, the **element** of **gold** is taken and fashioned into a **calf.** There is **one chemical** *EL- ement,* that is **gold.**

It: It is not **plural** which corresponds with **them. The gold** is absolutely **one** substance that makes **the** *image,* or *it,* or the *calf.* The object is **one.**

The Calf: The object that is *fashioned* is designated as the **calf. It** corresponds with the **pronoun** *it.* The **singular** pronoun *'it'* is **transitive** to the singular noun **calf.** There is but **one calf** or **object of worship.**
These: The correspondence takes on a **new pronoun** that is not **transitive** to the other **pronouns.** This pronoun is **plural.** What happens to the **singularity** or **oneness** in the **whole matter?** It comes from the misunderstanding of the term GOD, which is **Elohim.**

Gods: This term brings us again to determine the right understanding of the name *Elohim*. This term is **translated** by the **King James Bible** as being plural. Hence, when their **translation** is reference to another *Elohim*, they make the term **plural** using small letter *gods*: Which in the **Hebrew stands for Elohim.**

The translators **take** this **object** to be **an idol**, and **it surely is**, and calls it *gods*. Because they, the translators, think the **term Elohim** to be the plurality of **personalities** rather than **attributes**, this term *gods* **does not correspond with the** object **designated**. There is but *one-calf* **made** and *one-altar* **built**. The **plural** translation is **incorrect**. The emphatic point that is spoken is that this is **Elohim;** He who brought you out of the land of Egypt. Since they made the **translation** to be **plural,** they use the pronoun **"These"** be the **Gods"** to correspond with the **plural term** *gods*.

LORD: **A** proper name is now given to the **object of worship.** They call Him *LORD*, (Jehovah). Jehovah is not TWO. **Jehovah is** *ONE*. **Jehovah is** One object/Person of **worship.** The first of all of the commandments is, "Hear, O **Israel: The** LORD OUR GOD IS ONE LORD." (Deu. 6:4) From the Hebrew *"Shema yisrael yehovah eloheenu yehovah echaD,"* the emphatic is, **"Hear, O Israel, Jehovah** (the self and **ever existing One),** our **Elohim,** is **"One Jehovah."**

This correspondence is reiterated in Mark 12:29: "And **Jesus** answered him, the first of all the commandments is, "**Hear, O Israel;** The **Lord** our **God is** ONE LORD:" [30]And thou shalt **love the** LORD **thy God** with **all thy heart**, and with all thy **soul,** and with all **thy mind**, and with **all thy strength:** this is the **first** commandment...." [32]And the scribe said unto Him, Well, Master, Thou hast said the **truth:** for there is ONE GOD; and there is none other but **He:**" (Mark 12:30, 32) How can we get **three** out of these statements? This is not talking about **one** out of three, one **out** of **two,** or one out of any other. This is an **absolute** ONE. This **is the numerical** ONE. **There** is **no other** number in ONE. It is **absolutely free** of any other **element.**

Jehovah, the only ONE GOD, can exist **universally** everywhere at the **same time.** Hence, Gen. 19:24 said, "Then the LORD,(Jehovah), **rained** upon **Sodom** and upon **Gomorrah** brimstone and fire **from the** LORD (Jehovah), **out of heaven;"**

Jehovah was on **earth** talking to **Abraham** at the time **He** rained down **fire** and **brimstone** from **heaven** (Gen. 18:1, 22–KJV), **Jehovah** is in **two places at once,** still remain ONE. **Deuteronomy 4:39** says, "Know therefore this day, and consider it in thine **heart,** that the LORD HE is GOD in **heaven above**, and upon the earth **beneath:** there is **none else."**

The name *Elohim* **does not** suggest a **trinity.** Its root name *El* **is the Strong** ONE.

EL (ALMIGHTY)

EL is the STRONG ONE, the ALMIGHTY. He is designated as the OMNIPOTENT. Essentially, He is the **All-Powerful** ONE. When compounded with other focal points, it gives other aspects such as **Elohim, "HE WHO IS"** strong enough to create. **El Shaddai,** means **"HE WHO IS"** Strong Enough **to Nourish. El** simply means **enduring** strength. It can be found at **the end** of many **Hebrew** words and names. **It's important to Note Genesis 33:20:** "And he erected there an **altar,** and called it **El-EL-ohe-Isra-El."**

ELOAH (IS ELOHIM)

He is the GOD Who is to be worshipped. He is **compared** with **idols,** which are **not** to be worshipped. Those idols are **inanimate** substances. They are **false gods.** ELOAH **is the** TRUE God who is to be **worshipped. Notice the sacrifice:** "They sacrificed unto **devils, not to God; (Eloah),** to **gods** whom they **knew not,** to new *gods that* came **newly** up, whom your **fathers** feared not." (Deut. 32:17–KJV)

ELYON (GENESIS 14:18)

Elyon is rendered as the **Most High God.** He is the **possessor of heaven** and earth, and is able to give **blessings** to the worshipper. He divides to the nations their inheritance. He is to be **worshipped** and **praised** as indicated in Psalm 7:17. Though He is *Elohim* **the Creator,** yet in the name *Elyon,* He is the possessor of heaven and earth and gives blessings to His subjects.

JAH (YAH)

This name *Jah* or *Yah* has a **distinct** meaning. The meaning has to do with the GOD who **exists. He Who IS, He Who Was,** and **He Who Shall Be.** In this name, He is the **everlasting** ONE. **He exists** in the **pass,** the **present,** and the **future.** This is **distinct** from what **He does.** It more so suggests His existence **without** exercising any relative **attributes.** This is the GOD, **who alone exists** in ETERNITY.

"LORD, Thou hast been our **dwelling place** in all **generations.** Before the mountains were brought forth, or ever Thou hadst formed the earth and the world, even from **everlasting** to everlasting, **Thou art GOD."** (Psalm 90:1-2–KJV)

"I said **O my GOD,** take me **not** away in the **midst** of **my days:** Thy years *are* throughout all generations. [25]Of old hast Thou laid the **foundation** of the **earth:** And the **heavens** *are* the work of thy hands. They shall perish, but Thou shalt **endure:** Yea, all of them shall wax old like a **garment;** As a vesture shalt Thou change them, and they shall be changed: But Thou *art* **the same,** And **thy years** shall have **no end."** (Psalm 102:24-27)

"Behold, GOD is my **salvation;** I will trust, and not be **afraid:** for the LORD (JAH) Jehovah is my strength and *my* **song;** he also **is become** my salvation." (Isa. 12:2)

This is YAH, the **self-existing ONE.** Who always Is, the **Great I Am.** This **name** is at the end of **Haleluyah. (Alelu-Yah! Praise "He WHO is" Worship Him!**

EL SHADDAI (ALMIGHTY BREASTED ONE)

El is again **compounded** with another **characteristic.** Why is such **a name** used? **We** must **examine** the **context** in which this name is used.

Genesis 17:1 says, "And when **Abram** was **ninety years old** and **nine,** the LORD appeared to Abram, and said unto him, I am the **Almighty God;** walk before me, and **be thou perfect."** God said, "I am the **Almighty** God" (*Heb. Ani El shaddai, I am God. I am* God *sufficient: from shadah to shed, to pour out. I am that* God who pours *out* blessings, *who gives them richly, abundantly, and continually*).

From this context, **God** is assuring Abram that **He is** the ALL-SUFFICIENT ONE. The **context** has in it the portion and the **incident,** as found in Genesis, chapter sixteen. **Sarai** had concluded that she was not a part of God's blessing **plan;** That is, to bless Abram with a child by her. For she had **passed the age** of child bearing and it **ceased** to be with **Sarah** after the **manner of women..** God had **not** mentioned that **Sarai** should be the one to bare **Abram's seed;** she suggested that **Hagar,** her handmaid, should be used to bare a child for her. **Abram** hearkened and **obeyed Sarai.**

He took her handmaid and she conceived a child to **help fulfill** God's promise. Under this **context,** God appeared unto **Abram** when he was **ninety-nine** years old. He informed him that regardless of **his age,** and **Sarai's condition,** he was well **able to nourish** both Abram and **Sarai back to strength,** so that they could produce the **promised seed.** Not only was Sarai's **body dead, Abram** had become **impotent.** He could **not** have **begotten** a child even if the woman was **young,** and in **childbearing age.**

EL SHADDAI now comes on the scene and says: He is ready to bless **Abram with** the seed. Neither Abram nor Sarai was able to perform and that is the reason **El Shaddai** said: I am the **Almighty God.** I will nourish both **you** and **Sarai** back **to strength:** both of you will have a child. Then **El Shaddai,** at this time, changes the **name** of Abram to **Abraham,** and Sarai to **Sarah.** Abraham means a **father of nations.** Sarah means a **mother of nations.**

All of this has to do with **God's timing.** The child was not to be born until the **appointed** time. God had **promised** Abram and his seed, (natural generation), the land of promise. [13]"And He said unto **Abram, know of a surety** that thy seed shall be a stranger in a land *that* is not theirs, and shall serve them; and they shall **afflict** them **four hundred years;** And also **that nation,** whom they **shall serve, will I judge:** and afterward **shall they come out with great substance."** (v.14) "And thou shalt go to thy fathers in **peace;** thou shalt be **buried** in a **good old age.** But in the **fourth generation** they shall come hither again: for the iniquity of the Amorites is not yet full."(Gen. 15:13-16)

This means that God would not bring forth the **seed child** until the **set time. Isaac** was not to be **born** until **Abraham** was **one hundred years old**. In the fullness of time, **Sarah** passed the **childbearing age** and **Abraham** also passed the **progenitor age;** He became **impotent.** Thus, God announced that he was ready to bless Abraham with a child by **Sarah**: "And **God said** unto **Abraham**, As for Sarai thy **wife**, thou shalt not call her name **Sarai,** but **Sarah** *shall* her name be. ¹⁶And I will bless her, and **give** thee a **son also** of **her:** yea, **I will bless her**, and she shall be a *mother* of **nations;** kings of people shall be of her." (Gen. 17:15-16—Kjv)

"Then **Abraham** fell upon his face, and **laughed**, and said in his **heart**, Shall a *child* be born unto him that is an **hundred years old**? And shall **Sarah, that is ninety years old, bear**? ¹⁸And Abraham said unto God, **O that Ishmael** might live before thee! And God said, **Sarah** thy wife shall bear thee **a son indeed;** and thou shalt call his name **Isaac**: and I will **establish my covenant** with him for an **everlasting covenant**, *and* with **his seed after him**…" ²¹But my covenant will I establish with **Isaac**, which **Sarah** shall bear unto thee at this **set time in the next year**." (Gen. 17:17-19, 21) The meaning of the Name **El-Shaddai** has to do with **nourishment**. God had to nourish **Abraham** and **Sarah** back to strength. They thought that Ishmael was to be the child of promise because of their age.

In the meantime, Genesis 18:9 tells us that **God** made another **visit** to **Abraham**: "And they said unto him, Where is **Sarah thy wife**? And he said, Behold, **in the tent**. ¹⁰And he said, I will **certainly return** unto thee according to the **time of life;** and, lo, **Sarah** thy wife **shall have a son.** And **Sarah heard** it in the tent door, which was behind him. Now **Abraham** and **Sarah** *were* old and **well stricken in age;** *and* it ceased to be with **Sarah** after the manner of women." (Vv. 9-11—Kjv)

¹²Therefore, **Sarah laughed within herself**, saying, After I am **waxed old shall I have pleasure,** my lord being **old also**? ¹³And the Lord said unto Abraham, Wherefore did **Sarah laugh**, saying, Shall I of a **surety** bear a **child**, which am **old**? ¹⁴Is any thing "**too hard**" for the Lord? At the 'time appointed' **I will return** unto thee, according to the **time of life**, and Sarah shall have a son." (Gen. 18:12-14—Kjv)

God had an appointed time for the birth of **Isaac**, and it had to be according to God's timing. This had to be **calculated** according to **400 years of affliction**, in order to bring them back to the **land of promise**.

Isaac was born according to the set time. He was named Isaac (*Hbr. Yischaq, meaning* laughter). Abraham was **now 100 years old**. He **lived 175 years** and **died** when **Isaac** was **75 years** old. **Jacob** was born when **Isaac** was **60 years old. Jacob** was **15 years old** when Abraham **died. Jacob** went down into **Egypt 115 years** later being **130 years old**. This being **215 years after Abraham** received the **promise at age 75**.

Israel **stayed** in **Egypt** for **215 years**. This is **equal to 430 years** of sojourning which **ended** on the **selfsame day they came out of Egypt**. The 400 years of affliction **began** when **Isaac** was **5 years old**. This being **30 years after** God **first** gave the **promise** to Abraham. **God began** reckoning the nation of Israel, from the time **Abraham** left his **father's house. God** considered **Abraham, Isaac**, and **Jacob as being a Nation. Ishmael** represented the **Nation of Egypt,** for **he was** an **Egyptian** (Gen. 21:9–Kjv).

Hence, the **Scriptures** said: "Now the **sojourning** of the children of Israel, who **dwelt in Egypt,** was **four hundred** and **thirty years**. [41] And it came to pass, at the **end** of the four hundred and thirty years, even **the selfsame day** it came to pass, that **all** the **hosts** of the Lord **went out from** the land of **Egypt**." (Exd. 12:40-41)

The background **context** of the name El-Shaddai is, that **God had to nourish Abram** and **Sarai** so that they may be **father** and **mother of many nations**. They needed him **at that time as** *El-shaddai*. This **name continued** through **Isaac** and **Jacob**.

EHE-YEH, ASHER, EHE-YEH
(Exd. 3:14)
I WILL BE THAT I WILL BE
AND NEVER CEASE TO BE THAT I AM.

This couldn't be explained any better than what **Dr. Adam Clark** wrote in his commentary: So **I quote** this passage from his **writing**:

"Exodus 3:14 [I Am That I Am] EHEYEH ASHER EHEYEH. These words have been variously understood. The *Vulgate translates EGO SUM QUI SUM*, I am who I am. The Septuagint, **I am He Who exists**. The Syriac, the **Persic,** and the **Chaldee** preserve the **original words without any gloss**. The Arabic paraphrases them, The Eternal, who passes not **away;** which is the **same interpretation given by Abul Farajius**, who also **preserves the original words**, and **gives the above** as their **interpretation**. The **Targum of Jonathan,** and the **Jerusalem Targum paraphrase** the words thus: "**He Who spake**, and the **world was;** He who spake, and **all things existed**" As the original words literally signify, **I will be what I will be**, some have supposed that God simply **designed to inform Moses**, that **what he** had been to his **fathers Abraham, Isaac,** and **Jacob,** he would be to him and the **Israelites;** and that he would **perform the promises** he had made to his **fathers**, by giving their descendants **the promised land**. It is difficult to put a meaning on the words; they seem intended to point out the **eternity** and **self-existence** of God" (Adam Clark, vol. 1 page 306).

Let us sum up this **name;** I am that I am, or *Ehe-Yeh-Asher-Ehe-Yeh*, simply describes God as the everlasting ONE, who exists from ETERNITY in the **past, present,** and the **future**. His existence does **not change**, though he reveals himself in other ways or characteristics. **He will be what he wants to be** and **never cease to be What or "Who He is"**. He was with **Abraham, Isaac,** and **Jacob**. He shall be with the nation of **Israel** in keeping **the promises** he made to **Abraham, Isaac** and **Jacob**. Hence, this brings us to the next name, **Jehovah.**

Jehovah (Yehovah)
(Exd. 6:3)

"And God spake unto Moses, and said unto him, *I Am The Lord*; And I appeared unto Abraham, unto Isaac, and unto Jacob, by the name of *God Almighty*, but by my name *Jehovah* was I not known to them." (Exd. 6:2, 3)

This name *Jehovah* has always been a highly debatable name as to what should be the correct pronunciation, and what is the true meaning of it? Before we deal with the true meaning of it, let us deal with the pronunciation of the name. How should we spell the name?

We must remember that in the Hebrew there are no vowels, but consonants, in the Hebrew alphabet. This does not aid us at all in the sounding of the phonetic' dialect. The sound of a word in the Hebrew was obtained through oral transmission. However, after a longtime the Massoretes gave vowel sounds to the Hebrew consonants. We must look at the four letter consonants that are contained in the name Jehovah. This is done in various ways that result in various syllables. These consonants are called in the Greek, Tetra-grammaton. Tetra meaning the four letter consonants found in the name Jehovah. The term grammaton mean letters in the Greek language.

JHVH

When determining the name Jehovah, the four letter consonants are made into syllables by taking three vowels and placing them between the letters. The vowels are, "E", "O", "A". They take the vowel "E", and place it between the consonants "J" and "H" and get the syllable (Je). They take the vowel "O", and place it between the letters "H" and "V" and get the syllable (Ho). They take the vowel "A", and place it between the letters "V" and "H" and get the syllable (VAH). This is how the name *Jehovah* is formed from the Hebrew four letter consonants. Some say that the Hebrew alphabet did not have a "J" in it, but rather a "Y". Therefore, the name should be pronounced with a "Y" instead of a "J". This results in the name being called *Yehovah*. This is true. The letter "J" is not a Hebrew original: But is a hybrid from another language.

YHWH

There are others, which say that the consonants that relate to the *Tetragrammaton* should be pronounced with the "Y" using only two syllables. This is done by taking the vowels "A", and "E" and placing them between the four letter consonants. This is done by taking the vowel "A", and placing it between the consonants "Y" and "H", and ending up with "YAH" as the first syllable. Then, taking the vowel "E", and placing it between the **consonants "W" and "H"**, and ending up with *"WEH"*. This then will cause the name to be pronounced with **two syllables** as *"YAH-WEH"*.

YHVH

The final approach that was taken is that the name should be **reflected without the "W" in the last syllables of** *Yahweh*, **because there was not a "W" in the Hebrew language, and only the "V" were used.** The *"W"* was formed by placing **two "V,Vs"** together, which were usually pronounced as the **same as "U". (W)** Medieval Scribes *"V V"*, 1,000 A.D., also written *"UU"*, became known as **double "U"**. The Hebrew did **not reflect a "W" in its alphabet**, so we could not use the **syllable "WEH"**, but more so the **syllable "VAH" or "VEH"**. The term Jehovah has the **syllable "Vah"**. This leans **more to the "V"**, rather **than the "W"**. For this reason, I think that the **most ancient way of pronouncing the** *Tetragrammaton*, **would be** *YAHVEH*.

Having dealt with the **pronunciation** of the name, let's deal with the **meaning**. The **meaning** is the **most important** of them all. Sometimes, the **sound** of a name changes when it is translated into another language. It is next to impossible **to know** the **exact** pronunciation of a **name** as we have **noticed** in the **aforementioned** discussion, but **a meaning** can be **obtained** from the use of the **context**.

The **meanings** of the **names** of **God** have to do with **what He does**. They are **not** primarily **what He** is called. He is **named** for what **He does** or **has done**, and what **He shall do**. When the **Scriptures** say that **Abraham, Isaac,** and **Jacob** did not know God as Jehovah, it does **not mean** that they did **not know** the **name** Jehovah. They did not know **Him** in the **fullness** of the **meaning** of that **name**.

The name **Jehovah** relates to the **covenant**. Jehovah **means: 'He who keeps His 'Covenant'** and **'promises'.** The promise was made to **Abraham, Isaac,** and **Jacob** that He would give to them the land of **promise**. During the **lifetime** of these **patriarchs, God did not** give them the **land** of promise. He gave them **nourishment as** *El-Shaddai,* but He did not give them the **promise land**. Abraham called the **name** Jehovah, when he **named** the place **Jehovah-jireh**. This shows the **title Jehovah was known**, but not the meaning **realized**. This is the reason **why God** said they did **not know Him as** Jehovah. God is **nothing to you** until **He performs a certain act** toward **you**.

The **time is ripe** and the **time has come** that the land that **Abraham, Isaac,** and **Jacob** were strangers is now ready to become the **children of Israel,** the natural **seed's inheritance. Jehovah** is keeping **His promises. This name** must **continuously** be **used until** all the **land** is **occupied** that Jehovah **promised to Israel. Jehovah kept His covenant,** but **Israel did not keep theirs.** The **Scriptures** said, this from the mouth of *Jehou-shua* (Jehovah-shua).

"And, behold, this day I *am* going the way of **all the earth:** and ye know in all **your hearts** and in **all your souls,** that **not one thing hath failed** of all the good things which the LORD your God spake **concerning you;** all are come to pass unto **you;** And not one thing hath failed thereof. ¹⁵Therefore it shall come to pass, that as all **good things** are come **upon you,** which the LORD your **God promised you;** so shall the LORD BRING UPON YOU ALL EVIL THINGS, UNTIL He have destroyed you from off this good land which the LORD your God hath given you." (Josh. 23:14, 15)

Jehovah brought Israel out of Egypt **not a day late according to His promise. Note the miraculous deliverance:** ⁴⁰"Now the sojourning of the children of Israel, (who dwelt in Egypt), was four hundred and thirty years. ⁴¹And it came to pass at the end of the FOUR HUNDRED AND THIRTY YEARS, EVEN THE SELFSAME DAY IT CAME TO PASS, THAT ALL THE HOSTS OF THE LORD went out **from** the land of Egypt." (Exd. 12:40)

In **Genesis chapter fifteen** we find the promise that Jehovah made to Abraham, that in the **fourth generation** He would **bring them out with great substance.**

"And He said unto **Abram** Know of **a surety** that thy seed shall be **a stranger** in a land that is **not** theirs, (and shall **serve them;** and they shall afflict them) **four hundred years;** And also that nation, whom they shall serve, will **I judge:** and afterward shall they **come out with great substance.** ¹⁵And thou shalt **go to thy fathers in peace;** thou shalt be **buried** in a good **old age.** ¹⁶But in the **fourth generation** they shall come hither again: for the iniquity of the Amorites is not yet full." (Gen. 15:13-16–KJV)

Jacob went down into **Egypt** when the **generation** of **Levi was named.** While Levi was in Egypt, he had a son by the name of **Kohath,** and Kohath begot **Amram,** and **Amram** begot **Moses.** Counting from **Levi to Moses,** we get **four generations.** The emphatic thing about this is, that Jehovah used the **fourth** generation, **namely, Moses,** to bring Israel out of Egypt. **Moses'** name means drawn forth (1 Chron 6:1-3).

Israel was brought into the **land of promise,** but they **did not keep** the **covenant** Jehovah made with them. **Carefully note the disobedience:** "And **an angel of the LORD** came up from Gilgal to Bochim, and said, I made you to go up out of Egypt, and **have brought you** unto the land which **I sware unto your fathers;** and I said, I will never break **my covenant** with you. ²And ye shall make no **league** with the **inhabitants** of this **land;** ye shall throw down their **altars:** but ye have **not obeyed my voice:** why have ye done this? ³Wherefore I also said, I will not drive them out from before **you;** but they shall be *as thorns* in **your sides,** and their **gods** shall be **a snare** unto **you.**" (Judg. 2:1-3–KJV)

Interestingly enough, this **disobedience** does **not** destroy the **promises** of **Jehovah;** neither does it negate **His name.** The name **Jehovah** must still be **exercised** until all the land is occupied. Jehovah is working on **Israel's** salvation to bring them back into **covenant** relationship. **Nevertheless, Note the faithfulness** of God: "Behold, the days come, saith the LORD, THAT I WILL MAKE A NEW COVENANT WITH THE HOUSE OF ISRAEL, and with the **house of Judah: Not** according to the **covenant** that I made with their fathers in the day *that* I took **them by the hand** to bring them out of the land of **Egypt;** which **My covenant** they **brake,** although I was **an husband** unto them, saith the LORD: (*Jehovah*)." (Jer. 31:31)

The full meaning of the Name of **Jehovah** is, HE WHO KEEPS HIS COVENANT. This name Jehovah is still the name to be used to **recognize** what **Jehovah** is **doing**. It is **associated** with many other **additives** while holding the root word JEHOVAH, and some of its consonants. The whole **purpose** of Jehovah is to **save Israel,** and to bring them back into the land wherewith **He** made a **covenant** with ABRAHAM, ISAAC, AND JACOB.

The **Book of Isaiah** gives the full range of the **salvation of Jehovah.** The mere **meaning** of the **name** of Isaiah is THE SALVATION OF JEHOVAH. *In the Hebrew it is, YESHA YAH, The Salvation of Jehovah. (Yahveh Salvation Yahveh)* Isaiah's writings are directed to the **restoration** of **Judah** and **Israel. Note Isaiah's vision as follows:**

"The **vision of Isaiah** the son of Amoz, which **he saw** concerning **Judah** and **Jerusalem** in the days of **Uzziah, Jotham, Ahaz,** and **Hezekiah, kings** of **Judah.** "**Hear, O heavens,** and **give ear, O earth: for the** LORD **hath spoken**, I have **nourished** and brought up children, and they have **rebelled** against **Me.** ³The **ox** knoweth **his owner,** and the **ass his master's crib:** *but* **Israel** doth **not know, My People** doth **not consider.** ⁴Ah **sinful** nation, a people laden with **iniquity**, a **seed** of **evildoers,** children that are **corrupters:** they have **forsaken** the LORD, (Jehovah), they have **provoked** the HOLY ONE **of Israel** unto anger, they are gone away backward." (Isa. 1:1-4—KJV)

I **believe the focus point is found in Isaiah, chapter twelve:** "And in that day thou shalt say, **O** LORD, (Jehovah), I will **praise thee:** though Thou wast angry with me, Thine anger is turned away, and Thou **comfortedst** me. ²Behold, GOD (El) is my **salvation (El-Shua);** I will **trust,** and **not be afraid:** for The LORD JEHOVAH (Yah-Jehovah) is my **strength** and my **song;** he also is **become my salvation."** (*Jehosua-Jesus*) (vv. 1, 2)

Jehovah will save them. He will **recover Israel.** He remains with the **name** Jehovah through which He will save them. Israel is His witness. **He saith:** ¹⁰"Ye are **My witnesses,** saith the LORD, (*Jehovah*), and **My Servant** whom **I have chosen:** that ye may **know** and **believe Me,** and **understand** that I *am* **He: before Me there was no GOD** (El), **formed,** neither shall there **be after Me.** ¹¹I, even I, am the LORD; and **beside me** *there* is **no saviour."** (Isa. 43:10, 11—KJV)

JEHOVAH ALONE IS SAVIOUR. "**The voice** of him that crieth in the wilderness, prepare ye the way of the LORD, (Jehovah), **make straight** in the **desert a highway** for **our God.** ⁴Every **valley** shall be **exalted,** and **every mountain** and **hill** shall be **made low:** and the **crooked shall be made straight,** and the **rough** places **plain:** ⁵And the **glory of the** LORD **shall be revealed,** and all flesh shall see it **together:** for the **mouth** of the LORD (Jehovah), hath **spoken it."** (Isa. 40:3-4)

Jehovah is destined to come himself and **save.** This is mention again in Isaiah chapter Forty. ⁹"O Zion, that bringest good tidings, get thee up into the **high mountain; O Jerusalem,** that **bringest good tidings,** lift up thy **voice** with **strength;** lift it up, be **not afraid;** say unto the cities of Judah, **Behold your God!** ¹⁰Behold, the LORD GOD (*Adonai Jehovah*), **will come with strong** *hand,* and **His arm** shall **rule for Him:** behold, **his reward is with Him,** and His work before Him." (Isa. 40:9, 10)

The person who comes to **save** us must **bear** the **name** and person of **Jehovah,** or he **cannot** be the **saviour.** This is why the **Scriptures** said, in Matthew 1:21-23; Isaiah 7:14 concerning the **saviour** that was **to be born:** [21]"And she shall **bring forth a Son,** and thou shalt call **His name Jesus: (*Jehovah Shua*),** for he shall save his people **from their sins."** [22]Now all this **was done,** that it might be fulfilled which was **spoken** of the LORD by the **prophet** saying, [23] "Behold, **a virgin** shall be with child, and shall bring forth a Son, and they shall call His **name, Emmanuel,** which being interpreted is, **God with us."**

The child that was to be born is called **Jehovah** saves. JESUS **is Jehovah,** who came in the **flesh** to save his people from their **sins.** According to the gospel of St.Luke 2:11, "For unto you is born this day in the city of David a **Saviour, (shua),** which is **Christ the LORD."** (*Meshia Jehovah*) **Christ is Jehovah.** Jehovah is Christ. He is the **personal** manifestation of Jehovah. We must **confess** that Jesus is Jehovah (1 Cor. 12:3).

Let me show by the **Scriptures** that **Jesus is Jehovah,** who came into the world. There are **two** great passages of Scripture found in Isaiah 40:3 and St. John 1:19-29, which verify this truth. **Note the following process of determining** this **great truth:**

Isaiah 40:3, writes: "The **voice** of him that **crieth** in the wilderness, Prepare ye **the way** of the LORD, (*Jehovah*) make **straight** in the desert a **highway for our God** (*Elohim*)."

We must **compare** this Scripture with St. John 1:19-29, and see in the **context Who** this Scripture is **talking about.** [19]"And this is the record of John, when the **Jews** sent **priests** and **Levites** from Jerusalem to ask him, **Who art thou?** [20]And he **confessed,** and **denied not;** but confessed, **I am not the Christ.** [21]And they asked him, **What then?** Art thou **Elias?** And he saith, **I am not,** Art thou that **prophet?** And he answered, **No.** [22]Then said they unto him, **Who art thou?** That we may give an **answer** to them that sent us. **What** sayest thou of **thyself?** [23]He said, **I am the voice** of one crying in the **wilderness, Make straight the way** of the LORD, (Jehovah), as said the prophet **Esaias."** (v. 23)

"And they which were sent were of the **Pharisees.** [25]And they asked him, and said unto him, **Why baptizest** thou then, if thou be not that **Christ,** nor **Elias,** neither that **prophet?** [26]**John** answered them, saying, I baptize **with water:** but there standeth **One** among you, whom **ye know not;** [27]**He it is,** Who coming **after** me is **preferred** before me, Whose **shoe's latchet** I am **not worthy** to unloose." These things were done in Bethabara **beyond Jordan,** where John was baptizing."

The next day John seeth Jesus coming unto him, and saith, **Behold the Lamb of God,** which taketh away the **sin of the world.** [30]This is He of Whom I said, **After** me cometh a **Man** which is preferred **before me:** for He was before me." (St. John 1:19-30) **These two passages declare that Jehovah was coming:** the **voice** in the wilderness prepares a way for him. John **confessed** that he was **that voice crying** in the **wilderness.** Jesus was the LORD, (*Jehovah*) which came after him, though he was before Him.

247

This shows that the **name of Jesus in the Hebrew is Jehovah saves.** Everyone must **confess** that Jesus **is Jehovah:** Who came in **the body,** or be **classified** as an **Anti-Christ.** It is the **spirit of Anti-Christ,** who **does not** give Jesus the full **credential;** that He is the **God of the Old Testament,** who came in the **flesh,** into the world. **Note the following Scriptures carefully:**

"Beloved, **believe not every spirit,** but **try** the spirits, whether they are of **God:** because many **false prophets** are gone out into the world. ²Hereby **know ye the Spirit** of **God:** Every spirit that confesseth that **Jesus Christ is come in the flesh** is of **God:** ³And every spirit that **confesseth not** that **Jesus Christ** is come in **the flesh** is **not of God:** and this is that *spirit* of **anti-Christ,** whereof ye have heard that it should **come;** and even now **already is it in the world.**" (1 John 4:1-3—Kjv)

"Wherefore God also hath **highly exalted Him,** and given Him **a name** which is **above every name:** ¹⁰That at the **name of Jesus** (*Jehovah-Shua*) every knee should bow, of things in **heaven,** and things in **earth,** and **things under the earth;** And that **every tongue** should confess that **Jesus Christ is** Lord (*Jehovah the Messiah*), to the glory of God the Father." (Phil. 2:9-11)

This Scripture is the quotation of Jehovah from the Old Testament. "Tell ye, and bring *them* **near;** yea, let them take counsel **together:** who hath declared this from ancient time? *who* hath told it from that time? have not I the Lord (Jehovah)? and *there is* no God else beside **Me;** a just God and **Saviour;** *there* **is none beside Me.** ²²Look **unto Me,** and be ye saved, all the ends of the **earth: for I** *am* God, and *there* **is none else.** ²³I have sworn by **Myself,** the **Word** is gone out **of My mouth in righteousness,** and shall not **return,** That **unto Me** every **knee** shall **bow, every tongue** shall **swear.** ²⁴Surely, shall one say in the Lord (*Jehovah*) have **I righteousness** and **strength:** even to Him shall men **come;** and all that are incensed against Him shall be ashamed. In the Lord (Jehovah), shall **all seed of Israel** be justified, and **shall glory.**" (Isa. 45:21-25)

The Scriptures in the New Testament, Philippians 2:9; Romans 14:11, refer to **Jesus** (*Jehovah-save*). Both the **Jews** and **Gentiles** must acknowledge that **Jesus is Jehovah. Jesus** is Jehovah from **heaven.**

The underlying reason **Israel** rejected **Jesus** is because he did not appear like the **Old Testament** Jehovah that appeared unto Abraham in a fleshly body (Genesis 17:1; 18:1). **Jehovah,** from time to time, appeared in **human form.** The **Messiah** was to come as Jehovah in a **body.** That is the reason He was called **Jesus** or Jehovah the **Saviour** (St. Luke 2:11).

In fact, Matthew 23:39 says, **Israel** will **not see** him **again** until they **say that Jesus is the** Lord. Thus, the Scriptures said, "For I say unto you, Ye shall **not see Me henceforth,** till ye shall say, **Blessed is He** that cometh in the Name Of The Lord **(Jehovah)."** St. John 5:43, **Jesus said,** "I am **come in my father's name,** (*Jehovah*), and you **received me not.** If another will come in his own name, him you will receive."

JEHOVAH JIREH
GENESIS 22:14 - - KJV
(THE LORD WILL PROVIDE)

We will now examine the various **compounds** that are **associated** with **Jehovah's** name. [14]"And Abraham called the **name** of that place **Jehovah-Jireh:** as it is said *to* this day, In the **mount** of the LORD, (*Jehovah*), it shall be seen." *Yehovah-yireh,* or as it is said to this day *"behar Yehovah yerach",* on this **mount** the LORD **shall be seen.**

This **compound** goes far **beyond** the phrase the LORD **will provide.** This takes us back to **verse seven** when Isaac asked, "Behold the **fire** and the **wood:** but where is the **Lamb for a burnt-offering?"** [8]And Abraham said, My son, **God will provide himself a lamb** for a **burnt-offering:** so they went both of them together." (Gen. 22:7, 8–KJV) *Elohim yireh,* **God will provide.**

JEHOVAH ROPHEKA
(GOD WHO HEALS)
(Exd. 15:26)

"And said, If thou wilt diligently hearken to **the voice** of the LORD THY GOD, and wilt do that which is right **in his sight,** and wilt give ear to his commandments, and keep all his statutes, I will put none of these **diseases upon thee,** which I have brought upon the **Egyptians:** for I am the Lord **that healeth thee."** (Ex. 15:26–KJV)

There are three conditions that Israel **must meet** to have this promise Number: They must hearken to **the voice** of the LORD their God. God knows what's best for you. God knows that long-established **practices** regulate our social lives. Sometimes our **habits** and **diet** have an effect on our well being. Much of our conditions are derived from one's ancestors' **cultural practices** that is an **ill fate** to **our health.** Israel just had been brought out of Egypt, but **Egypt must be** brought **out of them.** They must acknowledge the LORD as their God (*Elohim/ Creator*).

They must acknowledge the words of Jehovah as being the revelations of truth. This truth will **heal** and **keep them healed.** "He sent his **Word** and healed them, and delivered *them* from their destructions."(Psalm 107:20–KJV)

Psalm 12:6 says, The words of the LORD *are* **pure words: They will purify seven times,** and **heal all.** *"My son, forget not my law; but let thine heart keep my commandments: For length of days, and long life, and peace shall they add to thee...[8]It shall be health to thy navel, and marrow to thy bones."*(Pro. 3:1-2, 8–KJV) Your blood supply shall be rich with nutrients.

They must continue to adorn themselves in a holy life, if they do so, God would be their constant healer. [22]"For I spake not unto your fathers, nor commanded them in the day that I brought them out of the land of Egypt, concerning **burnt offerings** or **sacrifices:** [23]*But this thing commanded I them, saying, Obey my voice, and* I will be **your**

God, and ye shall be **my people:** and **walk** ye in all the ways that I have commanded you, that it may be well unto you." ((Jer. 7:22, 23–KJV)

JEHOVAH NISSI
THE LORD MY BANNER (HE WILL BE YOUR WARRIOR)
(Exd. 17:15, 16)

"And Moses built an **altar,** and called the name of it JEHOVAH NISSI: For he said, Because the LORD hath sworn *that* the LORD *will have* WAR with Amalek from generation to generation." (Ex. 17:15–KJV)

This **name** was used by **God,** because of His declaration of **war against Amalek,** the enemy of **Israel.** When **Jehovah** is our NISSI, there is **no need to fight,** for **Jehovah** will **fight for us.** [15]"And he said, Hearken ye, all Judah, and ye inhabitants of Jerusalem, and thou king **Jehoshaphat,** Thus saith the LORD unto you, **Be not afraid** nor **dismayed** by reason of this great **multitude;** for the **battle is not yours,** but **God's."** [16]To morrow go ye down against them: behold, they come up by the cliff of **ziz;** and ye shall find them at the end of the brook, before the wilderness of Jeruel. [17]*Ye Shall Not Need To Fight In This Batle: Set Yourselves, Stand Ye Still, And See The Salvation Of The Lord* With You, **O Judah** and **Jerusalem: fear not,** nor be **dismayed;** to morrow go out against them: for the LORD *Will* be with you." (2 Chron. 20:15-17) For an **outstanding example,** (Compare Exd. 15:3–KJV).

(JEHOVAH MEDKADISKIM)
(Exd. 31:13)
(THE LORD THAT SANCTIFIES)

"Speak thou also unto the children of **Israel,** saying, Verily **My Sabbaths** ye shall **keep:** for it is **a sign** between **Me** and **you** throughout your **generations;** that ye may **know** that I am the LORD that doth **sanctify** you." (Exd. 31:13)

Medkadiskim (Hebrew qudash, kaw-dash') To set aside, **to make holy.** To be used **only for the LORD.** As the **Sabbaths** were to be kept **holy:** He that is sanctified must be **kept holy.** The **underlying** point **is,** I have **prepared** you for myself.

Jehovah Medkadiskim is the name of sanctification. It is demonstrated by the use of the **Sabbath,** which was set **apart** from the other **days** of the week. It was to be **observed** to **note** that **Israel** was set apart from the rest of **the nations.** Hence, the **meaning** of sanctification is **to be set apart** for the **master's use.** Israel became God's **peculiar** treasure. Special commandments were given to **reflect** that standing. More importantly, **note God's chosen treasure as follows:**

*"Ye are **the children** of the LORD **your God:** ye shall **not cut yourselves,** nor make any baldness between your eyes for the dead. For thou art an holy people unto the LORD*

thy God, and the L<small>ORD</small> *hath chosen thee to be a peculiar people unto Himself, above all the nations that are upon the earth."* (Deu. 14:1-2–K<small>JV</small>)

I<small>SRAEL</small> W<small>AS</small> N<small>OT</small> S<small>ANCTIFIED</small> U<small>NTIL</small> T<small>HE</small> **LORD** C<small>LEANED</small> T<small>HEM</small> U<small>P</small> F<small>OR</small> H<small>IMSELF</small>.

"Now **when I passed by** thee, and **looked upon thee**, behold, thy time was the time of **love;** and I spread **My skirt over** thee, and **covered** thy **nakedness:** yea, I sware unto thee, and **entered** into **a covenant** with thee, saith the Lord God, and thou becamest mine." (v. 8)

"Then washed **I thee with water;** yea, I thoroughly **washed away thy blood from thee,** and I **anointed thee with oil.** ¹⁰I clothed thee also with **broidered** work, and shod thee with **badgers' skin,** and I girded thee about with **fine linen,** and I **covered thee with silk."** (Eze. 16:8-10–K<small>JV</small>)

God does this same thing for his church. He **sanctifies** it. "Husbands, **love** your wives, even as **Christ** also **loved** the **church,** and gave **Himself for it;** That He might **sanctify** and **cleanse it** with the washing of water by the Word." (Eph. 5:25, 26)

1 Corinthians 6:11 Paul writes: "And such were **some of you:** but ye are **washed,** but ye are **sanctified,** but ye are **justified** in the name of the Lord Jesus, and by the Spirit of our God."

Israel became God's wife. She was set **apart** for Him. The same thing is with the church. "But ye are a **chosen generation,** a royal **priesthood,** an **holy** nation, a **peculiar people;** that ye should show forth the **praises** of Him Who hath called you out of **darkness** into **His marvelous light:** Which in time past were **not a people,** but are now the people of **God:** which had **not obtained mercy,** but now have obtained mercy." (1 Pet. 2:9, 10)

"If a **man** therefore **purge** himself **from these,** he **shall be** a **vessel unto** honour, **sanctified,** and **meet** for the **Master's use,** and **prepared** unto every **good work."** (2 Tim. 2:21)

Sanctification is not just a state of holiness, but rather a **separation** for the **master's use.**

JEHOVAH SHALOM
(JUDGES 6:24)
"THE LORD WILL SEND PEACE"

"Then Gideon built an altar there unto the LORD, and called it Jehovah-**shalom:** unto this day it is yet in Ophrah of the Abiezrites." (Judg. 6:24) **The Jehovah-shalom** means, **God will send peace: Or peace be unto you from the Lord.** This greeting is so common in that part of the world. This **term Shalom** carries with it a **profound** meaning. It goes **beyond the point** of greetings, and **lends** more to **the wisher** of the greeting. That is; May it be well with your family, may it be well with thee, and

251

may it be well with thy business. If none of those **provisions** were **present** with the person who was being greeted, the **greeter** was **responsible** for **making** those things to come to **pass that day.**

It is prompted from the custom of doing some good deeds for a person that day. It is said that if a person had **not done any good deeds** for **anyone that day**, he would go out into the streets and say to a **passer-by:** Ho! Such an one, have you had your **provision for the day?** If not, come in and have **supper with me.** For it is now at **the end of the day,** and I have not had the occasion **to do any good deeds** for anyone this day.

Whenever anyone came to **the home** of a person, **the owner** felt **obligated** to **show kindness** unto him. This is the **reason** why **Abraham entertained** the **three visitors** who came to him in **Genesis, Chapter eighteen. Note the following remarkable episode:**

"And the LORD appeared unto him in the plains of **Mamre:** And he sat in the tent **door** in the **heat of the day;** and he lift up his eyes and looked, and, lo, **three men** stood **by him:** and when he saw them, he ran to **meet them** from the tent door, and bowed himself toward the ground, (v.2) And said, My Lord, if now **I have found favour** in **thy sight,** pass not away, I pray thee, from thy **servant:** Let a little water, I pray you, be fetched, and **wash your feet,** and **rest** yourselves **under the tree:** (v.4) And I will fetch a morsel of **bread,** and **comfort** ye your **hearts;** after that ye shall pass **on:** for therefore are ye come to your servant. And they said, So do, as thou hast said." (See Genesis 18:1-5; 19:1-3)

This is the **example** of how **the greeting of shalom** proceeds. **Strangers** were looked upon as the **possibility** of being **an angel.** In this case, these men were **heavenly visitors,** who **came by.** "Be not **forgetful** to entertain **strangers:** for thereby some have entertained **angels** unawares."(Heb. 13:2)

It is said, that once in an **Arab village,** a young man **killed a person. While the witnesses** ran to apprehend him, **he ran into a tent for safety. The owner** of the tent allowed him to come in, but would **not allow** the pursuers to come in. He felt **obligated** to **protect** whoever came into his **tent:** For **he was a stranger** who came **in.** When he **refused to allow** the pursuers to come in, they said unto **him:** Sir, you don't understand, this **person** just **killed a man. The man** that was killed was **your son!** He said, I would now take this person who **killed** my son to **become my son! This is** what is **meant** by the term **Shalom!**

JEHOVAH TSIDKENU
(THE LORD OUR RIGHTEOUSNESS)
(Jeremiah 23:6)

In his days **Judah** shall be **saved,** and Israel shall dwell **safely;** and this *is* His name whereby He shall be called, "THE LORD OUR RIGHTEOUSNESS." (v. 6)

This has to do with the state of holiness. This has to do with justification. We that were sinners have been **made righteous**. This was presented **first to Israel** and then to the **Gentiles**. Israel **rejected** the righteousness of God and God turned to the **Gentiles.**

This righteousness was **given unto us** by the act of God **without** meritorious work on **our part**. We became righteous in a **justified** manner. One man put us into sin, and **one** man took us out of sin. We became the "**righteousness of God**" in Christ Jesus. In Adam, **all die**. In Christ, all are made **alive** (Rom. 1:16, 17; 5:14; 6:17).

The unfortunate thing about the children of Israel is that they **sought** to be **righteous** through **keeping the law**. The **opportunity was given them** to obtain righteousness **by the law**, but **they did not** obtain it. Deuteronomy 6:25 says, "And it shall be **our righteousness**, if we **observe to do all** these commandments before the LORD our God, as He hath commanded us."

Israel failed to exemplify the righteousness of God: Romans 3:20 tells us, "Therefore by the **deeds of the law** there shall **no flesh** be **justified** in **His sight:** for by the **law is the knowledge of sin**. But now the righteousness of God **without** the law is **manifested,** being witnessed by the law and the **prophets;** Even the righteousness of God *which* is by **faith of Jesus Christ** unto all and upon **all them** that **believe:** for there is **no difference:** For **all have sinned,** and **come short** of the **glory of God;**" (Romans 3:21-23)

Being justified freely by His grace through the redemption that is in Christ Jesus: Whom God hath set forth to be a propitiation through faith in His blood, to declare His righteousness for the remission of sins that are past, through the forbearance of God; To declare, I say, at this time **His righteousness:** that He might be just, and the justifier of him which believeth in Jesus." (v. 26)

The Jews continuously **rejected the Gospel of God,** which **contains** the **righteousness** of God. **Paul** speaks about them by **saying:** "Brethren, my heart's **desire** and **prayer** to God for **Israel** is, that **they might be saved**. For I bear them record that they have a **zeal** of God, but **not** according to **knowledge**. For they being ignorant of God's **righteousness,** and going about to **establish** their **own** righteousness, have **not** submitted themselves unto the **righteousness** of God. For **Christ** is the **end** of **the law** for righteousness to **every one that believeth.**" (Rom. 10:1-4)

The entire **Book of Romans** is the **Hermeneutical** approach to the study of the **righteousness of God.** This then, is the **teaching** of the **Go**

JEHOVAH SHAMMAH
(THE LORD IS THERE)

"It was round about **eighteen thousand measures:** and the **name of the city** from that day shall be, **The LORD is there.**" (Ezekiel 48:35) This **name** simply **means** the LORD (Jehovah) **is there.** It is a city described by **Ezekiel.** By the way, of **social** application, **Jehovah** is a **present help** in trouble.

JEHOVAH ELYON

"I will praise the LORD according to **His righteousness:** and will sing **praise** to the name of the LORD MOST HIGH." (Psalm 7:17)

This name signifies a call to **praise** the **most high God, a time** for **jubilant praises to the Lord** for His **excellent greatness.** "I will bless the Lord at **all times:** his **praise** shall continually **be** in **my mouth.** My **soul** shall make her **boast** in the LORD: the **humble shall hear** thereof, and be **glad.** O **magnify** the LORD with me, and let us exalt **His name** together." (Psalm 34:1-3—KJV)

JEHOVAH ROI
THE LORD IS MY SHEPHERD
(Psalm 23:1)

This **name comforts** the soul. It shows the **relationship of Jehovah** as a **shepherd** attending his flock. Taken from the 23rd Psalm, as presented by David, who had **experience** in shepherding his **flock.** There are various renderings of **relationships** in the following Psalm:

1. The Lord **is my shepherd** (*Jehovah Jared*).
2. He maketh me to lie down in **green pastures** (*Jehovah-jireh*).
3. He leadeth me beside the **still waters** (*Jehovah shalom*).
4. He **restoreth** my soul (*Jehovah Rophekah*).
5. He leadeth me in the **paths** of **righteousnes**s for His name's sake (*Jehovah Zidkenue*).
6. Yea, though I walk through the valley of the **shadow of death,** I will fear no evil: for thou art **with me** (*Jehovah Shammah*).
7. Thy rod and Thy staff they **comfort me** (Jehovah Shalom).
8. Thou **preparest a table** before me in the presence of mine enemies (*Jehovah Nissi*).
9. Thou anointest my head with oil; my **cup runneth over** (*Jehovah Jireh*).
10. Surely, goodness and mercy shall **follow me all the days** of my life (*Jehovah Jireh*).
11. And **I will dwell** in the house of the LORD: (*Beth- El*).
12. **Forever** (*El-Olam*).

ADON/ADONAI/ADONIM

These **three names** have to do with **God ruling** over **various ones:** His LORDSHIP.

ADOM, ADONAI
(Gen. 18:3-KJV)

This is **God** who rules over others. God is **the ruler** of the earth. "God is the **Judge:** He putteth down one, and sitteth up another." (Psalm 75:7) "...The **heavens do rule"** (Daniel 4:26).

ADONIM

God as Adonim, rules over His own. This is God's special relationship with **His people.** It is the **plural form** of the name Adon. Adon is **ruler,** but Adonim is ruler over **his own.** These names **contrasted are:** Adon is Lord as **overlord,** or **ruler. Adonai** is the Lord **as blesser,** and Adonim as **the Lord who rules** his own.

NAME OF BOOKS

There are very **interesting** accounts realized when we **study** the books of the Bible. Some of the **names** suggest the **meaning** of the book. The same is **true** as it relates to **persons** that are **named** in the Bible.

The **Bible** itself has a meaning from a **connotation** rather than a denotation. What I mean by this is, the usage of the name bible is derived primarily from which the bible is associated. In other words, the **Bible** is so named or famed because it was associated with the **biblus plant** in the port of **Syria.** The **leaves of the biblus** plant were used to write on. This was not restricted for the bible only, but also for other books and writings. Because the **Bible** was the book most written on the biblus plant it became **synonymous** with the **plant** that is called biblus.

Now we have the transliteration of the word **biblus** for Bible, meaning the **Book,** because of the connotation associated with the plant on which it was written. Now the Bible is the book made from the collections of other books into one harmonious book. **Note, in particular, the Book: "Seek** ye out of **the book** of the LORD, and **read:** no one of these shall **fail, none** shall **want her mate:** for My **mouth** it hath commanded, and His **Sprit** it hath **gathered** them." (Isaiah 34:16)

GENESIS
(Gen. 1:1–KJV)

This book is named because of the **message given in its composition**. The name **Genesis is taken from the Greek term** *"Genaeo,"* meaning generation. There are **twelve generations noted in the Book of Genesis**. These terms are realized when the Scriptures say, **"These are the Generations"** starting with the **Generations** of the **heavens** and **the earth:** (Genesis 2:4). These are the Generations of **Adam,** (Genesis 5:1-KJV). These are the **Generations of Noah**, These are the **Generations** of the **Sons of Noah,** (Genesis 10:1) Etc. Therefore, when the term Generation is **continuously** mentioned, it corresponds with the **meaning** of the **name** of the **book**. This is found **throughout the Book of Genesis** when it is **rightly divided**.

EXODUS
(GREEK EX-HOUS-DUS: TO GO OUT)

This **name** is given by the Septuagint to suggest the **going out of Egypt**. The **Hebrew** name is not so, but denotes more of the **contents** of the **book**. Hence, "The book of names," for it starts out with the names of the **sons of Jacob** as they go down into **Egypt**. In addition, this book **reveals** various **names** of God as follows: Eh yeh Asher-Eh-yeh, (Exodus 3:14), **El-shaddai),** (Exodus 6:3), **Jehovah,** (Exodus 6:3), **Jehovah Ropheka,** (Exodus 15:14), **Jehovah Nissi,** (Exodus 17:15), and **Jehovah Medkadiskem** (Ex. 31:13).

(LEVITICUS)
(JOINED UNTO)

The **root meaning** of this name is joining unto (Gen. 29:34). The significant part of this is that this book **establishes the Levitical priesthood**. This priesthood joined God and Israel together by **sacrifices**. This established the atmosphere of **worship**. Hence, the Hebrew meaning is: (vayyikra) called contained in the first sentence. This gives a **summoning to worship**, but only through **blood sacrifices**.

NUMBERS

This name is primarily rendered by the **Greek** translators because of the **two numberings** carried on in this book. However, the Hebrew **meaning is:** Be midd-bar, in the wilderness, because it records what took place there.

DEUTERONOMY
(REHEARSAL OF THE LAW)
(HEBREW HAD E BARIM THE WORDS)

THIS IS PRIMARILY THE 'MEMOIRS' OF MOSES. THE KEY WORD IS REMEMBER.

JOSHUA
(HEBREW: JEHOVAH SAVES; GREEK JESUS/JEHOVAH SAVES)

JOB
HEBREW IYYOB)
MEANING: AFFLICTED
THIS BOOK POINTS MORE TO THE END OF SUFFERING (JAMES 5:11).

PSALMS
(GREEK PSALMOI SONGS)
(HEBREW TEHILLIM, MEANING PRAISES)
(THE ROOT WORD IS HALAL, TO MAKE A JUBILANT SOUND)

ISAIAH HBR. YESHA-YAH
(Meaning the **salvation** of Yahveh)

(JEREMIAH Heb. Y'IRMEYAHA)
Meaning, **He who Jehovah raises** up

(EZEKIEL Heb. YE HAZZEK-EL)
(Meaning, **El strengthens**)

(DANIEL Heb. DANI-EL)
(Dani means Judge, El is God)

This is demonstrated throughout the **book of Daniel**. The time will not suffice to continue in all of **the books** of **the Bible**.

PERSONAL NAMES

ADAM, HEB. ADAMAH
(MEANING, RED EARTH)

ELIJAH HEB. ELI YAH
(MEANING, MY GOD IS YAHVEH)

ELISHA, HEB. ELI SHUA
(MEANING, MY GOD IS SAVIOR)

NAMES OF GOD IN THE NEW TESTAMENT

The New Testament was written in the **Greek** Language. It does not always give the **Hebrew flavor** that is so relevant in the Old Testament. The **Old Testament** language **derives** from **God** Himself, while the **New Testament** language **originates** from **mankind.** Therefore, the great force given in the **Hebrew** is not as **BOLD,** in the Greek. The **Hebrew has distinctive usage**, especially in the **various names** of God. **This is also true** in the various **translations** of the **Bible, both** in reference to the **Hebrew** and in reference to the **Greek**. Let's **examine** this in the various titles given to God or **His names.**

GOD

The usage of the Name *GOD,* has more or less generalized God as being someone who is **divine** or a **person of deity**. So the term is used not to denote any **distinctive** characteristic, but rather to show **a supreme being**. For that reason, much force and **meanings** are **lost;** or are **not even recognized**.

In **Hebrew**, the Name God is ELOHIM. This shows God as **Creator**. While in Greek, the **Name** God, is **Theos**. In the Greek, it does give the **distinctive** character, but rather shows **divinity,** or a divine person.

There are **three other words used for God, or deity** such as:

1. **Theotes**, rendered **Deity** and used of **Christ** found in **Colossians 2:9**, this is shown in **the term, "Godhead."**
2. **Theiotes**, rendered in the **abstract** found in **Romans 1:20**.
3. **Theios,** rendered **Divine** and used of **Christ** (2 Peter 1:3, 4; Acts 17:29).

This title varies in its meaning. It is not speaking of **characteristics,** as the term Elohim does, but rather a **person of deity.** The thought is **Grecian,** for they would use **objects** for worship without **proof of deity.** The **Hebrew** used the character of the being, which **depicts what he does**, or has done to **merit worship.**

On Mars Hill, Paul confronts the Greek culture and worship. They had many objects **inscribed for worship.** Paul's **focus** was placed on the altar "To The Unknown God." The emphatic **point** is that they **did not know Him;** neither did they know the others to be Gods. **None of those deities was proven as God.** They were only **created objects** in the **minds** of the worshippers or **admirers carved** by **man's arts** and **crafts.** They **did not** have the **right** to be **called God (Elohim),** for they had **not created anything.** They were created **in the minds of men,** and made into an **object of worship.**

They violated the very principle of the Greek culture, which **boasted** in **Philosophy,** and is governed by the **quest to prove** all things. The three classifications of **Philosophy** are **as follows: Idealism, Realism, and Pragmatism.** They were trying to put to the Idea a **pragmatized** result, which had **not passed the test** of the **second** classification to prove the **idea to be true.**

Paul argues that the **Deity** that you worship should be **proven** that it is **real** from the **things** that **it has done.** Upon that note, he brings the **Hebrew** definition into **fruition** by saying:

"Ye men of **Athens,** I **perceive** that **in all** things **ye are too superstitious.** For as I passed by, and beheld your **devotions,** I found **an altar with this inscription, "To The Unknown God."** Whom therefore **ye ignorantly worship,** Him declare I unto you. **God** that **made the world** and **all things therein,** seeing that **He is Lord of heaven** and **earth,** dwelleth **not in temples made** with **hands;** Neither is **worshipped** with men's hands, as though He needed any thing, seeing He giveth to all life, and breath and **all things...;"** [29]Forasmuch then as we are the **offspring** of **God,** we ought **not** to **think** that the **Godhead** is like unto **gold,** or **silver,** or **stone,** graven by art and **man's device."** (Acts 17:22-25, 29)

In the **Greek,** they considered **God as an object.** In The **Hebrew, Elohim, (Grk. Theos) is a living, creating,** and **sustaining God,** who should be **worshipped** by His **creation** Revelation 4:11, **He is our Sir.**

I Am (Eh-Yeh)

He who always **was**, but is willing to enter into a changing relationship with others. Hence, **"I will be that I will be**, and never cease to be **what I AM."** (Ex. 3:14; St. John 8:58)

FATHER
(GRK. PATER)
Matthew 23:9—KJV

This expresses a **relationship** to a **begotten son.** With man, it denotes parentage and not an **ancestor.** It also means **a Sir, senior, an author, or spiritual father** (1 John 1:14, 15; 1 Cor. 1:15).

ALMIGHTY
(GRK. PAN-TOKROTOR: HEB. EL-SHADAI)

The **Prefix** (Pan), in the Greek, **means all.** The Suffix, **tokrator** means **powerful.** The Prefix **El** in the **Hebrew** means **All Powerful**, and the suffix in the Hebrew means **nourisher.** This name shows God as the **All Powerful Sufficient One** (2 Cor. 6:18; Rev. 1:18, 21, 22).

POTENTATE
(GRK. DUNASTES)

THIS IS GOD AS THE ALMIGHTY KING, OR RULER (1 TIM. 6:15; REV. 19:15, 16).

LORD
(GREEK KURIOS, DESPOTES)

Kurios in the Greek is used in many cases to **represent the name Jehovah**, as in Mark 1:3, 11:9, 10. This is a quotation from the **Old Testament** found in these verses, and many others when it shows the **divinity of Christ.** "For unto you is born this day in the city of David **a Saviour**, which is **Christ** the LORD." (Jehovah The Mashiah—Luke 2:11)

The **powerful thrust of this name** is seen in **Acts 2:36.** "Therefore let all the house of Israel know **assuredly**, that God hath made that **same Jesus** (*Jehovah the Savior*), Whom ye have **crucified, both** LORD (Jehovah) **and Christ"** (Mashiah). This Jesus, whom you have crucified, is Jehovah the Messiah!) ³⁷"Now when they heard this, they were **pricked** in their **heart,** and said unto **Peter** and to the rest of the apostles, Men and brethren **what shall we do?** ³⁸Then Peter said unto them, **Repent,** and **be baptized** every one of you in the **name of Jesus** (*Jehovah the Saviour*) Christ, (*Mashiah*) for the **remission of sins,** and ye shall **receive** the gift of the **Holy Ghost."** (Acts 2:36-38)

Despotes, which also means owner and **absolute authority,** is taken from *deo,* which means **to bind,** and *pous,* (foot).

EMMANUEL
(HEB. IMMANUEL)

This **name** in the **Greek** and **Hebrew** means **God with us** (Isa. 7:14; Matt. 1:13). **This shows the deity of Christ.**

MESSIAH

This is the Greek transliteration of the Hebrew *Mashiah- anointed.* This transliteration is spoken **twice in the New Testament** (St. John 1:41, 4:25).

CHRIST
(*Grk.Cristos-from crio anoint*)
(Heb. Mashiah)
(St. John)

Jesus is the Messiah. The **term** Messiah means **anointed by God.** The sense gives us to know that **this person** is **approved of God. Peter** spoke concerning Him by saying, "The **word** which **God** sent unto the **children of Israel,** preaching **peace by Jesus Christ: (He is Lord of all:)** That word, I say, ye know, which was published throughout all **Judea,** and began from **Galilee, after the baptism** which **John preached;** How **God anointed Jesus of Nazareth** with the **Holy Ghost** and **with power:** Who went about doing good, and **healing all** that were **oppressed** of the **devil;** for **God was with Him.**

And we are **witnesses** of all things which **He did both** in the land of the **Jews,** and in **Jerusalem;** whom they **slew** and **hanged on a tree:** Him **God raised up the third day,** and **shewed Him openly;** Not to all the **People,** but unto **witnesses chosen** before of **God,** *even* **to us,** who did **eat** and **drink** with Him **after He rose from the dead.** And He commanded us to **preach** unto the People, and to **testify** that **it is He** which was **ordained of God** *to be* the **Judge** of **quick** and **dead."** (Acts 10:36-41)

In this statement of **Scripture alone**, we see the **holistic intent** of the **Messiah-ship** of Jesus. He is **the ONE chosen by God** to be the **Savior** of the **World.**

This is also seen in **Phillip's** testimony unto **Nathanael** when he **said:** "Philip findeth **Nathanael,** and saith unto him, **We have found Him,** of Whom **Moses** in the Law, and the **Prophets,** did write, **Jesus of Nazareth**, the son of **Joseph....**" **Nathanael** answered and saith unto Him, **Rabbi,** Thou art the **Son of God;** Thou art the **King of Israel."** (St. John 1:45, 46, 49)

The Messiah-ship is further attested by **John the Baptist** when he bare record of Him. 29 "The next day **John seeth Jesus** coming unto him, and saith, **Behold the Lamb of God**, which taketh away **the sin** of the world. This is He of whom I said, **After me** cometh a Man which is preferred **before me:** for He was before me. And I **knew Him not:** but that He should be made **manifest to Israel,** therefore am I come baptizing with water. 32And John bare record, saying, I **saw** the **Spirit descending** from heaven like a **dove,** and it **abode upon** Him. 33And I knew Him **not:** but He that sent me to **baptize with water,** the same said unto me, Upon **whom** thou shalt see the **Spirit** descending, and **remaining** on Him, the **same is He** which **baptizeth** with the **Holy Ghost.** And I saw, and bare record **that this is** the **Son of God."** (St. John 1:29-34—Kjv)

The **whole point of the anointing** is primarily **to show** that this is the **person,** this is the **time,** and this is the **place,** for the **long expected deity to come.** The **approval** and **anointing** is the **divine stamp** that this **person,** this son of **Joseph,** this son of **Mary,** and the **lineage** He came through, is **absolutely** the personal manifestation of God in biological **human form. God** had **come** into the **world.**

This **answers** the questions of **John:** "Art thou He that should come or **do we look for another?"** (Matt. 11:3) The **divine** credentials are given as quoted from **Isaiah 35:3-6**. The **LORD** (*Jehovah*) was to come. Not a **Son** of God coming in the flesh, but rather, **God** the Father **is come** in the flesh **as the Son of God.** This **Messiah is God the Father.** Christendom wants all to believe that the **deity** of Jesus is his **Son-ship** and not Him being **God the Father manifested** in **the flesh.**

Believing **Jesus is Christ** goes far **beyond** the idea that Jesus is the **Son** of God. **Jesus is God the Father!** To say that **Jesus is God** the Son goes beyond biblical teachings. **The son side of Jesus** is **not** his **God** side or **deity side.** It is **His fleshly side.** "That Holy Thing that shall be **born of thee** shall be called the **Son of God."** (Luke 1:35) Remember, that which is born of **flesh is flesh.** The **son side** of Jesus is **not equal** with **the Father.** St. John 14:28, For Jesus said, **"My Father is Greater than I."** This is to say that the **(Spirit)** is **greater** than **the flesh** (Son). **Jesus** and the **Father** is the **selfsame person** as it **relates to the Spirit.** For He said in another **place:** "I and **my Father are One".** This makes **Him God the Father,** for the **term equal** means the **same** (St. John 10:30; Phil. 2:5)

Here is the great ploy concerning **Jesus the Christ: He is God the Father who came in the flesh.** No wonder **the Scriptures said:** "Hearby **know ye the Spirit of God:** Every spirit that **confesseth that Jesus Christ is come in the flesh** is of **God:** And every **spirit** that confesseth **not** that **Jesus Christ is come** in the **flesh** is **not of**

God: and this is that **spirit of antichrist**, whereof ye have heard that it should **come; and even now already is** it in the **world**." (1 John 4:2-3) The **antichrist** spirit **denies** the **deity of Jesus**. It **denies** that **Jesus is** Jehovah **who came** into the **world**.

The **name of Jesus Christ** must be better **understood** as not being **a type** or a figure of **Jehovah**. It must be understood **as being** the **fulfillment** of that **name Jehovah**, the **Messiah**. **Messiah** is **Jehovah** and in **Him dwells all the fullness** of the **Godhead** bodily. We are **complete in Him, and** beside **Him, there is no saviour**.

In the **Old Testament** the One who was to come was **Jehovah** the **Father. The Scriptures said**: "For I am the Lord thy God, the **Holy One** of Israel, thy **Saviour**." (Isa. 43:3) "Ye are My witnesses, saith the Lord, and My servant whom I have **chosen:** that ye may **know** and **believe Me**, and **understand** that I am **He:** before **Me** there was **no God formed**, neither shall there be **after Me. I, even I, am** the Lord**;** and **beside Me** there is **no saviour.**" (Isa. 43:10, 11)

"Say to them *that are* of a **fearful** heart, **Be strong**, fear **not:** behold, **your God** will come *with* **vengeance,** *even* God *with* a **recompence;** He will come and save you." (Isa. 35:4, 40:3; St. John 1:23, 29-30)

It is **scriptural clear** that the person, **who is Christ**, is Jehovah Himself, manifested **in the flesh**. Whosoever denies that Jesus is Jehovah who came in the flesh is of the **spirit of antichrist**. To make it plain, **Jesus is the Father** who came in the **flesh:** And if you **deny this**, then you are the **spirit of antichrist**.

When **Jesus came** into the coasts of **Caesarea Phillipi**, he asked his disciples, saying, Whom **do men** say that I the **Son of man am?** [14]And they said, Some *say that thou art* **John the Baptist:** some, **Elias;** and others, **Jeremias**, or one of the prophets. [15]He saith unto them, But **whom say ye that I am?** [16]And Simon **Peter** answered and said, **Thou art the Christ**, the **Son of the living God**. [17]And **Jesus** answered and **said unto him**, Blessed art thou, **Simon Bar-jona:** for **flesh** and **blood** hath not revealed it unto thee, but **my Father** which is in heaven...."

"Then charged he his disciples that they **should tell no man** that he was **Jesus the Christ.**" (St. Matt. 16:13, 14, 16, 20) **The focus point of Peter's confession** was **not** that **Jesus** was the **Son** of God, but that **Jesus** was **the Christ** (St. Matt. 16:16). **The King James Version** in the **1611 Edition does not** have the **term Son of God**. In the gospel of **St. Luke,** "He said unto them, But whom **say ye that I am?** Peter answering said, **The Christ of God.**" (St. Luke 9:20; 2:11)

JESUS

(Grk. Iesous, Heb. Joshua)
(Meaning Jehovah The Saviour)

This name Jesus is associated with the **name** of God in **His relationship** to **Israel,** as it relates to the **promise land.** This is especially, **the Jehovah,** without the part **(shua)** meaning **Saviour.** The **compound Joshua** became necessary when **The

Isralites **broke** the **covenant** of the land. The Patriarch **Joshua** divided the land to the **Israelites,** but they **forsook** the God of the **covenant.**

It's **interestingly enough, to note the following visit:** "And an Angel of the Lord, (Jehovah) **came up** from Gilgal to **Bochim,** and said, I made you to go up out of Egypt, and have brought you unto the land which I sware unto **your fathers;** and I said, **I will never break My covenant** with you. ²And ye shall make no **league** with the inhabitants of this **land;** ye shall throw down their **altars:** but ye have **not obeyed My voice:** why have ye done this?" (Judges 2:1-2)

Jehovah fulfilled the **meaning** of this **name** when he **gave Israel** the land. The whole land was **never conquered** because **Israel broke off** the **covenant relationship with God.** The name Jehovah is still wanting or waiting **to be fulfilled** in its **completion.** While this wait is going on, Jehovah has become **Shua.** That is **Jehovah** has become Jesus. Since Israel should be **saved,** Jehovah must come to **save them!** Hence, the **Scriptures must denote Israel's salvation:**

"Say to them *that are* of a fearful heart, Be strong, fear not: behold, **your God** will **come** *with* **vengeance,** *even* God *with* **a recompence;** He **will come** and **save you."** (Isa. 35:4) **Jehovah** must come and **save them.**

"**Comfort** ye, comfort ye **My People,** saith **your God.** Speak ye **comfortably** to **Jerusalem,** and cry unto her, that **her warfare is accomplished,** that her **iniquity is pardoned:** for she hath received of the Lord's **hand double** for all her **sins."**

The voice of him that crieth in the wilderness, **prepare ye the way** of the Lord, **(Jehovah) make straight** in the desert **a highway** for our God." (Isa. 40:1-3) Jehovah is coming to **save** his people **from** their **sins.**

"For I am the Lord **(Jehovah), thy God,** *(Elohim),* the Holy One of Israel, thy **Saviour:** I gave **Egypt for thy ransom, Ethiopia** and **Seba** for thee." (Isa. 43:3)

"**O Zion,** that bringest good tidings, get thee up into the high **mountain;** O Jerusalem, that bringest good tidings, **lift up** thy **voice** with **strength;** lift it up, **be not afraid;** say unto the cities of Judah, **Behold your God!** Behold, **the Lord God,** *(Adonai Jehovah),* will come with **strong** *hand,* and **His arm shall rule for Him:** behold, **His reward is with Him,** and His **work before Him. He shall feed His flock like a shepherd:** he shall gather **the lambs** with **His arm,** and **carry** *them* **in His bosom,** and shall gently **lead** those that are with **young."** (Isa. 40:9-11)

This depicts the salvation of Jehovah. Jehovah will be the one who will come and save them. Jehovah is the only Saviour. "Ye are **My witnesses,** saith the Lord, *(Jehovah)* and my servant Whom I have **chosen:** that ye may **know** and **believe Me,** and **understand** that **I am He: before Me** there was **no GOD** *(EL),* **formed,** neither shall there **be after Me. I, even I,** am the Lord; *(Jehovah),* and beside Me **there is no Saviour."** (Isa. 43:10, 11) This means that **He is Jehovah** the **Saviour,** Or **Jehovah is salvation,** Or **Jehovah is Joshua,** Or **Jehovah is JESUS!**

"Behold, **GOD,** (El) **is my salvation;** I will **trust,** and **not be afraid:** for The Lord Jehovah, (Yah Yehovah), is **my strength,** and **my song;** he also is **become** my **salvation."** (Joshua, Jesus)–Isa. 12:2

The long **awaited salvation by Jehovah is anticipated by the Scriptures.** From **Adam** to **Christ** a parade of **names** and quotations **predicts** the coming savior and **salvation. Jacob** struggled with an angel whose name was **not revealed.** For when he asked him of, his **name:** "...And he said, Wherefore is it that thou dost ask after **My name?** And he blessed him there. [30]And **Jacob** called **the name** of the place **Peniel:** for I have **seen God** face to face, and **my life** is preserved." (Gen. 32:29-30) The name is **not** then **revealed.**

"And **Manoah** said unto the Angel of the LORD, (*Jehovah*), **What** is thy name, that when thy sayings come to pass we may do thee honour? [18]And the Angel of the LORD (*Jehovah*) said unto him, **Why** askest thou thus after **My name,** seeing it is **secret?**" (Judges 13:17-18) This then was a visit from **Jehovah** in a **theophany.**

A search is required in **Scripture to find the saving** name of **God,** or what **name** does He use **today to save his people?** Psalm 22:22 says, "I will **declare** Thy **Name** unto **my brethren:** in the midst of the congregation will **I praise** Thee." There **is a need** for that **name** to be made **known.** Isaiah, chapter 49:1, **"Listen, O isles, unto Me;** and hearken, ye people, from **far;** The LORD (*Jehovah*) hath **called** Me from **the womb;** from the **bowels of my mother** hath He **made mention** of My **name."** The name is **mentioned** but **not made known.**

Isaiah 7:14 says, "Therefore the LORD (*Jehovah*), Himself **shall give** you **a sign;** behold, **a virgin shall conceive,** and bear **a son,** and shall call **his name Immanuel."** (*being interpreted is, God with us*) The **person** who **carries** this **name** must be designated as **God with us.**

Isaiah 9:6, "For unto us a **Child** is **born,** unto us a **Son** is **given:** and the **government** shall be upon **His shoulder: and His name** shall be called **Wonderful, Counsellor, The Mighty God,** (*El-Gibbor*), The **everlasting Father,** (*El-Olam*) The **Prince of Peace."** (*King of Salem*)

"And the LORD, (*Jehovah*) shall be **King** over **all the earth:** in that day shall there be **One** LORD, (*Jehovah*) and his **name One."** (Zach. 14:9)

There is a biblical list of **names** which are mentioned from **Adam to Jesus.** "Genesis 1:1 and St. John 1:1 says, "IN THE **beginning."** In the beginning, God **made man,** and at **the ending,** God **became man.** At the first **"He Who is" God** as **Creator;** in the ending **"He Who is"** God as **redeemer.** In order to redeem man, He had to have **blood,** so that He could **taste death** for **every man.** The **price** of redemption **is obtained** through his **Name.**

The Scriptures have shown plainly that Jehovah was coming to save his **people** from their sins. **After Israel is** redeemed; the **prevalent** name and action **must be** attached to that covenant name. **Since** the covenant name **of God was** and **is** Jehovah, that name **must remain until** the restoration of the Land to Israel **is completed. Therefore,** when the first begotten is **brought into** the world, **His** name **must** be called JEHOVAH SAVES OR JOSHUA.

The ostensible approach to this is, when the **Name Jehovah is attached** with the **compound (shua) he saves Israel** and makes them fit to **return to the land** or even heaven itself. The **unfinished work** that Jehovah had to do for them **will be completed** and they may join the church **which is** the **uttermost purpose** of **Eloheen** (Eph. 1:4, 10; Rom. 11:25-36). This **prevalent name is** the name also used to save **any people** from their sins. Instead of a **promised land,** we have the **promise of the Spirit** (Joel 2:28; Lke. 24:49; Acts 2:14, 39; 10:44-48; 11:15; 15:8).

This is from the **Hebrew Jehovah saves. This name,** in a compound way, **is Joshua,** which is Jesus in the **New Testament.** When Jesus was born he had to bare the **name** of **Jehovah-the saviour. It is extremely important to note** the following **prophecy:** "And she shall bring **forth a Son**, and thou shalt call **His name JESUS:** for he shall save **His People** from their **sins.** Now all this was done, that it might **be fulfilled** which was spoken of the LORD, (*Jehovah*) **by the prophet** saying, Behold, **a virgin shall be with child**, and shall bring forth **a Son**, and they shall call **His name Emmanuel**, which being interpreted is, **God with us**...25And knew her not till she had brought forth her **firstborn Son:** and he called **His name JESUS.**" (Heb. **Jehovah the Savior)**—Matt. 1:21-23, 25

St. Luke 2:11, "For unto you **is born this day** in the city of **David a Saviour**, which is **Christ the Lord.**" (*Heb. Jehovah the Messiah*). This is the **name,** which is **contained** in the **formula** for **Salvation.** There is **no other name given** that could be used to **save.** Without **this name,** there is **no healing.** Without **this name,** there is **no baptism** for **remission of sins. Without this name** the Holy Ghost would not come. **Without** this **name, no one can be saved!**

A great mistake is made when one fails to **rightly interpret the baptism** of the **Great commission.** Jesus **commanded** His **disciples by saying:** "Go ye therefore, and **teach** all nations, **baptizing** them in **the name of** the **Father,** and **of** the **Son,** and **of** the Holy Ghost." (Matt. 28:19)

This baptismal formula does not refer to the **titles** of the **Father,** of the **Son,** and of **Holy Ghost,** which are **common nouns. The preposition** "of" the **father** does not mean **baptize** in the **titles—Father, Son,** and **Holy Ghost,**—but rather the **Name** of the **Father,** and the **Name** of **the Son,** and **of the Holy Ghost.** The term name is **singular,** meaning, the **same must** be **associated** with **each title.**

THE SON'S NAME

A search must be made to find the NAME **of the Father, Son, and Holy Ghost.** Let's use a simple process by considering the **naming** of the **Son** found in **Matthew, Chapter one** and **examine explicitly, verse 21:** "And she shall **bring forth a Son**, and thou shalt **call His** NAME **JESUS**, for He shall **Save His People** from their sins." We have here the **term** SON, and the **term** JESUS. The **term** Son **is** NOT **the name,** but the **term** JESUS **is the name.** Therefore, if a person was to **baptize,** he would **not use** the term **son,** but, the **term** JESUS (*Jehovah savior*) For JESUS **is the name** of the **Son.**

THE NAME OF THE FATHER

We must now determine the NAME of the Father. In St. John 5:43 Jesus said, "I am come in My Father's name, and ye receive Me not: if another shall come in his own name, him ye will receive." Jesus declares that he came in his Father's name. This certainly is true, for the Father's name is Jehovah. In fact, He is Jehovah saving his people as we mentioned above. Therefore, the NAME of the Father in Hebrew is *JEHOVAH SAVES (Grk.* Iesous- *(Ee-ay-soouce).*

THE NAME OF THE HOLY GHOST

The name of the Holy Ghost must also be examined. Jesus said, that the Holy Ghost would come in His name. It's also interesting to note St. John 14:26, "But the Comforter, Which is the Holy Ghost, Whom the Father will send in My name, He shall teach you all things, and bring all things to your remembrance, whatsoever I have said unto you." This means that the Holy Ghost bears the name of JESUS (*Heb. Jehovah Saves*)

This plainly shows that the formula for baptism must be done in the NAME of Jesus! Furthermore, Jesus sums up the command in St. Luke 24:47 by saying: "And that repentance and remission of sins should be preached in His NAME among all nations, beginning at Jerusalem." This is one singular name: His name is JESUS.

In St. John 17:26 Jesus made sure that the disciples knew what the NAME was by saying: "And I have declared unto them Thy name, and will declare it: that the love wherewith Thou hast loved Me may be in them, and I in them."

On the day of Pentecost, we see the actual carrying out of baptism in the NAME of Jesus. This is the name of the Father, Son, and Holy Ghost. The disciples were not confused over which name or formula to use. They said, irrevocably that the NAME, which was to be used, was none other than the name of JESUS. Peter preached: "Therefore let all the house of Israel know assuredly, that God hath made that same Jesus, Whom ye have crucified, both LORD and CHRIST." (Heb. *Jehovah The Messiah*) His name is: LORD, (Heb. *Jehovah*), JESUS, (*Heb. Jehovah the Savior*) Christ, (*Heb. Messiah*).

The formula that was introduced for baptism was as follows: "Repent, and be baptized every one of you in the NAME of JESUS CHRIST for the remission of sins, and ye shall receive the gift of the Holy Ghost." (Acts 2:38) The baptismal formula in the Name of Jesus is practiced throughout the Book of Acts. In Acts 8:12, we find this formula being exercised: "But when they believed Philip preaching the things concerning the kingdom of God, and the name of Jesus Christ, (*Heb. Jehovah the Messiah*), they were baptized, both men and women...." [14]Now when the apostles which were at Jerusalem heard that Samaria had received the Word of God, they sent unto them Peter and John: [15]Who, when they were come down, prayed for them, that they might **receive the Holy Ghost:** (For **as yet he was fallen upon none of them:** only they were **baptized in the name of the Lord Jesus.**)" (*Heb. Jehovah, Jehovah the Saviour,* Acts 8:12-15–JKV)

The practice of baptism in the NAME OF JESUS CHRIST was the only name the **Apostles knew.** Peter said: "Be it **known unto you all,** and to all the **People** of Israel, that by THE NAME OF JESUS CHRIST, (*Jehovah the Saviour, the Messiah*), of Nazareth, Whom ye **crucified,** Whom **God raised from the dead,** even by him doth **this man** stand here before you whole. This is the **Stone Which was set at nought** of you **builders,** Which is become the **head of the corner. Neither** is there **salvation** in any **other:** for there is **none other name** under heaven **given** among **men,** whereby we **must** be saved." (Acts 4:10-12)

The name of Jesus was not restricted to the Jews only, but was also **practiced** on the **Gentiles as well.** It's interesting to **Note this experience:** "While **Peter** yet spake these words, the **Holy Ghost fell on all** them which **heard** the **Word.** And they of the circumcision which **believed** were astonished, as many as came with Peter, because that on the **Gentiles** also was **poured out the gift of the Holy Ghost.** For they **heard** them **speak with tongues,** and **magnify God.** Then answered **Peter,** Can any man **forbid water,** that these should not be baptized, which have **received** the **Holy Ghost** as **well as we?** And he commanded them **to be baptized in the name** of the LORD." (*Heb. Jehovah*)

See, the **Gentiles also received the Holy Ghost,** and were **baptized in the name** of the LORD (*Heb. Jehovah Saves*). The Ephesian **Gentiles were baptized in the Name of Jesus. Note the following conversation:**

In as much as the name of Jehovah is **a covenant** or **a promise** to Abraham and his seed, concerning the land of promise, the **Gentiles** also received the **benefit of** the **covenant** not as it **relates** to the **land,** but as it **relates** to the **promise of the Spirit.** This is also the **uttermost plan** for **Israel** that they are **filled with the Spirit.** This **promise** goes **far beyond** any **limited scope** of the land (Eze. 11:19; 36:23-26; Gal. 3:7-14).

"And it came to pass, that, while **Apollos was at Corinth,** Paul having passed through the upper coasts came to **Ephesus:** and finding certain disciples, He said unto them, **Have ye received the Holy Ghost since ye believed?** And they said unto him, we have **not so much as heard** whether there be any Holy Ghost. And he said unto them, **Unto what then were ye baptized?** And they said, Unto John's baptism. Then said Paul, **John** verily **baptized with the baptism of repentance,** saying unto the People, that they should **believe on Him** Which should come after him, **that is, on Christ Jesus** (*Heb. Messiah Jehovah the Saviour*). When they **heard this,** they were **baptized in the name of the** LORD **Jesus.**" (*Heb. Jehovah, Jehovah the Saviour*) (Acts 19:1-5)

Paul was baptized in the name of Jesus. Acts 22:16 says, "And now **why tarriest thou? Arise,** and **be baptized,** and **wash away thy sins, calling on the name of the** LORD (Heb. Jehovah).

Being baptized in the name of Jesus is alluded to in the epistles. Romans 6:3 states: "Know ye not, that so many of us as were **baptized into Jesus Christ** were baptized **into His death.**"

Galatians, 3:27 says: For as many of you as have been **baptized into Christ** have **put on Christ**.

In **Colossians** 2:11, 12: "In Whom also ye are circumcised with the circumcision made **without hands**, in putting off the body of the sins of the flesh by the circumcision of **Christ: Buried with Him**, (*The person him is synonymous with the name of the one who dies on the cross*). In baptism, wherein also ye are **risen with Him** through the **faith** of the operation of God, **Who** hath **raised** him **from the dead.**"

IN CHURCH HISTORY

JUSTIN MARTYR, A.D. 156 is the first to have **mentioned** the **Trinitarian Formula** of Baptism, that is, in the name of the **Father,** and of the **Son,** and of the **Holy Ghost.** They began to use this method instead of the **formula in the name of** Jesus Christ, which is **considered by almost all historians** as being the one **practiced** by the **Apostles** and the **early Church**.

From the **Encyclopedia Britannica, the Eleventh Edition Vol. 3, Page 365,** section 5, on the **Baptismal formula**, it said: "The **Trinitarian** formula and Triune Immersion **were not uniformly used** from the beginning, nor did they always go together. The teaching of the **Apostles** indeed prescribes baptism in the **name of Father, Son,** and **Holy Ghost,** but on the next page speaks of the name **of** the Lord, the normal formula of the **New Testament**. In the third Century, baptism in the Name of Christ was still so widespread that **Pope Stephen**, in Opposition to Cyprian of Carthage, declared it to be Valid. From **Pope Zechariah**, we learn that the Celtic Missionaries in baptizing omitted one or more persons of the Trinity, and this was one of the reasons why the Church of Rome anathematized them."

From the foregoing reading, we see that a **conflict** had arisen over the **formula** of baptism. There is a difference between **Pope Stephen** and **Pope Zechariah.**

Pope Stephen was Bishop of the Church of Rome from A.D. 253-257. Baptism in **Jesus' name** was still **practiced.** However, **Pope Zechariah**, who was Pope over the **Roman Church** from A.D. 741-752, rejected those that baptized in the **Name of Jesus only.** We see then, that between **A.D. 253-741**, there had been a drastic **change** from the **formula of baptism** in the **Name of Jesus Christ**, to the formula **in the name of the Father, Son,** and Holy Ghost. This **influence** came chiefly from the **Nicene Council**, where they **officially adopted the Trinity** of God in three **distinct Persons.**

The name of **Jesus** is proven the **main name** that **God is using today.** Do you **believe** in the **Name of Jesus Christ?** Have you been **baptized** in the **Name of the** LORD JESUS CHRIST according to **Acts 2:38? Amen**

THE NAMES OF GOD
(Examination)

1. Quote at least ten Names of God. Give their meanings and scripture reference.

_____

2. Write the name Yahveh in ancient Hebrew characters.

_____

3. What scripture is it to show that God have revealed Himself in various names

_____

4. Who were the Massoretes?

_____

5. Does God recognize other languages?

_____

6. How many languages was the name of Jesus written in, and what are they.

_____

7. Do names sometimes have different sounds in other languages? Give Example.

_____

8. What name is God using today?

_____

9. How does this name relate the name Jehovah of the Old Testament?

_____

10. Research the various names of God as they are used in the twenty- third Psalms.

_____

Printed in the United States
By Bookmasters